Early Larkin

Early Larkin

James Underwood

BLOOMSBURY ACADEMIC
LONDON • NEW YORK • OXFORD • NEW DELHI • SYDNEY

BLOOMSBURY ACADEMIC
Bloomsbury Publishing Plc
50 Bedford Square, London, WC1B 3DP, UK
1385 Broadway, New York, NY 10018, USA
29 Earlsfort Terrace, Dublin 2, Ireland

BLOOMSBURY, BLOOMSBURY ACADEMIC and the Diana logo are trademarks of Bloomsbury Publishing Plc

First published in Great Britain 2021
This paperback edition published 2023

Copyright © James Underwood, 2021

James Underwood has asserted his right under the Copyright, Designs and Patents Act, 1988, to be identified as Author of this work.

For legal purposes the Acknowledgements on pp. viii–ix constitute an extension of this copyright page.

Cover design: Namkwan Cho
Cover image © The Society of Authors as the Literary Representative of the Estate of Philip Larkin

All rights reserved. No part of this publication may be reproduced or transmitted in any form or by any means, electronic or mechanical, including photocopying, recording, or any information storage or retrieval system, without prior permission in writing from the publishers.

Bloomsbury Publishing Plc does not have any control over, or responsibility for, any third-party websites referred to or in this book. All internet addresses given in this book were correct at the time of going to press. The author and publisher regret any inconvenience caused if addresses have changed or sites have ceased to exist, but can accept no responsibility for any such changes.

A catalogue record for this book is available from the British Library.

A catalog record for this book is available from the Library of Congress.

ISBN: HB: 978-1-3501-9712-1
PB: 978-1-3501-9721-3
ePDF: 978-1-3502-0118-7
eBook: 978-1-4411-9713-8

Typeset by Deanta Global Publishing Service, Chennai, India

To find out more about our authors and books visit www.bloomsbury.com and sign up for our newsletters.

*For my parents Allison and Steve,
and for Emily*

Contents

Acknowledgements	viii
List of abbreviations	x
Introduction	1
1 A portrait of the artist as a young man: The Larkin-Sutton letters	13
2 Larkin's short fictions	33
3 Brunette Coleman: Experiments in genre	51
4 Brunette Coleman: Experiments in gender	71
5 The outward turn: Larkin's novels	93
6 The Coleman effect: *Sugar and Spice* and Larkin's early poems	119
7 Larkin's first great poems	141
8 *The Less Deceived*	159
Conclusion	187
Notes	189
Bibliography	203
Index	209

Acknowledgements

This book began as a PhD undertaken at the University of Hull between 2012 and 2015. I am immensely grateful to my supervisor, John Osborne, for his brilliant and inspiring guidance, and for the many large coffees in the old Arts Café. It is no overstatement to say that John's work has revolutionized Larkin Studies, and, in so many ways, this project would not have been possible without him. My thanks also go to Daniel Weston and Sam Perry for their supervision. My examiners, Seamus Perry and Jane Thomas, were generous in their encouragement and feedback; Jane's support during my whole time at Hull and since has meant a lot. I'm grateful to other Hull colleagues, especially Sarah McKeon and Richard Meek. I'm also grateful to the university for awarding me a doctoral scholarship, without which I could not have undertaken a PhD.

The book has been significantly developed during my time at the University of Huddersfield, where I have been extremely fortunate to work with outstanding colleagues in English Literature and Creative Writing. I am indebted to several in particular for their support, direct and indirect, and their friendship: Merrick Burrow, Heather Clark, Steve Ely, Jessica Malay, Jodie Matthews and David Rudrum. I could not hope for better colleagues.

The Philip Larkin Society, and its journal *About Larkin*, have been excellent sources of information and exchange, and I have benefited greatly from conversations and collaborations with many individuals, especially James Booth, Rebecca Devine, Kyra Piperides and Philip Pullen. Archival research for this project was undertaken in the Larkin collections at the Hull History Centre, an incredible and invaluable resource; my thanks to all the staff there, and particularly to the former university archivist, Simon Wilson. Thanks also to my editor at Bloomsbury, Ben Doyle.

Over the years I have worked on this project, I have enjoyed the support, interest and encouragement of many friends – too many to mention here, but every one of them hugely appreciated. This book is dedicated to my parents Allison and Steve, and my partner Emily.

James Underwood
Huddersfield, August 2021

The third-party copyrighted material displayed in the pages of this book is done so on the basis of 'fair dealing for the purposes of criticism and review' or 'fair use for the purposes of teaching, criticism, scholarship or research' only in accordance with international copyright laws, and is not intended to infringe upon the ownership rights of the original owners.

Abbreviations

References to these works by Philip Larkin are cited in-text using the following abbreviations:

AGW	*A Girl in Winter*
FR	*Further Requirements*
J	*Jill*
LH	*Letters Home*
LM	*Letters to Monica*
OBTCEV	*The Oxford Book of Twentieth Century English Verse*
RW	*Required Writing*
SL	*Selected Letters*
TCP	*The Complete Poems*
TWG	*Trouble at Willow Gables and Other Fictions*

Archival sources in the Philip Larkin collections, University of Hull Archives, Hull History Centre:

U DPL	Papers of Philip Arthur Larkin
U DP/174	Letters from Philip Arthur Larkin to James Ballard Sutton

All other references are given as endnotes, in full on their first appearance, and in short thereafter. Insertions in square brackets are mine unless otherwise indicated. All URLs last accessed March 2021.

Introduction

This book tells the story of Philip Larkin's early literary development. It is not a biography, but the first book-length critical study of Larkin's early work: his poetry, novels, short fictions, essays and letters. It begins in the late 1930s, with the remarkable correspondence with Jim Sutton and Larkin's earliest literary efforts, and ends in the 1950s, with the publication of *The Less Deceived*, his first truly mature collection. Although Larkin's biographers have looked at this period of his career, no one has yet undertaken a comprehensive and systematic critical study of it.

This is unsatisfactory for a number of reasons. The first is a problematic narrative at the heart of Larkin Studies, which John Osborne calls the 'theory of the rupture'.[1] Osborne summarizes this as being 'between the prose works of the 1940s (bad) and the poems of the 1950s (good)', a distinction he sees as 'self-evidently reductive and implausible'. In fact, the problem is worse than Osborne suggests: the 'rupture' which critics identify runs much deeper, isolating almost all of Larkin's work of the 1940s, and fencing it off as a curiously bad false start. In a review for the *Times Literary Supplement*, Adam Kirsch described the publication of Larkin's *Early Poems and Juvenilia* as 'strictly unnecessary, and potentially damaging to his reputation'.[2] Richard Palmer is equally dismissive about Larkin's early work:

> until the late 1940s Larkin's poetry and prose fiction are almost entirely without distinction. . . . [W]hat is extremely unusual – possibly unique – about Larkin's early work is not just its mediocrity but the fact that it does not remotely telegraph the poetry that would ensue, either in quality or in the specifics of style, tone, choices of form, governing preoccupations and subject matter. I can think of no other writer of the first rank of whom something analogous could be said.[3]

Palmer is too impatient and too sweeping to detect any important continuities between the early and mature work. That said, there is little doubt that a massive transformation of Larkin's art did take place somewhere between the composition of the poems which comprise *The North Ship* and the publication of *The Less Deceived* a decade later. This introduces the second problem prevalent in Larkin Studies, namely the ways in which that transformation is explained. By and large, critics have followed Larkin's lead in proposing that the change is best understood as a trading of influences, swapping Yeats for Hardy. Having rediscovered Hardy's poetry in 1946, the story goes, Larkin realized the potential of writing about his own life, and disavowed Yeats, whose addictively bardic work had dominated his verse for several years. Central to this book's counter-narrative is an insistence on the significance of Brunette Coleman, the heteronym Larkin invented in 1943. Three years before his reassessment of Hardy, Larkin wrote a series of works in prose and poetry which led him not only away from Yeats and other unhelpful influences but also away from himself. This argument is controversial because whereas the Yeats-to-Hardy narrative emphasizes the autobiographical qualities of Larkin's mature verse, my account proposes that Larkin's breakthrough was a result of his burgeoning 'interest in everything outside himself', a phrase taken from an early short story, 'The Eagles Are Gone', and one which reverberates throughout this book.[4]

'The Dixon problem'

Establishing Brunette Coleman as a key influence on Larkin's development is also controversial because of the critical consensus which either diminishes or outright dismisses her importance. Once again, Palmer epitomizes this best when he writes that 'in all conscience, the Coleman stuff is feeble'.[5] He considers her work 'prolix arch nonsense', and argues that 'nobody would read such ephemera were it not for the "laundry-list syndrome", i.e. the compulsion to devour every last thing composed by a man who went on to become one of the twentieth century's greatest writers'.[6] But Coleman was essential to becoming that writer. Not only did she distract Larkin from his imitative and immature self-investigations in prose and poetry, but an unprejudiced consideration of her work reveals that many of the key ingredients for Larkin's mature work are present there – especially in her poems, where a recognizably Larkinesque aesthetic can be glimpsed for the first time.

Given the fundamentally unserious way in which the Brunette Coleman project has been framed – in short, as titillation for Larkin and undergraduate friends like Kingsley Amis – this argument may be too much of a stretch for some readers. Indeed, one reader of the manuscript of this book commented the following: 'Kingsley Amis might have thought, had he lived to see this, that it was another manifestation of the kind of article Jim Dixon struggles to write to keep his job' ('But it is much better than that', they hurriedly added). In fact, Jim Dixon, protagonist of Amis's *Lucky Jim*, occupies much safer ground, academically speaking, with his work on '*The Economic Influence of the Developments in Shipbuilding Techniques, 1450 to 1485*'.[7] But it is a good point: few critics agree that Coleman's work deserves the same kind of serious scholarly treatment. Of course, part of the charm of the Coleman writings is their fun – which means that an entirely po-faced analysis of them is bound to appear absurd and suffer from what that reader described as 'the Dixon problem'. But dismissing Coleman's significance raises more questions than it purportedly answers, such as why, in private, Larkin took them so seriously. These questions are explored in subsequent chapters, which adopt a broader, more open-minded approach to the *oeuvre*. Almost two decades after their posthumous publication, the time is right for a fresh look at Brunette Coleman's writings.

Indeed, the time is right for a fuller reconsideration of early Larkin. Scholarship on this poet has undergone a significant shift in the twenty-first century, and in doing so exposed the limitations of much of the scholarship of the late twentieth century. When Larkin died in 1985, his stock could not have been higher. Peter Levi, then the Oxford Professor of Poetry, wrote this in his obituary tribute for the *Sunday Telegraph*:

> Philip Larkin, until his death on 2nd December 1985, was the funniest and most intelligent English writer of his day, and the greatest living poet in our language.
>
> It is possible to feel about him, as people felt about Eliot, that he was the last great poet. . . . No new poet in English will be so well remembered for a long time to come.[8]

Thirty years later, however, Geoffrey Hill used his valedictory lecture as Oxford Professor of Poetry to disparage Larkin:

> Let me become a little aggressive towards you . . . by the easy expedient of introducing the name of Larkin. . . . *The Complete Poems* . . . contains fine poems, *fine* poems, and poems that are average, and poems that are even below average. His work is rated so highly across the literary board, because a large consensus has been persuaded by critical opinion that certain mediocre poems are outstanding.[9]

On the subject of Larkin's popularity, Hill was facetious:

> I would wish to say that if you find it very, very gratifying indeed when quite ordinary people – i.e. not reviewers – tell you 'that's just what I felt', I think you would be far better employed, you would be bringing far more delight to a far

wider variety of audiences, you would obtain far greater job satisfaction, if you were to sign up to appear as a regular expert on the *Antiques Roadshow*.

The attitudes of these two Oxford Professors of Poetry neatly bookend Larkin's fall, perhaps the most dramatic in twentieth-century British literature. Elsewhere, Hill has argued that 'During his lifetime Larkin was granted endless credit by the bank of Opinion'.[10] This is not true – there were always detractors – but the 1990s saw a very rapid withdrawal of credit. What caused opinion to shift from Levi's warmth in 1985 to Hill's severity in 2015, and where is Larkin Studies now?

Twentieth-century Larkin

Jake Balokowsky, the fictive biographer in Larkin's poem 'Posterity', describes his subject as 'One of those old-type *natural* fouled-up guys'; but Martin Amis argues that such biographical details are unimportant (*TCP*, 86). Introducing his selection of Larkin's verse, Amis writes with straightforward conviction: although 'what rivets us [is] the mystery story of Larkin's soul', there is a 'simple truth that writers' private lives *don't matter*; only the work matters'.[11] Still, as he admits, 'Every serious devotee' will have read not just the *Collected Poems* but also the *Selected Letters* and Andrew Motion's biography. The reaction to the last two publications was, he writes, 'prodigiously ugly and violent', a 'bovine' ideological stampede led by Tom Paulin.[12] Yet Amis seems confident that Larkin's reputation has been restored. There was an 'historical explanation' for the downturn, namely the 1990s zeitgeist, 'the high noon, the manly pomp, of the social ideology we call PC'. But with that chapter of Western history having been closed, Larkin is 'back to being what he was Before: Britain's best-loved poet since World War II'.[13]

Amis writes as though this is a case closed, but still his thinking appears more wishful than truthful. One critic reviewing the 2012 *Complete Poems* thought that 'The only thing we're reminded of is what a shit Larkin was in real life', and Blake Morrison, in his review of the most recent Larkin biography, argued that 'there's no doubt that a corrective is needed before the myth of Larkin as monster (misogynist, racist, porn addict, gin-swilling Thatcherite bigot) hardens into fact'.[14] Writing in *The Guardian*, Sean O'Brien criticized Amis's easy distinction between the life and the work:

> This kind of thing may not 'matter' to some presumed eternity of true judgment, but it propagates itself. Amis's own distinction between what we attend to (the

work) and should set aside (the private life) is not one that he himself is able to observe: see the absorbing and chilling biographical sketch with which he concludes his introduction.[15]

O'Brien is right: Amis introduces that sketch as 'a personal assessment of Larkin's character, and one that reflects a preoccupation that can fairly be described as lifelong'.[16] In this fleeting dispute between Amis and O'Brien, we find the essence of a debate which now divides scholarship on Larkin.

Biography – or more specifically, biographical reading practices – is the issue. Osborne estimated in 2008 that 'Of the twenty to thirty critical books and sixty or so worthwhile essays on Larkin, well over ninety per cent employ the biographical approach'.[17] This mainstream interpretive framework has enabled critics to falsify Larkin's work, and then brand it 'rancid', 'insidious' and 'minor', to quote Peter Ackroyd's assessment.[18] Amis's identification of three key publications between 1988 and 1993 helps explain much of this. When Anthony Thwaite's edition of the *Collected Poems* appeared three years after Larkin's death, bad feeling could already be detected. For some critics, the eighty-three previously unpublished poems were simply underwhelming. Ian Hamilton, for instance, disagreed with the idea that 'adding means increase', commenting that 'Kilograms aside, the plumpened Larkin *oeuvre* does not carry a great deal of extra weight'.[19] A deeper problem, however, was Thwaite's decision to arrange the poems in chronological order of composition. Larkin took 'great care' in arranging collections, telling John Haffenden that 'I treat them like a music-hall bill: you know, contrast, difference in length, the comic, the Irish tenor, bring on the girls. . . . The last one is chosen for its uplift quality, to leave the impression that you're more serious than the reader had thought' (*FR*, 55). In breaking this, Thwaite's intention may have been to chart the poet's development, but an unforeseen consequence was to make the poems readable in relation to the life.

This facilitated major problems when, in 1992, Thwaite published a selection of Larkin's letters. Littered with obscenities, many of them misogynist and racist in nature, the volume shocked a hitherto adoring public. Readers now eagerly awaited Motion's biography, released the following year, and consolidating the revelations of the *Selected Letters*, with added cause for concern. No longer merely interested in 'That vase', readers were fascinated by that wind-up, saluting model of Hitler which Larkin's father had displayed on the mantelpiece (*TCP*, 54–5). They were also absorbed by Larkin's pornographic habits, heavy drinking, sexual infidelities, and his slurs against women, ethnic minorities and the working class. When Larkin died in 1985, his popularity largely rested on the achievement of three slim volumes of verse. Just eight years later, readers could access a fat wad of private correspondence, an equally hefty biography, and an expanded poetic corpus arranged in chronological order of composition, allowing the *Letters* and the *Life* to be tacked onto it. Cultural commentators instantly seized upon these sordid details, in what Clive James has called 'a rush of dunces'.[20] Tom Paulin described the *Selected Letters* as 'a distressing and in many ways revolting compilation which imperfectly reveals and conceals the sewer under the national monument Larkin became', whilst Lisa Jardine, lambasting Larkin's 'Little Englandism', announced that 'we don't tend to teach Larkin much now in my Department of English'.[21] In his afterlife, Larkin had become the literary scandal of the decade.

Larkin and personae

That scandal was political in nature, but it also entailed a literary-critical debate about authors and personae. For obvious reasons, it was an attractive strategy for Larkin's defenders to simply cordon off the poetry from the biography, as Martin Amis insists should be the case. Insofar as clear differences between the man and his poems exist, this is an important and necessary strategy. But what Larkin's private, biographical writings and his public, literary ones have in common is their use of personae. Sometimes these are easy to pick out in the poems, such as when Larkin writes from the perspective of a bride, a disenchanted biographer or a jet-setting academic. In other, more seemingly autobiographical poems, the personae are subtler. Even more complex, however, was Larkin's use of personae across his different correspondences, and generally in his relations with people. As evidence of this, witness the personal pronouns which feature in the titles of relevant memoirs: *Philip Larkin, The Marvell Press and Me* and *The Philip Larkin I Knew*. In the former, Larkin is Jean Hartley's cynical but hilarious and kind acquaintance; in the latter, Maeve Brennan's deeply romantic, borderline religious companion. Since the appearance of the *Selected Letters* and Motion's biography in the early 1990s, new archives and publications have added substantively to the roll of Larkins. *Letters to Monica* (2010) suggested his lack of interest in party politics, his preoccupation with the domestic and, most interestingly, a feminine, almost spinsterish identity.[22] More recently, the publication of *Letters Home* (2018) presented Larkin the dutiful son. Other archives, such as Bruce Montgomery's in the Bodleian, will almost certainly add new Larkins to the record when they become available in the future.

What relation, then, does the highly sensitive aesthete of the Sutton correspondence have to the grumpy and stringent university librarian encountered by many students? What relation does the feminine and queer Larkin of the Monica Jones letters have to the laddish misogynist of the Kingsley Amis correspondence? What relation does the bigot of the Colin Gunner letters have to the gentle lover of Maeve Brennan? It is tempting to conclude none, except that the diverse personae Larkin developed in his different correspondences and relationships all helped with the business of being a writer. These were identities which, in collaboration with others, he constructed and explored, rather than simply expressed; and whether Larkin the private individual, Larkin the poet, or Larkin the public figure, they were constructed assiduously and self-consciously: 'Quite a Larkin afternoon', he told Jones after exploring a Victorian cemetery (*LM*, 437). Some acquaintances, including Brennan and Amis, were surprised and upset to discover, after his death, the existence of other Larkins: 'I sometimes wonder if I ever really knew him', Martin Amis recalls his father saying; others, like Gunner, always suspected they were getting a particular performance.

This emphasis on the multiplicity and relativity of Larkin's personae can be frustrating for readers, who understandably want to get at 'the real Larkin'; and various friends, critics and readers have indeed claimed to 'know' that Larkin. It can also look like a theoretical sleight of hand, conveniently allowing Larkin off the hook for his more troubling statements. But if we embrace the uncertainty, or negative capability, about what might constitute the real Larkin, then we can properly appreciate what makes him a great writer: his complexity, range and the attention he pays to the inner lives of other people. As will be seen throughout this study, Larkin's construction of personae was fundamental not only to how he presented himself, but also to his art.

Twenty-first-century Larkin

If conversations about Larkin in the late twentieth century were dominated by biographical revelations, in the twenty-first century the critical landscape is altering. Outrage at aspects of Larkin's life is being met with a staunch determination to return to his work. Two publications in particular have thrown the field wide open for new kinds of investigation: John Osborne's polemical monograph, *Larkin, Ideology and Critical Violence: A Case of Wrongful Conviction* (2008), and an authoritative edition of Larkin's *Complete Poems* (2012) by

Archie Burnett of Boston University's Editorial Institute. Osborne's study has revolutionized the field with its wholehearted rejection of biographicalism, a methodology which replaces '*the hermeneutical quest for textual meaning* [with] *a biographical quest for the moment of origination*' (original emphasis).[23] By substituting a text-centred approach for the author-centred one, Osborne makes close reading key to the process of interpreting Larkin's work: 'Once the meaning of an artefact is no longer regarded as having been nailed to the floor of the author's intentions, a limited plurality of interpretations is generated relative to different reading perspectives.'[24] His study identifies countless misreadings of Larkin's work in which narrators are 'sexed', 'raced' and so on, in order to make their identities fit with the poet's:

> The stark truth is that the overwhelming majority of the poems tell one nothing about the gender, race, class or nationality of either their narrators or their addressees, but that both the poet's champions and detractors fill in the missing information by jumping to the conclusion that the protagonist is always and only a white, male, middle-class Englishman named Philip Larkin.[25]

Osborne wipes clean this slate of presuppositions, approaching each poem afresh with the intention of reading *out* of it rather than *into* it. The Larkin who emerges is a stranger and more subversive writer, and one who has plenty in common with the younger author discussed in the present study. One particularly sharp example of Osborne's approach is his reading of 'MCMXIV', a poem often cited as an example of misty-eyed pre-war nostalgia: simply by shifting the emphasis of the poem's final line onto the word 'Never', Osborne turns it into an anti-nostalgic myth-buster: 'Never such innocence again, *please God!*', as he puts it.[26] In other words, a single verbal shift by the reader can transform the poem's politics entirely. More generally, Osborne revamps Larkin's relationship to modernism, and argues that the poet anticipated deconstruction by decades; he concludes by demonstrating Larkin's influence on a generation of younger British postmodernists. He has since followed this up with *Radical Larkin* (2014), a study of seven radical techniques used by the poet, including ellipsis, deterritorialization and de-essentialism. His fierce countering of the critical violence done to Larkin's work has cleared the way for new and more open-minded studies of this writer, the present one included.

The publication of *The Complete Poems* was another landmark moment for Larkin Studies. Burnett's edition expands the corpus by including all accessible poems, with newly interrogated print and manuscript sources, Burnett having found more than 100 errors in A. T. Tolley's edition of the *Early Poems and Juvenilia* alone. Most impressively, Burnett provides a comprehensive commentary on the poems, including Larkin's extensive intertextuality. The consequences of his editorial scholarship are substantial and manifold. Larkin's corpus is not just larger but more accurate. Perhaps more significantly, Burnett has strengthened the case for a more textual approach. Although there is far more biographical information than in any previous edition, Burnett's commentary also presents summaries of divergent critical interpretations, non-biographical contexts and Larkin's many citations and allusions. In other words, his commentary encourages readers to look within the poems in order to better understand them. As the dustjacket states, 'Larkin played down his literariness, but his poetry enrichingly alludes to and echoes the writings of many others; Archie Burnett's commentary establishes him as a more complex and more literary poet than many readers have suspected.'

Prospectus

It is with this complexity and literariness in mind, as well as the possibilities demonstrated by Osborne's text-centred ethos, that I have approached Larkin's early work afresh. It seems to me that another way to prove the multifaceted brilliance and subversiveness of Larkin's mature work is to show the early development and influences required to write it. The cradle-to-grave biographies have naturally explored the years before Larkin became a major poet. They have also explored a range of his writings from that period, though with varying degrees of coverage, patience and critical acumen. This study takes a more systematic approach; because it is not a biography, it also takes a distinctly different methodological one. Biographies necessarily weave a writer's work into the bigger life story being told, whereas this study only calls upon the life where it helps to clarify a particular point in some way. Biographies tend to have a narrative arc; this study does too, but it is one focused on texts rather than life events: what is being traced is Larkin's *literary* development, rather than psychological, sexual, professional and so on. The main methodological approach is that of close reading and literary analysis, even when what is being read seems to be biographical in nature, such as Larkin's letters. Though no theoretical or methodological approach can claim to be somehow 'pure', close reading at least has the virtue of not going looking for something particular in a text, instead allowing the text to speak on its own terms – a method Larkin's work has come to require. By working through Larkin's early writings with an openness to the ways in which meaning is textually constructed, this study presents an original and often surprising account of his literary development.

Chapter 1 of *Early Larkin* explores Larkin's vivid correspondence with his friend, Jim Sutton. In doing so, the chapter establishes a meta-narrative for the entire study, namely Larkin's sustained and self-conscious search for a writerly identity. This is a highly aesthetic and citational correspondence, which shows Larkin's early influences. Throughout the 1940s, Larkin used it to dialogically construct an artistic identity for himself and for Sutton. Searching for common artistic ground, he found it in the form of D. H. Lawrence. However, Lawrence's model of an artistic life, whereby the life and the art are one, was not something Larkin could replicate; this chapter shows how he adopted and then adapted the Lawrentian model.

Chapter 2 looks at Larkin's earliest prose, written between the late 1930s and the invention of the Brunette Coleman heteronym in 1943. Much of this represents an exercise in genre, contributing to Larkin's writer's education. The chapter offers a flavour of these early writings, and thinks through their implications for his development. It shows how Larkin's short fictions gradually moved away from narrowly autobiographical fantasies of male homosociality and authorship, towards an interest in other people that would come to define his mature work. The chapter draws particular attention to a 1943 short story, 'An Incident in the English Camp', which for the first time shows Larkin parodying, rather than imitating, genre fiction, exploring a female centre of consciousness and experimenting with a surrogate model of authorship.

Having tried his hand at this surrogate mode of authorship, Larkin expanded the practice by inventing Brunette Coleman, the lesbian heteronym whose work is the subject of Chapters 3 and 4. Coleman's work in and on the schoolgirl story genre has baffled, and in some cases irritated, critics; for the few sufficiently interested in them, Larkin's sexual psychology has offered the most obvious explanation. These chapters decline to take such an approach, instead reading them as a coherent *oeuvre*, and on their own terms, thereby allowing their preoccupation with genre and gender to emerge. Chapter 3 looks at Coleman's subversive approach to genre, reading her essay on the schoolgirl story as a remarkably expert analysis with some important ideas about the interaction between genre and gender. These are then related to her schoolgirl novella, *Trouble at Willow Gables*. Chapter 4 extends the discussion, looking at Coleman's narratological treatment of gender across her prose works and revealing a radical approach to sex and sexuality. Though Larkin eventually abandoned the heteronym, Coleman took his writing into new territory and enabled him to produce his most original and intriguing work to date. Her example showed him the possibilities of breaking rules and conventions, and of sensitively exploring the lives of others, rather than his own autobiography.

After Coleman, Larkin went on to produce more 'serious' fiction. Chapter 5 shows Coleman's influence on the two published novels, *Jill* and *A Girl in Winter*. *Jill* is the most obvious successor to the Coleman works: its protagonist, John Kemp, invents a fantasy sister, even acting as the surrogate-author of her letters and diaries. Though critics have read the novel biographically, this chapter shows how Larkin continued his sensitive exploration of difference, something he amplified in *A Girl in Winter*, with its female protagonist exiled to wartime Britain. It is in this novel that Larkin most successfully applies the lessons learned from his Coleman phase, writing a subtle and empathetic account of a foreign woman's experience.

Having traced Larkin's development in prose, this book then turns to the poetry. The standard narrative of Larkin's poetic development views *The North Ship* as a false start that would be corrected by his conversion in 1946 from a Yeatsian to a Hardyesque poetic. Chapter 6 challenges this narrative with its focus on the *Sugar and Spice* poems written by Coleman three years earlier. Against a backdrop of critical dismissal, the chapter argues that these poems represent some of the best of Larkin's writings that decade, and that they both resemble and influence his later poetic achievements. The chapter teases out from the *Sugar and Spice* poems a number of textual echoes of later, major poems, and also locates moments in *The North Ship* when Coleman's presence can be felt. Reading 'Femmes Damnées', one of Coleman's 1943 poems, the chapter asks how Larkin could publish this under his own name thirty-five years later, without it seeming out of place in his *oeuvre*.

In 1950, Larkin wrote 'Round the Point', a dramatic piece in which two characters debate the reasons for his stalling career as a novelist. Its prescient analysis returns us to the meta-narrative established in Chapter 1, showing that Larkin was now on the cusp of realizing his writerly identity. Chapter 7 looks at this and the significant changes occurring in his poetry workbooks. Having abandoned the novels he had worked on since *A Girl in Winter*, Larkin used the first weeks of the new decade to write his first two great poems: 'At Grass' and 'Deceptions'. Both are acts of poetic calibration, testing and respecting distance and difference, and therefore finally realizing Coleman's influence, and the achievement of *A Girl in Winter*, in his verse. The chapter presents close readings of these first two major poems, showing the distance Larkin had travelled during the preceding decade.

Chapter 8 completes the study by turning to *The Less Deceived*, Larkin's first truly mature collection. Reading a representative selection of poems from the volume, it shows how Larkin finally achieved maturity as a poet by continuing to practise ideas developed in earlier writings, especially those of Brunette Coleman. In *The Less Deceived*, Larkin continues to demonstrate his sensitive preoccupation with gender, and the lives of others more generally; he also follows Coleman in using personae to drive poems which upset genre, orthodoxy and cliché. These are poems expressed in a voice and manner definitively Larkin's own, finally enabling him to make his mark on literary history.

The poems Larkin wrote during the first weeks of the 1950s show that he had at last achieved poetic maturity. But it was during the 1940s that Larkin grew as a writer, discovering his 'interest in everything outside himself', and establishing a poetic that would make him famous. Larkin's major poetry – the poetry that is widely read and studied today – is the result of a decade's experimentation with ideas, influences, forms, genres, subjects, voices and personae. In his correspondence with Sutton, Larkin set out to attain literary greatness, but the journey he went on to achieve it was not the one he imagined. As he would later remark in 'Round the Point', 'A writer's development is a slow approximation to his fated position. . . . [D]iscovering what one writes about best is a slow business' (*TWG*, 481). If we are to truly appreciate Larkin's art, and continue to push back against reductive readings of it, we need to better understand the slow journey he undertook in order to produce it. This book tells that story.

1

A portrait of the artist as a young man
The Larkin-Sutton letters

This book is about the journey Larkin undertook to become a mature and original writer and one of the major poets of the twentieth century. Larkin's correspondence with James (Jim) Ballard Sutton is an important place to begin, because it was there that Larkin constructed and negotiated his artistic identity – an identity that was forced to adapt to the changing circumstances of his life and his growing acceptance of his own character and art. It is there that we can first begin to see the shape his literary development would take and the various roads not taken, a narrative pursued across subsequent chapters.

The friendship between Philip Larkin and Jim Sutton began at Coventry's King Henry VIII School. Their extant correspondence starts in 1938 with a letter Larkin wrote from a family holiday in Sidmouth, and trickles to a halt in the early 1950s.[1] It therefore spans the entire decade of the 1940s, and, as a running commentary on these formative years, is one of the most important available to Larkin scholars. This correspondence also contains some of the best writing Larkin produced that decade. These are vivid and lively letters, often deeply amusing, and electrified by playful language and obscenities. Such qualities are absent from much of the literary work Larkin produced during the 1940s, but would, during the course of the decade, gradually find their way into his writing and form part of what we now recognize as 'Larkinesque'. Critics were quick to point out the value of these letters: Andrew Motion has described them as 'extraordinary . . . intimate, spontaneous, vital', whilst Anthony Thwaite argues that 'They are very much a portrait of the artist as a young man' (SL, xii).[2] These are common means of characterizing the correspondence. The intimacy which Motion describes makes this correspondence stand out, particularly from more perfunctory or excessively performative correspondences, like those with Kingsley Amis and Colin Gunner, which were in many ways conducted from a sense of social obligation or guilt. The letters to Sutton are full of longing and exhilaration:

> Your word revived me like a warm fire, solid, sincere, deepest I wished more than anything else that rather you were here or I was in Coventry. (1 April 1941)[3]
>
> Permit me to observe that during the last eight days I have received 6 (six) letters from you . . . . In other words, I resemble a man who has consumed 6 bots [sic] of beer in swift succession. (12 April 1943)

The language of warmth and intoxication is perhaps more redolent of love letters, and at times, the sense of yearning arguably borders on the sexual: 'Ah, if only we could get together again and you stuff my poems in your cavernous pipe, and I put my feet through your canvases two at a time as of old' (5 August 1942). 'I long for you to come back', he wrote the year after; 'I feel you are a particularly good book or record I have voluntarily locked away and some time in the future shall take out and read or play again – if you see what I mean. Of course you are much better than a book or record. But it's almost the sense of something saved up. I hope you come back, soon' (12 August 1943).

Epistolarity

Letters occupy an unsound theoretical relationship to literary studies. As Hermione Lee writes, they are 'dangerous, seductive, and invaluable for biographers'.[4] That much may be obvious, but critics producing ostensibly less biographical scholarship are not immune to their seductions. Though some work has been done to theorize epistolarity, and literary correspondence is beginning to receive the more sophisticated attention it demands, a much older and more naïve notion of letter-writing continues to exercise a pull on the imagination of literary scholars and lay readers. As the historian Rebecca Earle points out, 'Personal letters . . . have often been read as windows into the soul of the author. The ancient trope that views the letter as merely a conversation in writing lent particular force to this idea, whereby the letter becomes as unmediated as a casual conversation.'[5] Larkin has been a notable victim of this approach, since it was his letters – and a sometimes wilfully simplistic way of reading them – that were responsible for the backlash of the 1990s. As Amanda Gilroy and W. M. Verhoeven argue, however, this view of letter-writing as a casual, unmediated form of expression involves two acts of erasure, namely the 'dialogic construction of identity' and the independent 'textuality' of letters.[6] These aspects must surely be even more acute in the case of a writer's letters. For Hugh Haughton, a poet's letter 'is not only a source of information but a *form* of information, a literary performance with a bearing on poetry'.[7]

In this chapter, however, I am less interested in the possibility that Larkin's letters represent early rehearsals for poems than in the idea that they represent early rehearsals of a writerly identity. Larkin used this correspondence as a space in which to construct and negotiate his identity as a writer – the '*form* of information' Haughton describes. In this sense, I concur with its characterization as a 'portrait of the artist as a young man', but complicate the implications of that phrase: declining to treat the correspondence as biographical plunder, a source of information *about* the young artist, I instead interpret it as the place where he first *became* a young artist. From the displays of power in early modern royal portraiture, to the carefully composed twenty-first-century 'selfie', the history of the portrait and self-portrait teaches us that this genre is fundamentally about the construction and projection of identity, not the naïve recording of it. If the Larkin-Sutton correspondence is a portrait of the artist as a young man, then it is only because the correspondence itself is the process by which the young Larkin constructs and projects himself as artist.

War and letter-writing

This correspondence was at its most intense during the Second World War. In 1940, Larkin and Sutton both went to Oxford, Larkin to study English Language and Literature at the university, and Sutton to study art at the Slade, recently relocated from London in order to avoid German bombing. Sutton, however, would only enjoy two terms, being called up into the Royal Army Service Corps in the spring of 1941. Larkin, whose exemption from military service due to poor eyesight had been confirmed earlier that year, was able to continue his studies. This distanced, wartime context is crucial to understanding the correspondence.

A casual reference in December 1940 – 'My bloody Uncle is convinced that the invasion will start tomorrow' – reminds us just how much the threat of disaster and defeat loomed over the country during these years (20 December 1940). However, references like this to the war are relatively scarce: it seems Larkin was largely uninterested in the subject, seeing it more as an interruption to the relationship and their artistic destinies (explored later in the chapter). His letters show almost no interest in nationalist sabre-rattling, the implications of the war, or its specific battles and developments. Even on 8 May 1945 – the day after Germany signed an act of military surrender – Larkin's mind was elsewhere: 'I hope the end of the European War means that we shall meet again soon, and be able to get going on affairs of mutual and eternal interest. By this I mean the appreciation and creation of temporal and timeless ART.' As the nation erupted in euphoric relief, Larkin wrote this:

> I listened to Churchill blathering out of him this afternoon, and the King this evening. But all day I have had a headache and felt despondent. The second draft of the novel has reached p.22. I have had some bad meat for supper which gives me a thoughtful expression. And the weather has turned enervatingly warm. (8 May 1945)

Here, the great war leader Churchill is 'blathering', the king is no better and the Allies' victory is narrated as casually as Larkin's headache, the drafting of his novel, his evening meal and the weather. For Larkin, there are concerns more personally significant than the fate of Europe.

One such concern is to keep Sutton's 'mutual and eternal interest' in art alive throughout the war. Jenny Hartley has argued that 'During a war letters assume a heightened significance, and the Second World War can be seen as the last golden age of letter-writing'.[8] She goes on to discuss the important role women, and particularly mothers, played as letter-writers during this conflict:

> In their letters, mothers reproduced the kind of dailiness we find in women's fiction. The creation of the everyday, the 'study of provincial life', to borrow *Middlemarch*'s subtitle, is a project which the letter-writing mother shares with the writer of domestic fiction. . . . If mothers were the domestic realists of the war, they also had to practise the novelist's arts of editing and selecting. Letters might offer space for creativity and enable the writing self to gain in confidence, but they had to be carefully angled and controlled with the reader in mind. Mothers could not forget for long the function of their letters as surrogate maternal comfort.[9]

Larkin, though neither a woman nor a mother, was in the privileged position of remaining at home and at Oxford, thanks to his exemption. In this context he seems to have assumed a similarly 'surrogate' role. This partly manifests itself as chatter about jazz, books, mutual friends and so on, but often also as scene-setting – presenting Sutton with vignettes of the 'provincial life' from which he has been torn. There is both an Englishness and a strong verbal-visual quality to these efforts. In one fascinating letter, penned in rich present tense from the gardens of St John's College, Larkin writes:

> Round the base of a treetrunk there is a wooden circular seat. The tree (unknown tree) lets its branches fall around on all sides so that anyone sitting on the seat is mainly obscured. A thin veil of ~~green and~~ sungreen leaves flick and mottle in the wind: this page is shadowed by endless changing. Farther, bells debate the exact moment of 2 o'clock. Due to the wind and the curious tree there is always a rustling, like constantly blowing leaves in Autumn streets, or, on a scorched headland, the distant sound of the sea. (21 May 1941)

This is impressive prose, and edited to achieve maximum impact. The passage shows genuine poetic promise: 'flick and mottle... shadowed by endless changing' is redolent of Gerard Manley Hopkins, and 'bells debate the exact moment' is a strong metaphor, which would find its way into a later poem, 'Livings III': 'The bells discuss the hour's gradations' (*TCP*, 78–9). The letter seems designed to put Sutton back in touch with home – with the city and the country he has had to leave behind. Having been sent away to fight a war, a letter such as this one carries him, for the moment, out of his present reality and into another. But Larkin's letter-writing goes beyond the mere provision of 'comfort'; convinced, as Larkin was, that Sutton was the art world's Next Big Thing, passages like this also seem to have been written to appeal to his friend's visual imagination, lest it wither away in an unconducive military environment. Often, then, Larkin's letters self-consciously participate in a version of *ekphrasis*:

> I saw a horse last night, standing at the edge of a field, being patted on the nose by some people, and lifting its long proud head away, again & again, proudly; but gently the shape of its skull surprised me. It was a black one. And then the fields, in slopes and little hills, sunlit and hedged. And the clouds, small, pearly blue-grey sea-shells, drifting along the blue horizon, like Paul Nash. And the feeling of people out in their Sunday things on a summer evening. (6 July 1942)

Such passages represent a kind of *ekphrasis* because of the way they render visual experience into words, passing on those words for Sutton to re-produce as something visual again, whether in his imagination, or with pen and paper (this particular passage was prompted by a sketch of a horse which Sutton had sent). Larkin himself compares the scene to a Nash painting, so that life imitates art and becomes art again. What purpose could this serve, other than to keep Sutton's painterly imagination kindled? This is much more than keeping his friend's spirits high during testing times: letters like these represent a more significant project – the most important of this correspondence – which is the mutual construction of the pair's artistic identities.

A shared artistic identity

When Larkin and Sutton arrived in Oxford in 1940, each man knew where he wanted his life to go: Larkin was determined to be a great novelist, and Sutton to be a great painter; and each one had confidence in the other's abilities. Sometimes Larkin jokingly addresses Sutton as 'Wotto Giotto' or 'Ello Angelo, Michael' (respectively, 16 September 1941 and 5 October 1941), but is deadly serious about their mutual greatness:

> Yes, I look forward to our meeting again, I do really. . . . I need someone who consciously accepts mystery at the bottom of things, a person who devotes themself to listening for this mystery – an artist – the kind of artist who is perpetually kneeling in his heart – who gives no fuck for anything except this mystery, and for that gives every fuck there is. Is this you? I believe it is. (16 August 1945)

This is perhaps the most explicit instance of Larkin constructing a narrative of shared artistic promise: in his directness – 'Is this you? I believe it is' – Larkin leaves no room for doubt that he and Sutton are both 'artists' in the deepest sense. He is also serious about Sutton's talent:

> By the way, the drawings you sent impressed me. There has always been something about your style of drawing that I only vaguely identify as 'lower class'. By this I mean primarily the people you draw are l-cl, but there is also something about your 'line' ('in two yahs from now, Sutton, you'll draw as well as you evah will!') which is rough, crude and fundamental, vivid and earthy. There is great hope for your painting. (23 June 1941)

In another intriguing letter, Larkin gives Sutton a tantalizing glimpse of the kind of work he might go on to produce:

> I think you might make a name as 'the painter of the brickyards' – blue sky, red bricks, yellow sun. Scaffolds, shadows, comic labourers, brown tea, and the rarified ice-wind blowing through the grass. Or just one enormous . . . picture entitled 'The Builders' with about 50 builders running & jumping and falling and shouting and building and climbing and conveying with the wind against them. It would be richly beautiful and also richly humourous [sic]. (12 April 1943)

Larkin's vision for Sutton's aesthetic seems to be a blend of Ford Madox Brown's *Work* (1852–63) and Stanley Spencer's Cookham paintings. This is not simply a case of friendly encouragement. The visual stimuli, the provocations and inspirations, the reminders of home and of normality – all this must have been life-affirming for an aspiring painter stuck in a martial environment that, when it was not horrific, was downright banal. This is borne out by one of Larkin's sketches, discussed by Julie Maylon, which shows him sending a literal 'lifeline' from England all the way to the Middle East, where Sutton was based.[10]

Again and again, Larkin presents himself and Sutton as the next generation's Great Artists, working in the novel form and painting respectively:

> [T]here has been a change in English psyche. The wind is blowing 'in a new direction of time', and I feel that you & I, who will be if anyone the new artists, are onto it. I am not confident about this, nor am I prepared to argue about it, but it seems likely to me. (6 July 1942)

This shared artistic destiny becomes something of an obsession for Larkin: 'Together, we shall be no more successful materially – if I am ever famous it will not be for ages, probably till I am dead because I will not push myself – but we shall do better work. We shall become more faithful artists', he wrote on 16 August 1945. With an almost outrageous sense of arrogance, Larkin told Sutton that 'I was not meant to study, but to be studied' (12 April 1943). This was, admittedly, during the midst of his dreaded Finals; but one gets the impression that he was only half-joking. His letters are full of epigrammatic, often pretentious statements about art; given his confident and powerful sense of his own future, it is easy to feel these have been put down for the benefit of posterity, secure in the faith that scholars would pore over these letters for signs of early genius. They have, of course – indeed, this chapter is dedicated to them – but so many of the ideas Larkin sets down in this correspondence bear little resemblance to his more mature literary practice, or his more mature temperament. This shows the extent to which Larkin used the correspondence in order to test out ideas, theories, voices and identities. It is highly unlikely, for example, that he would have much sympathy with any of the following principles even a decade after he wrote them down:

> As for the vision itself, it's got something to do with sex. I don't know what, & I don't particularly want to know. . . . I should think poetry & sex are very closely connected. (20 December 1940)

> What a poet has to do is to create a new language, for himself. (11 April 1942)

I was thinking that every man should at some point in his life voluntarily abandon himself to the spirit of journeying. (22 July 1944)

The point is not to criticize Larkin's aesthetic inconsistency but to demonstrate the function of this correspondence as a kind of holding place for potential voices and identities to be worked out.

Writerly anxieties

That said, for all the gusto and self-promotion, there is much more anxiety about Larkin's ability to live up to his own expectations. Even as a teenager, Larkin possessed enough self-reflexivity to describe one of his poems as 'Full of gloom and adolescent self-conceit and windbag sentimentality and pseudo-Keatsian mush' (6 September 1939). He is aware of the self-absorbed moaning that takes place in his letters, often apologizing to Sutton for the 'mental pyrotechnics' and 'gabblings of a demented megalomaniac' (respectively, 21 May 1941 and 6 September 1939). He is also acutely conscious that such 'demented babblings' are 'badly written'. In other words, Larkin's concern is with the aesthetic quality of his emotions rather than the emotions themselves. If writing is at the very core of his identity, then an inability to write, or to write well, represents a serious existential crisis. This results in countless letters of agonizing self-analysis and reproach. One device Larkin sometimes employs is a dialogue between different parts of himself: the 'Self' and the 'Better Self', or the 'Mind' and the 'Bowels':

> God, I can't possibly write letters.
> Mind. Don't 'write letters'. Write!
> Bowels. Aw fuckin' 'ell, I can't.
> Mind. Tee-hee! I know you can't! That [sic] just the point, isn't it? Look at that book on the table! Know what it is? Shall I read the title to you?
> B. Aw, fuck off!
> Mind. 'The Letters of DH Lawrence'. He he! That shits you up a little, eh? One thing a pseudo Lawrence can't do, eh? Achilles' heel, eh?
> B. 'Aw, fuck, Achilles' tits!'
> Mind. Vulgar abuse gains no advantage to you. Why not admit that you are a complete sham? Why not realise that your natural laziness and incompetence, coupled with an absurdly inverted inferiority complex, has led you to assume a role for which you are peculiarly fitted but for the reality of which you are quite unsuited? (16 June 1941)

The mind/bowels dichotomy is amusing, but reveals a particularly interesting concern of Larkin's, which is his ability (or not) to write letters. This anxiety shows Larkin's perception of letter-writing as an art in itself, rather than a straightforward transmission of information and gossip. He yearns to be a writer, but does not think he can write letters; ergo he is not a writer. Ironically, passages like this represent a far more idiosyncratic and entertaining style than the one he was carefully curating in his poetry and prose in 1941. This is a lesson he would have to learn; but in 1941 Larkin was too preoccupied with emulating his personal pantheon of literary influences. He could, at least, recognize this problem, but for various reasons spent much of the 1940s repeating it. A highly representative example of the misery this caused him can be seen in the following letter:

> I am continually examining myself for signs of literary ability. This in itself is a bad thing. And there is a point of view that is always present in my mind and to which in moments of extremer gloom like this I tend to adhere. This is:
>
> 1. I want 'to be a writer', not 'to write'.
> 2. The kind of writing (scrabbles, scratchy nonsense) I have perpetrated up to now has been entirely derivative and imitative.
> 3. There has been in it no 'unknown quantity', such as abounds in Lawrence and all writers worth admiring.
> 4. It is merely a symptom of youthful onanistic egoism, of which there are far too many examples.
> 5. Look at Isherwood! By the time he'd finished his 2nd university year he'd written Lions, Shadows – a 100,000 words novel. Length, boy, length!
> 6. Look at Auden, and his superb early poems! . . .
> 7. Look at Dylan Thomas! (Just look at him).
>
> . . . There are times when I absolutely pray for the power. (1 April 1942)

Larkin's self-examination generates a remarkably prescient assessment of his weaknesses, all of which would need to be resolved: his desire to act out the identity of a 'writer' being stronger than his desire to earn the identity by actually writing; the derivative nature of his attempts at writing so far; the consequent lack of originality, or 'unknown quantity' as he puts it; a juvenile obsession with himself ('onanistic egoism'), and with especially dominant models and influences – Lawrence, Isherwood, Auden, Thomas – which stifle his attempts to produce anything original. That Larkin was able to recognize these problems allowed him to eventually address them; they are explored in greater depth throughout the course of this study. For the moment, however, it is worth interrogating the function of some of these influences in this correspondence and in Larkin's identity formation.

Influence

Larkin's writing under the influence of particular artists is a major theme of this study. If, as I have argued, this correspondence constructs Larkin's identity as an artist, then it partly does so by using other artists as building blocks. In other words, Larkin's identity is performed through a series of repeated references to specific artists. In one letter, Larkin tells Sutton he is 'content not to be able to "appreciate" Shakespeare & Beethoven, preferring Isherwood & Armstrong. People of 19 who say they can appreciate the former are liars and cunts. No one of 19 – unless they are genii of course – can be expected to' (24 September 1941). His preference for Isherwood and Armstrong over Shakespeare and Beethoven is symptomatic of a very contemporary taste. As well as a number of jazz artists, the most frequently cited figures in the correspondence include Lawrence, Isherwood, Auden, Joyce, Mansfield and Woolf: all modern, if not modernist, artists; many of them radically experimental; many of them controversial, who suffered censorship; and much of their work either explicitly or implicitly feminist.

These things are important to note. During his lifetime and after his death, Larkin was criticized for a number of political and aesthetic reasons: for enjoying a narrow, unambitious, mostly white and male set of influences (Hardy, Betjeman, etc.); for his professed dislike of modernism; for the conservative and reactionary nature of his 1973 *Oxford Book of Twentieth Century English Verse*; and for the racist, misogynist and class-conscious attitudes revealed in his *Selected Letters*. Each one of these is at least unsettled by the radical, diverse, subversive and contemporary influences present in this correspondence, which Larkin used as the basis of his writerly identity. This was not just performance; later chapters show the positive impact writers like Woolf had on his work and on his development. Whilst simply imitating those writers was unwise, it is true that many of their concerns were also the concerns of the early Larkin, and of the mature one.

As will be seen in Chapter 2, Isherwood and Auden were particularly significant – and particularly hindering – influences for Larkin. In 1942, Larkin sent Sutton five typed-out poems from Auden's *Look, Stranger!* (1936) without comment – the sheer brilliance of the poems apparently speaking for itself. Larkin repeatedly points to the presence of Auden in his verse, sometimes boastfully, sometimes in acknowledgement that it is holding him back, and sometimes both simultaneously: 'My poetry – my thin trickle of cindery shit – has changed too. I write about big things nowadays – quite in Audenish, I'm afraid' (5 April 1943). Given Larkin's ambition at the time was to be a novelist, Isherwood is perhaps the more significant influence. We have already seen him express envious admiration for *Lions and Shadows* (1938) – not only for the book itself but also because Isherwood wrote it at an impressively young age. Elsewhere, in another letter seemingly written for the benefit of posterity, Larkin writes: 'I know I am a mirror – a curious concave mirror that makes everything small and distinct – a mirror that must be polished by ceaseless artistic creation' (22 March 1944). Larkin's 'I am a mirror' echoes the famous line on the opening page of Isherwood's *Goodbye to Berlin* (1939): 'I am a camera with its shutter open, quite passive, recording, not thinking.'[11] His identity as a novelist is, then, self-consciously modelled on Isherwood. But the comparison is problematic: 'I'm feeling a bit Isherwoodish myself', he told Sutton on 16 December 1940, 'but being far too conceited on the (arse) hole for self hatred am dissolved in maudlin self-pity'. As a description of 'the education of a novelist', much of *Lions and Shadows* is taken up by expressions of the author's literary frustrations; but what Larkin seems to imply here is that Isherwood's 'self hatred' proved a far more superior means of overcoming these than Larkin's 'self-pity', which achieves very little.[12]

In April 1941, he informs Sutton that he has

> been employing my time by making a selection of my poems into another book. 'Chosen Poems'. 35 in all – from '38 to '41. Typing them out depressed and impressed me. Depressed me because they were just like any other shit by Day Lewis or anyone else: impressed me because the words seem to come so easily ('My fatal gift for pastiche' – Ch. Ish) – odd phrases just like Auden.
> pastiche means copying, youse iggerant cunts. (16 April 1941)

Once again, Larkin is discerning in recognizing his own strengths and weaknesses: he is sufficiently precocious and technically adept to write in the manner of the Thirties Poets he so admires, but not writing with enough originality to distinguish himself from them. There is an irony in the fact that Larkin chooses to diagnose his 'fatal' attraction to pastiche by echoing Isherwood's own self-diagnosis in *Lions and Shadows*. Even in writing this letter, Larkin performs an act of Isherwoodesque authorship: by telling his artist-friend about the poems he has been working into a book, Larkin mirrors the passage in *Lions and Shadows* where Isherwood shows Chalmers (a version of Edward Upward) the manuscript of his book, describing how he 'envied my fatal facility for pastiche'.[13] In case 'pastiche' seems too sophisticated in Larkin's case, however, he lands a final and honest blow on himself by deflating the term: 'pastiche means copying'. Isherwood may indeed have enjoyed such a 'fatal facility', but the novel in which he acknowledges this is itself evidence of an original talent. Larkin understood that, and he also understood that he would have to offer the literary world more than just imitation if he was to break into it. Chapter 2 further explores the ways in which Larkin performed an Isherwoodian identity, a behaviour he would have to abandon in order to make progress in his prose. There is, however, an even more significant and even more disabling influence in this correspondence than Isherwood. The single most important lodestar in these letters – and the figure with whom Larkin would have to wrestle most fiercely – is that of D. H. Lawrence.

Lawrence

For much of the 1940s, Larkin worshipped Lawrence. Though his letters to Sutton are full of farts and belches, sundry obscenities and irreverent comments on writers and other public figures – all part of what gives this correspondence its vitality – such vulgarity is notably absent from the many passages concerning Lawrence. For Lawrence, Larkin reserves his most emotional, reverential, religious language. Quoting Hesketh Pearson on Shakespeare's plays, Larkin writes:

> He says 'they . . . contain all the humour, all the beauty, and the feeling, and all the wisdom that ever mattered on this earth'. Now, I do not screw up my mouth & make a farting noise. But I do say that I say the same thing of 'Lady Chatterley' (the real one), 'Sons and Lovers', 'Kangaroo', 'Aaron's Rod', 'Pansies', and 'Collected Letters'. (6 July 1942)

In an extraordinary passage, he declares Lawrence 'England's greatest writer' on the basis of just one or two of his works:

> I have been reading 'Sons and Lovers' and feel ready to die. If Lawrence had been killed after writing that book he'd still be England's greatest novelist. If one knocks out all his books except 'S&L' and 'Lady Ch.' he is still England's greatest writer. Cock me! Nearly every page of it is absolutely perfect. . . . Lord, I pray power of thee! (20 March 1942)

Year after year, month after month, Larkin and Sutton return to Lawrence: 'You say "Lawrence is the only man I can wholeheartedly admire." I agree'; 'I fully agree about the importance of Lawrence. To me, Lawrence is what Shakespeare was to Keats and all the other buggers'; 'I am reading a lot of DHL – praise the Lord! – and feel like renouncing all other modern writers' (respectively, 16 September 1941, 6 July 1942 and 7 January 1943). It is Lawrence, then, who provides the ultimate yardstick against which Larkin measures his own literary ability: 'Having read Lawrence, I know what shit is, and won't write it: on the other hand, I can't write anything else' (19 June 1942). If Lawrence is Larkin's chief influence, he is also the chief obstacle to his success as a writer. Even more so than Isherwood or Auden, the mismatch between their personalities, their temperaments and their worldviews was massive. However much Larkin might worship Lawrence's work, with hindsight we know that he was never going to lead the kind of life that allowed Lawrence to write it. The main reason for this is the very different approach to art and life which Larkin would come to represent.

Art and life

For Lawrence, art and life were one: his vocation as an artist was powerful, and he could let nothing get in the way of it; everything he did, he did as an artist. According to F. R. Leavis, 'the man created out of the intensity of his living', whilst John Middleton Murry went further, arguing that Lawrence 'gave up, deliberately, the pretence of being an artist. The novel became for him simply a means by which he could make explicit his own "thought-adventures".[14] As a young man, Larkin could not predict precisely what shape his life would take, but could use this correspondence to work out his relation to art. His vivid definition of a true artist – cited earlier as someone 'perpetually kneeling in his heart – who gives no fuck for anything except this mystery, and for that gives every fuck there is' – establishes the centrality of art as a consensus.

The entire correspondence can be read as an extended and collaborative essay on what it means to be an artist. Early on, he is keen to paint himself as a Dandy: in one very early letter, he tells Sutton about the sartorial purchases he has made on holiday in Jersey, including two bow ties – 'one a brilliant, eye-teasing orange, the other a sort of crafty maroon. . . . Also a beret. If I had a cigarette holder I should look quite French. Wait till I get back to Coventry!' (12 August 1939). The following year, he sent Sutton his poem 'Ghosts': 'I wanted to send it you to show you my real talent – not the truly strong man but the fin de siècle romantic, not the clinically austere but the Peg's Paper sonneteer, not Auden but Rupert Brooke' (20 December 1940). 'One thing I object to is having to earn a living', he wrote in 1942 (7 December). These are the cultivated poses of an Aesthete, and Edna Longley has used this correspondence to characterize Larkin as a *fin-de-siècle* romantic.[15] But as the correspondence progresses, such a pose becomes less tenable. This is a necessary consequence of entering adulthood: though easy for Larkin to play the Dandy at university, the closer he got to graduation, the more he was forced to grapple with the question of how his art would fit into his life; and once out of university, life's many impositions would render the question much more urgent. It became an economic and social question more than an aesthetic one. Though middle class, Larkin's family was not wealthy enough to indefinitely support him as a writer; nor did he have the financial stability to experiment with a series of part-time positions, as Isherwood does in *Lions and Shadows*. The world of work and social commitments – a world he would write about so memorably in his later poetry – was calling. In such a context, his relationship with Lawrence begins to alter. In the summer of 1943 – the summer he graduated – Larkin admitted to finding himself 'a bit tired of Lawrence' (9 July 1943). A few weeks earlier, he had told Sutton: 'Oh, and another thing about Lawrence. Lawrence has been the world to me. Now the world is beginning to enforce itself through experience, and Lawrence will have to go, or at least be modified by experience. S'obvious. Yersh' (23 May 1943).

It is surely no coincidence that Larkin put these thoughts down on paper just a few weeks after reporting to Sutton that he had made

> a new friend – 'Percival', in 'Lions & Shadows'. Or so he says, and I see no reason to doubt his word. He was certainly at Repton & Cambridge with Isherwood & Upward. His name is Vernon Watkins & he is a poet. He is nearly 40 & has just published a book of poems which I don't like an awful lot, but I like him enormously. (16 March 1943)

Vernon Watkins's impact on the early Larkin is considerable but also complex. Their first encounter came shortly before this letter, when Watkins addressed the English Club at Oxford. The subject of his talk was Yeats, whom he had known; Larkin recalled the talk as 'impassioned and imperative', and cites it as the moment he first became interested in the Irish poet (*RW*, 29). Watkins was also friends with Dylan Thomas, and, as Larkin tells Sutton, had been at Repton and Cambridge at the same time as Isherwood, appearing very briefly in *Lions and Shadows* as the character 'Percival'. He had, therefore, all the glamour of association with a number of Larkin's literary heroes, and his passion for

Yeats would infect Larkin for a number of years to come (discussed further in Chapter 6). In this way, Watkins represents another significant but also unhelpful influence.

However, something else about Watkins also affected Larkin. In getting to know him, Larkin was drawn to a particular version of the art/life relationship, which he remembered years later in his obituary for Watkins:

> Having spent all his adult life in a bank, he was now a flight sergeant, no doubt for the duration; after the war he would go back to being a bank clerk again. This in no way hindered his devotion to poetry, which in turn was quite unaffected by ambition . . . . Plainly he had not the slightest intention of 'living by writing'; he was not interested in journalism or reviewing . . ., and found banking much more acceptable than pot-boiling. At that time he was not married. The picture this built up was of a genuinely modest, genuinely dedicated person, who had chosen, in Yeats's phraseology, perfection of the work rather than of the life. To anyone who, like myself, was on the edge of the world of employment his example was significant. Indeed, it was almost encouraging. (*RW*, 42)

In a minor but revealing detail, Larkin also mentions how Watkins would 'listen patiently to my enthusiasm for D. H. Lawrence' (*RW*, 41). Until his acquaintance with Watkins, Larkin's correspondence with Sutton never seems to register the possibility of such a separation of the life and the art. And yet, with hindsight, we know this is exactly the approach Larkin would take, establishing himself not in banking but in the similarly nine-to-five world of librarianship. Larkin would also compartmentalize his life and art in other ways: unlike Watkins, he would never marry, keeping even his longest and closest romantic companion, Monica Jones, at arm's length. In other words, rather than combining his life and his art, Larkin kept them separate, so that the latter might have some space in which to grow.

But what might it mean to perfect the work and not the life? James Longenbach has challenged the neat binary of Yeats's 'The Choice':

> There is something wrong, something too ingeniously self-forgiving, about Yeats's distinction between perfection of the life and perfection of the work. Yeats was a formidable guy; he lived in a medieval tower, he talked with dead people, he wrote some of the most beautiful lyric poems in the language. But nobody has a perfect life. Every life is enriched by disappointment, driven by compromise, and to suggest that one might have been a good person if only one had not been a great artist is to diminish the integrity of art. It is to suggest that art is not fueled by human experience – from the aesthetic to the political to the apocalyptic – but somehow transpires beside or beyond it.[16]

One might make a similar comment about Larkin's life: he reached the top of his profession as an academic librarian; he experienced passionate and loving relationships with women; he got immense aesthetic enjoyment out of jazz music; and so on. His life was not perfect, but it was not exactly empty or completely wretched either. But to debate whether or not Larkin's life was well-lived is a distraction and a decision best left for the man himself. The important point is his decision to separate out the life and the work, in order to achieve the latter's perfection. Again, as Longenbach points out, there can be no clean division between the two: art inevitably arises from the life of the individual who creates it.

But that statement in itself does not really tell us all that much. Think of Eliot, the bank clerk and then publisher, and author of *The Waste Land* and *Four Quartets*; then think of Byron, joining the Greek War of Independence, and writing *Don Juan*; to say that their art and their life related hardly accounts for the very different relation which each of these poets represents. For Larkin, one of the great poets of the everyday, that he chose to order his life as 'ordinarily' as possible is surely no coincidence. But – paradoxically – he was only able to write that poetry once he had made the decision not to make his life the centre of his art. On this, the comparison with Yeats once again becomes illuminating. Denis Donoghue has written:

> What surrounds Yeats's name is not the aura of an achieved poetry, a body of work separable from its origins, but an impression of genius fulfilled chiefly in the multiplicity of its life. . . . I am not certain that it is entirely a question of choice. It is sometimes assumed that Yeats sought perfection of his work and did so at some cost to his life. In fact, he made the other choice. Perfection of the life is compatible, as a personal and profoundly accepted choice, with occasional perfections in the work. . . . My impression remains that Yeats made the choice in favor of his life rather than his art, and that he thought of perfection chiefly as a matter of diversity, multiplicity of interests and relations. We respond to the choice when we think of Yeats as a presence, a figure in the landscape, a force of attraction drawing to itself preoccupations mainly historical, biographical, political, aesthetic, theatrical, and psychological.[17]

It would be difficult to argue that Larkin too fulfilled his genius through a wilful attraction to 'diversity [and a] multiplicity of interests and relations'. Again, this is not to say that his life was somehow dull or misspent, or that he had no interests. But Larkin had no desire to mythologize his life or his world; he had no interest in politics; he did not experiment with theatre, with spiritualism or with automatic writing. Poems came into existence as acts of the imagination, conducted at his desk with pencil and paper. We know from his letters that an average day for the librarian involved getting up, going to work, coming home, cooking a modest meal, catching up on correspondence and then, maybe, sitting down to work on a poem. We might even register this transformation in artistic propensities by registering Larkin's change in attire: gone are the flamboyant, Yeatsian garments, and particularly the bow ties, of his undergraduate days, in favour of the suit and tie. One represents the Decadent, visionary artist, the other the 'nine to five man who had seen poetry', in Seamus Heaney's memorable words.[18] James Booth quotes one of Larkin's letters to Sutton in which he announces that 'I intend to devote myself to writing and doing my boring job without enthusiasm or slackness. I only took it on account of being able to write in the intervals'.[19] Elsewhere, he cites Larkin's reflection in a 1982 interview that 'I've never been didactic, never tried to make poetry *do* things, never gone out to look for it. I waited for it to come to me, in whatever shape it chose' (*RW*, 74). As Booth comments, 'Being a librarian enabled him to "wait for it to come".'[20]

In short, then, it was a separation of the life and the work which allowed Larkin to achieve perfection of the latter. And so many of Larkin's mature poems *are* perfect. Although the posthumously compiled *Complete Poems* is a tome, it should be remembered that the poetry Larkin published during his lifetime amounts to just four slim volumes. This might be taken as one indication of his opting for perfection of the work. Such a settlement would, however, be hard-won, or slowly realized. After 1943 – the year he met Watkins – Larkin's letters to Sutton begin to think more consistently about the art/life quandary. Sending Sutton a copy of his poem 'The North Ship', Larkin explained:

> It took a great hold on my imagination, and I planned some more poems to make it into a loosely-linked long poem. But I have tried hard at them without success, and I know why it is. Every now and then I am impelled to try to declare a faith in complete severance from life: and I can never quite do it. Perhaps it is as well, because who knows the consequences? and I always say that no one can write well if he does not believe what he is writing. (17 October 1944)

Though Larkin would go on writing in such a mode for months to come, and the poem in question would be published as the centrepiece of a collection with the same name, we can see here the beginning of his loss of faith in a falsely Romantic conception of the writer and the writing life. Though it is not completely clear what Larkin means by having to 'declare a faith in complete severance from life', he seems to realize that his approach to poetry is false and that however seductive, however much it appeals to his 'imagination', he 'does not believe what he is writing'.

Two years later, Larkin was mired in a problematic and unhappy relationship with Ruth Bowman – his first substantial relationship with a woman, and one example of the many ways in which life asserts itself. In a particularly extraordinary letter, he told Sutton:

> What mainly worries me, if you'll excuse my speaking on my own affairs for the moment, is a strengthening suspicion that in my character there is an antipathy between 'art' and 'life'. I find that once I 'give in' to another person, as I have given in not altogether involuntarily, but almost completely, to Ruth, there is a slackening and dulling of the peculiar artistic fibres that makes it impossible to achieve that mental 'clenching' that crystallises a pattern and keeps it still while you draw it. . . . Time & time again I feel that before I write anything else at all I must drag myself out of the water, shake myself dry and sit down on a lonely rock to contemplate glittering loneliness. (7 April 1946)

It is striking that Larkin chooses to frame his relationship problems in terms of the art/life debate. Though we might object to his conception of a romantic relationship as 'giving in' to someone, he is clearly concerned about the ways in which life can suffocate the artistic impulse. Like Cyril Connolly (another influence, discussed in Chapter 3), who wrote 'There is no more sombre enemy of good art than the pram in the hall', Larkin shows concern that in his case art and life may be incompatible.[21]

In other words, as Larkin made his way through life – or as 'the world [began] to enforce itself' – he continued to use the correspondence with Sutton in order to negotiate his fundamental relationship to art. Lawrence continued to be his point of reference, but his relationship with Lawrence itself had to evolve and eventually be abandoned. Larkin never lost his enthusiasm for Lawrence's work, but his ambition to emulate it had to be ditched. In the 1980s, Larkin would wear a t-shirt bearing an image of Lawrence whilst mowing the lawn: a wry gesture, referencing this most undomesticated of writers whilst undertaking a mundane domestic chore. Indeed, one sign of how far Larkin travelled during this decade can be found in the form of an unpublished essay he wrote in July 1950, titled 'A note on the freedom of D. H. Lawrence'.[22] Considering the reverence with which he discusses Lawrence in countless of his letters to Sutton, the essay is startling for its sarcasm and irritation; as he told his friend, 'The other night, like a curate in the depths of misery blaspheming against the Almighty, I wrote a short hostile article about D.H.L.'s "freedom"' (*SL*, 166). In it, Larkin accuses Lawrence of disingenuousness. He begins by quoting him: 'Thank God I am not free, any more than a rooted tree is free.'[23] 'But is it true?', Larkin asks, before discussing the ways in which 'a man's freedom is commonly curtailed'. He classifies 'necessity' into three types: 'economic' ('a man must eat, he must earn money by work'), 'social' ('he must come to some kind of terms with the society he lives in') and 'emotional' ('yielding to certain common human desires, principally the sexual'). Larkin then relates each of these to Lawrence's life:

> It is hardly necessary to point out how singularly free Lawrence was from the first of these necessities. After the age of twenty-six he never held a salaried position but lived entirely by his writing. This is much more remarkable than it sounds. . . . As a writer who could live modestly by his writing – and let it be noted that modestly was how he preferred to live – Lawrence could afford to dispense with society. It would be interesting to compile an itinerary of his life to discover what was the longest time he lived in any one place . . . . There is no need to pile up quotations to prove that, as a social animal, Lawrence did not exist. . . . It has to be admitted that Lawrence could not escape the third necessity, emotional necessity, as completely as he did the other two. In fact he could not escape it at all.

Larkin's conclusion, therefore, is this: 'In the face of the foregoing one can only think that Lawrence would have been honester if he had said "Thank God I am free, as free as a man can well be. I know my freedom is not complete, but I wish it were".' The sense of frustration is palpable: by 1950, Larkin was established in his career, struggling to protect his writing time from a range of social pressures, and had broken off his engagement to Ruth Bowman, but was now in another, not always easy, relationship with Monica Jones. He knows he cannot evade any of the three necessities he sets out in the essay; and Lawrence, who managed two out of three, is galling for his disingenuousness – 'the absurdity of it all struck me like a fist in the knackers', as he put it to Sutton (*SL*, 166). As will be seen in the final chapters, however, Larkin was by this point just beginning to write the kind of poetry which would mark him out as an exciting and original new voice in English poetry. He may feel frustrated by these facts of life, but his literary development had come a long way during the preceding decade. Part of the recipe for his success was an evolving understanding of how his life might relate to his art. Eventually abandoning the example of Lawrence, for whom there was no essential difference between the two, Larkin arranged his life in such a way that would keep his art separate but alive.

If there is no corresponding moment of realization about this in the letters to Sutton, this is possibly because the correspondence begins to thin at this time. This is no coincidence: by the early 1950s, Larkin was a published novelist and poet, and beginning to write the poems that would make his name; on the other hand, Sutton, for whom Larkin had held such high hopes as a future great painter, had gone nowhere in the art world and instead become a pharmacist and landlord. In other words, Larkin had rehearsed the discourse of the artist, and eventually fulfilled it; Sutton, who collaborated in that discourse, ended up far from it. This explains why their correspondence does not last beyond the early 1950s: the flame of the artist's discourse, with nothing to feed on, simply expires.

As far as Larkin is concerned, however, what this important correspondence shows is the way in which he constructed and negotiated his writerly identity during the 1940s, responding to a number of influences and events, before finally abandoning the model he had admired for so long in the form of Lawrence. By the end of the 1940s, Larkin had settled on a way forward in terms of the art/life problem; he had achieved his ambition to become a published author, with two novels and a collection of poems; and he was beginning to write his first major poems. His writerly identity was, after a protracted negotiation, in place; but what remains to be seen is how his actual writing developed – how he found his voice – a question the following chapters seek to answer.

2

Larkin's short fictions

This chapter looks at the short fictions Larkin wrote before inventing the Brunette Coleman heteronym in 1943. His earliest efforts represent exercises in genre, as he works through the mechanics of writing. Other stories explore characterization, with varying degrees of success. The stories Larkin wrote at Oxford act out a fantasy of male homosociality and Isherwoodian authorship, a model he would have to abandon in order to make progress. Eventually, in the 1943 short story 'An Incident in the English Camp', Larkin tries his hand at an alternative mode of authorship, a development that paves the way for the Coleman works explored in subsequent chapters.

Very early Larkin

In 'the winter of 1939–40', Larkin co-opted a manuscript book with a specific purpose in mind: having decided that his many writings produced so far, which he had kept 'religiously', were taking up 'an amount of space they do not justify in worth', Larkin chose to 'burn a great deal'.[1] But to prevent the loss of 'all memory of the kinds of thing I did', he decided to 'select and retain a few extracts from the best of the manuscripts and so on, and give a brief inventory of them'. This manuscript book, then, gives us a sense of Larkin's literary tastes and phases during the 1930s, and the earliest stages of his apprenticeship.

In many ways, Larkin's literary efforts are typical of a precocious and bookish child's ambitions, pretensions and humour. A controversialist schoolboy pose of anti-authoritarianism is represented by 'several diatribes against various things, such as Education and Christianity', but in turn soon replaced by a controversialist schoolboy pose of authoritarianism: in one story, he recalls, 'wireless propaganda was sent out in a manner reminiscent of the Nazi regime in Germany, which at the time (I was about fifteen) attracted me intensely'. That

Larkin, just two years later, describes these pieces with embarrassment shows how short-lived such poses were. Other themes, however, seem to be longer-lasting: Larkin preserves an extract from 'The Life of a Cog', a play in which a character called 'Larkin, the Successful Author' says: 'You were tied down by the school certificate you had. You wanted a safe job – you got it. And now the jobs [sic] got you, and won't let you go.' Sometime after curating this manuscript book, Larkin added a pencil annotation: 'Pretty good'. It seems he could hear the croak of toads as early as the 1930s.

Larkin's prose and dramatic writings imitated whatever he happened to be enjoying at the time. A 'wave of gangsters and America . . . found its way into my little world'; shortly after, he wrote 'nearly a full-length novel' called 'Death in Swingtime' about 'a great jazz saxophonist who is poisoned'. Then Larkin 'began to read seriously' (he later pencilled inverted commas around 'seriously' to signal contempt for the younger self who thought he understood 'Aldous Huxley . . . and the rest of the moderns, Lawrence, Aldington, and Maugham'). Here we learn only the briefest of details about the novels inspired by his new diet: 'Shapes of Clay', for example, whose 'general scheme was Huxleyan, but the writing was more individual, except when it approached Aldington' (Larkin's pencil strikes again: 'approached' is underlined, and he adds 'a long way off, old friend'). 'Present Laughter' was 'written in the style of Evelyn Waugh'; another story, 'Trio', was conceived with the Hogarth Press in mind. None survived the bonfire.

Nor did an erotic play with the title 'Teddy Bear's Picnic' (perhaps just as well), or a masque called 'One O'Clock Jump'. By the end of the decade, Larkin was also writing poems and short stories about 'brief emotions and interesting characters'. Thus, in 1940, at the age of '17½', and just a few months before he went up to Oxford, Larkin was in a position to review and curate a variety of writings in prose, poetry and drama. Many of these he destroyed, and the brief selections saved and pasted into the manuscript book were subjected to his sarcastic annotations. But the Larkin who would very soon be engaged in an intense correspondence with Sutton about his artistic destiny had at least made a start.

As well as giving us a sense of Larkin's writings during the 1930s, the manuscript book tells us two other things. Clearly it represents an exercise in stock-taking: approaching the age of eighteen and entry to university, Larkin used this transitional moment in his life to collate the work done so far as a means of bringing into focus his options for the work to be done in the future. With annotations in both pencil and ink, it seems he returned to this book more than once. The other aspect it reveals is Larkin's engagement with the nuts and bolts of writing: genre, plot, structure, characterization, mood. Most of the prose pieces which Larkin excerpts or describes are deliberate exercises in genre: schoolboy stories, detective fiction, gangster thrillers, political allegories and so on. This, of course, was a perfectly natural activity for a bookish child, trying his hand at the kind of stories he loved to read. Similarly, for an aspiring novelist, it was logical to serve an apprenticeship by systematically working through different genres. As this chapter and subsequent ones show, however, this close engagement with genre is particularly significant when seen within the wider context of Larkin's career: these exercises *in* genre during the 1930s led him to experiment *with* genre during the 1940s, paving the way for the mature poetry of the 1950s and onwards.

Larkin's exploration of the mechanics of writing can be perceived more clearly if a wider array of extant pieces is surveyed. He tore out and kept, for example, a page from his school exercise book containing an evocation of a pub atmosphere (his teacher wrote 'v good' in red pencil).[2] 'Vampire Island' is a handwritten story, thirty-five pages in length, about a young boy who discovers a treasure map, falls asleep and dreams he is a pirate in search of gold and silver. It has all the hallmarks of a boy who has read and loved *Treasure Island*, and the most recognizably adolescent of endings: 'He realised that it was all a dream!'[3] Other stories, however, already begin the trend of modifying generic conventions. 'Incidents from Phippy's Schooldays' is a farcical send-up of Thomas Hughes's *Tom Brown's School Days* (1857), another novel enjoyed by the young Larkin, but the story is inspired by his own grammar school experience rather than the hallowed Rugby School, setting of the source text.[4] 'Last Man In (or "How Allan Saved His Side")' takes place on the school cricket pitch, but its protagonist, Allan Grayham, is contemptuous about the sport and the boys who play it, and sneers at them as his mind tours Plato, Socrates and Bernard Shaw.[5]

Other pieces try to be more 'literary' and reflect Larkin's more serious reading, either by wearing their stylistic influences on their sleeves or by eschewing plot in favour of purer evocations of character and mood. A one-page fragment, presented as an extract from a bigger work called 'Portrait of the Artist as a Young Frog', tries to justify the literary credentials of its title with a number of Joycean overtones: the narrator is desperate to get away from his stultifying home; he experiences sudden memories triggered by the flux of his surroundings; and there are some nice Joycean phrases, such as 'shitspattered streets'.[6] In 1940, whilst engaged in war work at Warwick Fuel Office, Larkin wrote a 'Letter to Myself' on headed paper, using a novelist's eye to detail the events and characters of a single day: from waking up and eating 'Cornflakes, bacon and scrambled egg (from dried eggs)', to a conversation with colleagues about the impending Allied invasion of France; one colleague, the 'morose' Mrs Glencross, has recently given birth whilst her husband is in enemy captivity.[7] Alongside fragments like these are longer pieces, such as an unfinished and untitled short story with an extended description of a rough crossing from Ostend to Dover, evoking the ship's putrid smells of beef, oil and vomit.[8] After what seems like ages, we are introduced to the protagonist, Charles Hemingway, whose name is as unconvincing as the story. Already, however, Larkin's eye for the details of contemporary urban life is active: arriving at the train station, Hemingway notices a number of advertisements, including one imploring him to 'Come to Sunny Jersey' (a similar image resurfaces in the 1963 poem 'Sunny Prestatyn').

Another untitled story ('It had snowed in the night'), this time finished and in typescript, is described in the manuscript book as being 'in the style of Virginia Woolf'. Opening in the early hours of Christmas Day, Larkin's prose imitates Woolfian rhythms with its acutely sensitive description of a snowy night during which the protagonist's mother has passed away: 'Very carefully he slipped out of his bed and dressed, very carefully, for he must recapture what he had felt, obscurely, he must be careful not to lose the single thread he held to connect him with last night, because he knew last night had been very important.'[9] In fact, it is another modernist writer, Joyce, who casts a bigger shadow upon the piece:

> All over England the steeples were rocking, the notes rising to the pale clouds, sunlit overhead in the rarefied air. All over England, snow would tumble in a little as doors swung back, would lodged [sic] against windows when the curtains were drawn.

Syntactically, and in its use of a wintery landscape as objective correlative for death, the passage is an imitation of 'The Dead' (1914). Although not without faults, this story is one of the loveliest pieces written by Larkin in the 1930s, and an early stylistic rehearsal for *A Girl in Winter*, discussed in Chapter 5.

'Maurice' and 'The Eagles Are Gone'

Whilst early pieces like 'Vampire Island' may have fed Larkin's 1939–40 bonfire without causing literary historians too much sorrow, some of the stories he wrote just before and during his time at Oxford would have been a greater loss, given that they tell us much about his literary development. As the untitled 'It had snowed in the night' shows, not everything Larkin wrote before Oxford was merely generic. The remainder of this chapter discusses five short stories written between the late 1930s and 1943: 'Maurice', 'The Eagles Are Gone', 'Story I', 'Peter' and 'An Incident in the English Camp'. These stories are not offered up as contenders for the 'neglected masterpiece' category of literary criticism, but they are discussed as important transitional works, interesting as examples of what Larkin had to either ditch or amplify in his writing.

Larkin mentions 'Maurice' in his manuscript book as having been written in 1939. It is a strange story, in which two Sixth Formers, Dorning (the narrator) and Stephen Simmons, recognize a fellow drinker in the pub as Maurice, an alumnus of their school. He joins them for a drink. Maurice's build and demeanour are confidently masculine; despite his education, he has chosen to work in an armaments factory, and it is not long before Simmons tries to impress him: '"I want some skirt," remarked Stephen suddenly. . . . [W]hy he made the statement I have not the faintest idea, unless, of course, he was speaking the truth, which I considered unlikely', the narrator ponders.[10] Maurice relays his vast sexual experience, but in doing so reveals a nasty misogyny:

> There's a bloody lot of trash talked about women – about their beauty, for instance. Well, I've been to Paris, Ostend, Brussels, Hamburg, and Naples – and I've never seen a completely beautiful woman yet. Never. All ugly sods in one way or another. . . . A lot of them stink. Others have terrible voices, or stumpy fingers; some have bad breath or bite their fingernails. There's something wrong with every one of them, yet when one thinks how everyone talks about them.

The female body disgusts Maurice, but there is a faint sense of his physical admiration of the men who toil in the factory: 'The fellows are simply impregnated with filth. They've been brought up to think and act plain dirt, and they do'. This is delicately suggestive of a repressed homosexuality; indeed, Larkin's reflective account of this story in the manuscript book describes it as being 'rather like Isherwood'. As will be seen, this represents the beginning of a recurring trope in Larkin's short fiction.

In terms of characterization, 'Maurice' is an enigma. The narrator, Dorning, is the weakest presence in the story, and he focuses mainly on Maurice's speech and appearance, with the odd comment on Simmons's reactions. Consequently, it is difficult to pin down either the narrator's or the implied author's attitude to Maurice: Is he a captivating connoisseur of male animal roughness, or just a misogynistic bore? The ambiguity may be Larkin's artistic choice, but it seems more like an artistic failing. In this sense, 'Maurice' makes an interesting companion piece to 'The Eagles Are Gone', although the latter is difficult to date, and therefore to establish whether any connection was intended.[11] 'The Eagles Are Gone' reads more explicitly as an allegory of characterization. Its narrator, who is called 'Philip Larkin', visits the family home of an Oxford friend during the long summer vacation. Isherwood's influence emerges again, this time at the level of dialogue: Philip and his friend, Peter, engage in self-consciously effete banter ('I'm getting a bit tired of being a brilliant young man. It's so unoriginal.').[12] Although the Larkin character is visiting a friend's family, the descriptions of family life are remarkably similar to the actual Larkin's descriptions of his own: 'I never left the house without a sense of walking into a cooler, clearer, saner and pleasanter atmosphere', he wrote in an autobiographical fragment.[13] This is particularly true of the subtle warfare waged daily at the dinner table: 'For all their unending battle, Peter and his mother were not unlike at certain moments.' It appears that Larkin was exploiting narrative distance in order to explore his own home life.

In the end, however, the story does more than that. During his stay with Peter's family, Philip catches glimpses of the different characters' inner lives. Peter's father, Mr Canning, is a stoic and taciturn builder who spends as many evenings as possible in the pub. In this sense, he is a two-dimensional stock character. But when Philip learns more about Mr Canning's history, particularly his experience serving in the First World War, he begins to piece together a more vivid psychology:

> Peter had been born in 1916, Robert in 1920. Slowly, after the War, the household got under way. But Mr. Canning could never wholly resign himself to living in the present with his wife: the War was always lurking at the back of his mind, drawing his [sic] away into the past. Mrs. Canning resented this, and showed. it. [sic]. As a result, he retreated even further among his friends who understood him better, perhaps who'd been in the War themselves. Mrs. Canning was left more and more alone, left to a life that was increasingly unsatisfactory and dull.

Similarly, in describing Mrs Canning, there is a telling simile: 'As I held the door for her and the tray, the smell of cooking from the kitchen struck like a wave of unutterable boredom.' In passages like these, it is possible to see the two Larkins (the writer-character and the actual writer) becoming increasingly interested in the lives of others. Importantly, this is also otherness for its own sake. The characters are not mere ciphers for Larkin's own family; Mr Canning's life, for instance, has been shaped by war, whereas Sydney Larkin never experienced combat.

The most interesting character in the story, however, is Peter's younger brother, Robert. In some ways, the dynamic between Peter, Robert and their parents mirrors that of Larkin, his sister Kitty and their parents: Peter is transparently the favourite child; Robert is well-treated but not lavished with the attention given to Peter, and in consequence does not achieve the same success.[14] Robert seems set to be written off as a minor character until a series of earnest conversations, contrasting sharply with Peter's pose of insincerity, triggers Philip's interest:

> [R]ather unexpectedly, he began to talk to me . . . He told me of a fivevalve set he'd made . . . . After a time I began to enjoy it: previously I'd vaguely realised his frankness and so on was perfectly genuine, born not of a neurotic desire to put you at an immediate disadvantage, but from a perfect extravertist [sic] interest in everything outside himself.

Robert, and his 'perfect extravertist interest in everything outside himself', is a foil to the narcissistic Peter, whom Larkin cannot draw into conversation about the brother he considers 'an exceptional damned nuisance'. Later in the story, Philip encounters Robert and a girlfriend at the local fair. Robert has won several coconuts, and gives one to Philip, who 'guiltily' lodges it behind a washstand in the Cannings' home, not knowing 'what to do with it'. When Peter accompanies Philip to the train station for his journey home, the coconut reappears:

> The whistle blew at last and Peter got up, feeling in his mac pocket and grinning.
>
> 'You forgot something, you know,' he said, shutting the door.
> 'What's that?'
> 'Here you are . . . you might as well keep it as a symbolic souvenir.'
> And he handed me the coconut . . . .
>
> When I got home, I thought of tying the coconut up with a label and some pink ribbon and sending it back to him. But on the whole, I decided not to. However, when I see him again (probably at Oxford next term) I shall certainly ask him what he meant by it.
> And, meanwhile, the coconut rests on my bookcase, looking rather out of place.

This is how the story ends: like an object in a Katherine Mansfield story (another of Larkin's major influences at this time), the coconut is imbued with psychological symbolism. Philip's bemusement at the coconut mirrors the bemusement he felt when gently confronted by its gifter, Robert, whose intriguing character he had too easily overlooked in favour of the more obvious candidate for his attention.

The coconut, 'rest[ing] on my bookcase, looking rather out of place', functions as a legacy with which Philip must grapple, an exotic reminder that fascination can appear in unexpected places. (The story's title and epigraph, taken from Shakespeare's *Troilus and Cressida*, therefore subvert Pandarus's belief in the superiority of the aristocracy above commoners.) This is why the story may be read as a kind of allegory, in which certain characters – but especially Robert, and his strange gift – come to represent Larkin's burgeoning interest in other people, or, to borrow the phrase he uses to describe Robert, his 'interest in everything outside himself'.

'Story I' and 'Peter'

If in 'Maurice' the young Larkin writes 'rather like Isherwood', then the two short stories written at Oxford in 1941–2 adopt wholesale Isherwood's manner.[15] As discussed in Chapter 1, when Vernon Watkins visited the English Club at Oxford, part of the attraction for Larkin was that he was one of Isherwood's Repton and Cambridge peers, and had been fictionalized in *Lions and Shadows*. Larkin's excitable letter to Sutton, quoted in the previous chapter, was followed by one to Kingsley Amis:

> I rejoice to hear that you have got a copy of 'Lions and Shadows'. I like all the bits you mention, but I know the book so well that everything has assumed almost equal proportions. Do you notice how beautifully it is all constructed? He cuts out *utterly* home and sex, doesn't he? Those are reserved for his novels. I could read about his Cambridge days for ever, and the descriptions of Auden and the lunatic . . . and his holidays in the Scilly Isles. (*SL*, 78)

It should come as no surprise to find Larkin writing stories heavily influenced by Isherwood. One way in which Larkin mimics Isherwood is by making 'Story I' and 'Peter' tales of a young writer's education. This echoes *Lions and Shadows*, whose subtitle is 'An Education in the Twenties'. In his prefatory note to the reader, Isherwood writes:

> Its sub-title explains its purpose: to describe the first stages in a lifelong education – the education of a novelist. A young man living at a certain period in a certain European country, is subjected to a certain kind of environment, certain stimuli, certain influences. That the young man happens to be myself is only of secondary importance: in making observations of this sort, everyone must be his own guinea-pig.

> Because this book is about the problems of a would-be writer, it is also about conduct. The style is the man. Because it is about conduct, I have had to dramatize it, or you would not get farther than the first page. Read it as a novel. I have used a novelist's licence in describing my incidents and drawing my characters.[16]

Isherwood's 'environment' was Cambridge in the 1920s; Larkin's was Oxford in the 1940s. Isherwood's 'stimuli' and 'influences' included Auden, Upward and Spender; Larkin was a member of 'The Seven', a self-styled gang of undergraduates gathered around the 'idea that we should form some definite group with definite ideas, set against the college authorities and all the intellectuals and scholars we disliked'.[17] As for the 'style' being equal to 'the man', Larkin imitated the languidly camp quality found in so much of Isherwood's prose. This foreshadows the camp style Larkin would explore under the guise of Brunette Coleman, discussed in Chapters 3 and 4, but in these stories it has a distinctly male-homosexual emphasis. Motion argues that 'Both these stories, unsatisfactory in literary terms, have important things to say about Larkin's developing sexuality'.[18] Whether true or not, a psychological account such as this ignores their 'education of a novelist' function, not to mention Larkin's thrill at the absence of sex in *Lions and Shadows*, as expressed in his letter to Amis. It is surely more interesting and productive to read the two stories as literary exercises. After all, 'Story I' was by no means the first story Larkin wrote, but its title implies that it was the beginning of something. It is also typed out and dated, and as Booth has argued, this 'indicates that Larkin regarded it at the time as a significant start in his writing'.[19] Moreover, both David (in 'Story I') and Peter have ambitions to be writers, and both are very much aware of their literary ancestors: 'David liked Oxford, privately. It pleased him to think that so many people had walked as he was doing down this very street, who had later become famous by their writing: Shelley and W. H. Auden, Matthew Arnold, Gerard Manley Hopkins, Compton Mackenzie and all the rest.'[20]

Chapter 6 discusses Larkin's unsuccessful attempts in his early poetry to live up to a poetic identity modelled on Yeats. The same problem hinders his early fiction, but the identity being imitated is that of an upper-middle-class homosexual novelist. Because of this, the stories reveal interesting tensions between the kind of work Larkin was trying to write and the kind of work he would go on to write with greater success. His ability, for instance, to mimic the effete speech of Isherwood's characters is impressive and amusing, but not authentic: 'My dear fellow, I am very strongly in favour of the Boy Scout movement and give it all my immoral support.'²¹ Part of the problem is that Larkin and his gang were largely of the grammar school class, and therefore socially and culturally distinct from those who attended (in)famous English public schools like Repton and Rugby. Peter recognizes this, comparing his boarding school peers 'who had only had homosexual experiences' with himself and Edwin, grammar school boys and 'completely virgin', who 'felt very keenly their lack of social background'.²² As a result, there is something forced about these characters' ostensible homosexuality. This, too, is acknowledged by Peter:

> Peter imagined that with the possible exception of Geoffrey, the rest did not feel anything towards the society except a mild team-spirit. For himself at any rate it was an attempted expression of solidarity, of a cell of resistance against a college of intellectuals and stupid scholars. He felt that alone in his circle there was a gay spirit that he felt essential to his happiness. He felt that there existed an awareness of an indescribable portion of human life that he thought most important: a kind of regard for each other as humans and not as abstractions or purveyors of ideas. It was this awareness that was jokingly and half-ashamedly concealed under a common cloak of homosexuality cultivated by Edwin and Peter as a badge of unconventionality against the rest of the college, whom, they hoped, regarded them with shocked envy.²³

It is difficult to read these stories as outlets for repressed homosexual feeling, and not as anything other than a reflection of The Seven's anti-authoritarian stance – a pose 'cultivated . . . as a badge of unconventionality'.

This perhaps explains the melodramatic immaturity of some of Larkin's characterizations. In 'Story I', an inebriated Patrick Rush leaves a Bacchic student party, staggering through the 'utter blackness' of wartime Oxford:

> Quite naturally he began to cry, shedding tears of absolute shame as he recalled the evening and his actions, the loathsome rapid servility of his hands to execute the vapid mirages of mind. Hands swam before his eyes, grasping, touching, manipulating, cleverly overcoming obstacles so that the mind could gratify its absurd beliefs, half-desires, and hallucinations, conspiring like vicious and unimaginative courtiers to burden further the patient and ox-like peasantry of the body. . . . Horror, Horror. . . . He was foul. Foul. Foul.²⁴

The language is excessively baroque, and the echo of Kurtz in *Heart of Darkness* (1899) tips the passage into the ridiculous – Booth asks whether 'Larkin himself [was] perhaps drunk when he wrote this comic sub-Lawrentian farrago?'²⁵ But we might explain the poorly judged tone as a consequence of the mismatch between the identity Larkin wanted to adopt and the very different social circumstances in which he actually existed.

The theme of homosexuality, however, does have greater success when it comes to stand for the policing and precariousness of identity more generally. Homosexuality in these stories is framed by two important contexts: a legally heteronormative society, and a war threatening conscription or bombing. The main characters – all young men – cannot be anything but aware of this backdrop. In 'Story I', for example, David thinks he will be lucky to 'get in a year' at Oxford, 'if they don't start calling up the nineteens'; with military service 'like a blank wall before him, any sort of purpose in life seemed senseless'.[26] Towards the end of the story, he is woken from his drunken stupor by an air raid warning, and momentarily hopes for a 'good bomb' to put an end to it all.[27] It would logically follow, then, that characters might afford themselves some illicit end-of-the-world pleasure, sexual or otherwise; but war is a time for social norms to be reaffirmed. The Oxford of these stories never neglects to remind characters of its heteronormative expectations. When Patrick Rush departs after a particularly flamboyant conversation with his roommates, David and Christopher, the latter shows his homophobic relief and irritation: 'Does he act the pansy because he can't help it or because he thinks it's clever?'[28] Later, Christopher unenthusiastically leafs through 'the latest copy of *Men Only* . . . half-heartedly look[ing] at the nudes in it'.[29] Drunken brawls between men are common, and the vaguely menacing noise of masculine laughter from nearby college rooms is a recurring motif in both stories – usually at pivotal psychological moments for the characters.

Indeed, Larkin is much better at writing about delicate, potentially embarrassing and risky homosexual insinuations – what the narrator of 'Story I' calls 'hereditary implications and taboos' in the 'air' – than he is about self-loathing.[30] When Patrick Rush invites a fellow undergraduate to his rooms for coffee and biscuits (the man remains nameless throughout – a subtle means of signalling secrecy and shame), Larkin's prose shows greater sophistication in its attention to minute details as revelations of psychology:

'Do help yourself.'

His friend politely took a plainish one. Rush to liberate his next choice, took the second-best one on the plate – ornate, and with a candied fruit on it. He enjoyed eating it, but kept carefully one bite behind the other. Sipped his coffee, but always to an equal distance down the cup: sometimes lifted the cup without drinking.[31]

After the man leaves, Rush realizes 'he was sweating. Under the arms his shirt was coldly wet, and felt horrid. He walked over to the fire, and noticed the other had left nearly half a cup of coffee, on the arm of the sofa. He picked it up and drank it, putting his mouth where the other's had been. It was almost cold'.[32] Interestingly, in *Jill* (discussed in Chapter 5), John Kemp does the same with Gillian's cup. But in *Jill*, the homosexual element is absent; the fact that Larkin recycles this intensely intimate moment suggests that homosexuality in these stories provides a means of exploring more universal emotions of shyness and awkwardness rather than homosexuality per se. Many readers will be tempted to read the shift as evidence of Larkin's own transition from homosexual to heterosexual impulses. But his fictional works of the 1940s explore a wide taxonomy of different desires: repressed male-homosexual (the short stories), repressed female-homosexual (Brunette Coleman's writings), shy male-heterosexuality (*Jill*), harassed female-heterosexuality (*A Girl in Winter*). What all of these have in common is a general sense of awkward difference, arguably a more significant concern than Larkin's own sexuality, whatever that may have been.

This would certainly explain why Larkin cannot pull off the upper-middle-class camp of the Isherwood he admires and imitates, but can indeed write with great acuity about a more general condition of otherness. That Larkin also recycles other aspects of these stories further suggests that he was working up to something bigger than his own sexual revelation. In 'Story I', we learn from a stashed letter that Patrick has a stepsister: 'Of course, there were great jokes at school about the sister with a different name from mine', he says.[33] Not only does this once again evoke the period's social conservatism, it also shows Larkin entering new territory: Rush's family situation does not feature again in the story, but an epistolary stepsister does reappear in a much more significant way in *Jill*. Perhaps this, too, was a lesson in authorship learned from Isherwood, whose most famous character, Sally Bowles in *Goodbye to Berlin*, was first devised in an earlier, shorter work. More importantly, it again suggests literary development rather than sexual.

'Story I' differs from 'Peter' and its Isherwood intertext by exploring multiple points of view: David, Patrick and Christopher each get their own turns as the story's centre of consciousness. Whereas 'Maurice' and 'The Eagles Are Gone' explored the possibilities of character from the point of view of a singular first-person narrator, 'Story I' rotates this privilege. This means that other characters are permitted to be interesting in their own right, not simply in a way that is defined by the narrator. This too shows Larkin moving closer to an 'interest in everything outside himself', as suggested by the end of 'The Eagles Are Gone'. And it is an important move for his subsequent work: as will be seen, Brunette Coleman represents a sustained attempt to write from a perspective very much 'outside himself', and the two published novels are essentially studies in perspective. Many of Larkin's great poems, too, explore the experiences and emotions of others: 'Wedding-Wind', 'Deceptions', 'Mr Bleaney', 'Afternoons', 'The Explosion' and so on. Even the first-person lyrics readers have typically associated with Larkin himself tend to contain a kind of in-built dialectic which guards against solipsism: 'and both are satisfied, / If no one has misjudged himself. Or lied'; 'Struck, I leant / More promptly out next time, more curiously, / And saw it all again in different terms'; 'Or I suppose I can' (*TCP*, 30, 56–8, 58–9).

'Story I', therefore, warrants its numerical title because it is very much a transitional piece. Admittedly 'Peter', which Booth suggests may postdate 'Story I' 'by three months or so', returns to a single centre of consciousness.[34] But Larkin cannot seem to stop the narrative attention from wandering. Sitting in Hall, Peter finds himself wondering 'once again what [the servants] thought of the college, and in particular of his special circle of friends'.[35] There is also a degree of the self-reflexivity of 'The Eagles Are Gone': discussing a mutual friend with Edwin, Peter says, 'I like him all right. I don't think he means much to me, though', and is gently lambasted by Edwin: '"You're a silly shit. Can't you see him apart from yourself?" This was acute. Peter was slightly nettled'.[36]

Interactions like these reveal a significant tension in the stories: Larkin seems caught between writing about himself – and in doing so presenting himself in an artificial way – and being carried off in new directions. The end of 'Story I' demonstrates why this is a problem: David, standing on the college tower for fire-watching duties, considers jumping off; once again, the prose is immature and overly melodramatic: 'David sighed as he remembered all the everyday worries and nuisances to which he had now returned – to English Literature, to Elizabeth, to the Army and all the rest of it.' In the end, he loses his resolve: 'After all, he was only nineteen: in the next five years there would be more changes than he could possibly conceive. He would have to wait, and in the meantime not bother. "But if only I knew!" he thought impatiently'.[37] This reads like a teenager's diary. The reasons for David's suicidal thoughts seem largely inconsequential; having to complete an English Literature degree may be a nuisance, but it is hardly the stuff of great fiction.

This is Larkin's bind: to make himself appear more interesting, he portrays himself as a latter-day Isherwood; but in making himself the subject of his fiction, as Isherwood did, he is necessarily limited to writing about some pretty uninteresting and commonplace adolescent grumbles and anxieties. One passage in 'Peter' illuminates the point: when the protagonist attends a talk at the Literary Club, Larkin makes sure to achieve verisimilitude based on his own experience:

> Before I introduce you to the speaker tonight, I should like to ask all college secretaries to return all cards they have *not* sold to the treasurer as soon as they can, as there is still a great demand for membership and we're sure they haven't all yet been disposed of. So if you *have* any spare cards you haven't sold, could you let us have them as soon as possible.[38]

As Treasurer of the English Club, Larkin obviously knew its administrative workings – but this level of detail seems superfluous. Isherwood, in his preface to *Lions and Shadows*, explained that he has had to 'dramatize it, or you would not get farther than the first page'. But as these examples from 'Story I' and 'Peter' show, Larkin's primary material – his life at university – was not really interesting enough to benefit from the magic dust of dramatization. He was guilty of putting the cart before the horse: writing fiction about the life before the life demanded fiction to be written about it.

By this point in 'Peter', Larkin seems to have abandoned the idea of writing a good story, and instead uses it as another opportunity to be self-reflexive. The talk at the Literary Club is given by Mervyn Rimer, a conceited young poet who speaks in a pompous drawl – 'No age – except possiblah our own – has been without its great mastahs of the art of poetry . . .' – and closes 'with a vague oratorical appeal for a religious revival'.[39] Much like Larkin in his letters to Sutton, Peter knows that he is firmly opposed to such pretentious chatter, but also realizes that he has so far failed to offer anything better:

> He rarely specified his talents, even to himself; thinking vaguely of himself as 'a writer' he was alarmed to find on self-examination how flimsy his claims were to such a pretension. . . . He had few of the attributes of a successful writer: character interested him, but only as a means for purveying moral truth: he took no delight in it. He was incapable of inventing a plot – or indeed any situation that he had not himself personally experienced. . . . Altogether, he felt like a mule with a perverse and all-consuming desire to be a racehorse.[40]

If Larkin's 'transparently autobiographical' story suffers from being *too* personal, then at least his subsequent work would benefit from the honest auto-criticism he wrote here.[41] To his credit, Larkin accurately identifies some of the obstacles preventing his writing from developing into something more compelling, namely his lack of 'delight' in character, and his inability to devise a plot not based on personal experience. To look beyond one's personal experience does not necessarily mean writing books about dragons or alien invasions, but it does require recognition that it is hard to fashion great literature out of the melodramatic anxieties of a middle-class, nineteen-year-old Oxford undergraduate.

'An Incident in the English Camp'

Manifested within a number of these stories from the late 1930s and early 1940s, then, is a series of transitional tensions. That Larkin was able to recognize some of these afforded him the option of progressing – but how? The next two chapters answer that question by looking at the work he produced using the Brunette Coleman heteronym, but there is one story written in 1943 which allowed Coleman to emerge. This story appears to have been another conscious exercise as part of the 'writer's education'. Booth describes how the story seems

> to have been composed compulsively during the course of one day as a deliberate exercise, as if the author were setting himself a challenge. Larkin even calculated, as he went, exactly how many pencilled words would be needed to fill all the pages of the small lined notebook in which it is written. He missed one page in the middle, to which he returned for the final words of the story.[42]

In this sense, the story follows a pattern of behaviour also seen in the earlier pieces. But the results of this self-directed challenge are very different, and the story paves the way for a new approach to writing which, as will be seen, would ultimately lead to literary maturity and success. For the first time in Larkin's serious attempts at the short story form, the centre of consciousness is a woman. The setting is still 1940s varsity Oxford, but the male homosexual element no longer features. This does not mean, however, that the story is straightforwardly heterosexual. The work's full title is 'An Incident in the English Camp: A Thoroughly Unhealthy Story, by P. A. Larkin'. In it, Larkin adopts the genre of popular romantic fiction, but unleashes its kitsch potential to such an extent that it becomes parodic of that genre.

Returning to her college rooms from lunch, Pamela finds a male friend waiting for her: Robbie, previously a student at 'Judas College', now an officer in the British Army and currently on embarkation leave.⁴³ Pamela and her environment are described in typically feminine and domestic terms:

> Pamela glided swiftly along the passage and up the stairs to her little room, situated at the end of a wing, where the sun poured in from windows in two walls on her hearth rug, her books, the pussy willow catkins in her Poole vase, and her camouflaged divan-bed. And as she opened the heavy door, with her name slipped crookedly in the socket outside, the room burst upon her like a bomb of sunshine, streaming from the mirror and the backs of the hairbrush and handmirror on the dressing table.⁴⁴

Although some of the imagery ('camouflaged', 'bomb') draws the reader's attention to the war raging elsewhere, it also, as Booth points out, 'serve[s] merely to emphasize the innocuousness of the scene'.⁴⁵ Similarly, Robbie is a stock character straight out of the romantic fiction found in the period's women's magazines: plain but handsome, chivalrous, clean-living and utterly conservative. Surveying Pamela's room, he notices 'with some alarm a few new additions since he last inspected the shelf: *Fleurs du Mal*, by Charles Baudelaire. French, eh? He frowned.'⁴⁶ Later, he tells her

> of the study group he had organised on the British Empire, of lectures and manoeuvres, of a day's shooting he had got when stationed near a friend's estate, of the indescribable greatness of the Army, its intricacy, its formality, its luxuries and hardships, its traditions and innovations, and the strength which lay waiting in it like a coiled spring.⁴⁷

Robbie is, through and through, an officer and a son of the Empire.

The pair spend the day together: they play squash and enjoy afternoon tea and a show at the theatre before Robbie returns to the station. During this time, Pamela is shown to be a fantasist. Waiting on the platform, she imagines a marriage proposal: 'Supposing she drew his gloved hand from his pocket, and disclosed in the warm palm a shining ring! Her knees trembled at the thought.'⁴⁸ This is classic territory for the genre, of course, but much more intriguing is how her mind wandered during the show:

> As the curtain went up and the lights dimmed, she had found herself imagining a sunbaked Libyan plain, with a British gun crew frantically firing and reloading, led by a desperately handsome officer with a bloodstained bandage round his temples. Hear the whine of the approaching shell! A terrible explosion, clouds of smoke blocking the view. Gradually it clears! are they all dead? No! the officer rolls over with a moan of pain. Stay! What is this? A slim khaki figure is wriggling

swiftly over the sand, a red cross satchel on its back. Is it a drummer boy? Its cap is shot off by a bullet, the golden curls fall free – can it be – Pamela?[49]

This fantasy is soon dispelled by the show's 'vagaries of romantic passion', a stirring performance of 'There'll Always Be an England', and the rousing of the audience for the national anthem. In other words, a dose of solid English patriotism puts to bed the nonsense of her overactive brain. But the sense of something naughtier, something transgressively erotic and gender-bending, which pushes against the story's conformity, cannot be forgotten.

There is no sudden marriage proposal to end the story, but it does close with a *Brief Encounter*-style platform farewell (although the story predates the film by two years). Larkin's parodic intentions are revealed by the characters' dialogue and thoughts. Asked what he plans to do after the war, Robbie responds:

> 'You know I used to think I'd just fool around at Oxford a bit before going into the business. Well, I'm not so sure I want to, now. I feel more that I ought to go abroad somewhere and help keep the English tradition of fair ruling going. After all, that's what this war's for, to keep a bit of justice and freedom on the earth. Well, it's no good letting it slip once we've won, is it? Of course,' – he waved his hand – 'I don't say I shall come through this show: but if I do I'm jolly sure I want to keep England going *as England*, what she's been in the past and yet still keeping a firm hand on changing conditions. We've got to, you know.'[50]

Robbie's sense of English imperial exceptionalism is unironic, but articulated as it is in his upper-middle-class patter ('jolly sure'), the reader cannot share in it. When his train departs, Pamela's thoughts are similarly sincere but not credible:

> Pamela watched it go, without regret, almost with exaltation, for now she could face life alone again. She almost wished Robbie could be struck dead, his words would have been so beautiful, and then she could cherish his memory and live as he would have wished. She walked in exaltation through the black streets, her heart glowing like a coal with deep love.[51]

The story ends with her realization that she can truly understand 'the dying words of John of Gaunt' in Shakespeare's *Richard II*. Her thoughts, and Robbie's monologue, are so nauseatingly earnest and self-absorbed that they stretch and overcome the reader's capacity to take them seriously.

This is the 'Thoroughly Unhealthy' element signalled by Larkin's title. The story adopts many hallmarks of popular romantic fiction: purple prose; an unspoken but virtuous desire between a gallant man and a graceful woman; glorification of the Empire and the English way of life. But the authorial tone labours and finally mocks these aspects, and the text gestures towards something more subversive in Pamela's Libyan fantasy. This represents significant progress from Larkin's self-obsessed and unsuccessful Isherwoodian imitations of the past four or five years. In works like 'Story I' and 'Peter', he attempted to inhabit a style and a genre which, for various reasons, he could not make his own. Not only does 'An Incident in the English Camp' move Larkin away from the adolescent solipsism of male undergraduate protagonists, it also heralds a new approach to writing, for he both inhabits the language and conventions of a specific genre *and* pulls them apart from within, producing a work that is more transgressive, more original and more interesting. In 'An Incident in the English Camp', Larkin seems to have glimpsed, for the first time, the possibilities of textual drag. As will be seen in the next two chapters, this anticipates Brunette Coleman's work in a number of ways: the subversive power of books (Baudelaire); the internal pressures and slippages of otherwise po-faced prose (Pamela's fantasy); plots and characters largely unrelated to Larkin's own life; the subversion of gender and sexuality; and the exploitation of a kitsch, camp style. Indeed, it is possible that Larkin's title is a pun: the 'Incident' imagined by Pamela occurs in a military camp, but also (as does the wider story) in a kind of 'English Camp' style.

As Booth points out, the decision to name 'P. A. Larkin' as the author at least allows for the possibility that the author might be female (Pamela?).[52] Including this as part of the story's title ('by P. A. Larkin') certainly opens up some distance between the living, breathing Philip Larkin and the figure designated as the author. This again shows Larkin making a more serious attempt to explore 'everything outside himself'. He must have decided that the experiment in surrogate authorship should be taken further, since his next move was to invent a lesbian heteronym, Brunette Coleman. The following two chapters seek to demonstrate the revolutionary significance of that decision for Larkin's career.

3

Brunette Coleman

Experiments in genre

In 'An Incident in the English Camp', Larkin's early fiction experienced a series of breakthroughs. For the first time, he had written a story whose centre of consciousness was a woman; the story inhabits but then subversively disrupts a specific mode of genre fiction (popular romance); and there is a sense of self-conscious distancing between the author named in the title ('P. A. Larkin') and Larkin himself – indeed, the implied author could well be a woman. In other words, Larkin was beginning to experiment with authorial identities, with gender and with genre. From this experiment emerged the figure of Brunette Coleman, Larkin's lesbian heteronym.[1] This chapter looks at Coleman's interest in genre, and the ways in which it relates to her concern with gender. Chapter 4 then explores the treatment of gender and sexuality in Coleman's prose works. The most obvious novelty of these two chapters is that they elect to take seriously Coleman's work. The two lines of enquiry – genre and gender – are crucial in showing how Coleman first paved the way for Larkin's more serious, published fiction, explored in Chapter 5, and then for the poetry that would finally see his literary ambitions realized, the subject of Chapters 7 and 8.

Who is Brunette Coleman?

Brunette Coleman is the seemingly prolific English author of stories for schoolgirls. Larkin told Amis she was the 'sister' of Blanche Coleman, leader of one of the first all-women bands in the 1940s, and a 'natural ashblonde'.[2] Coleman is unmarried, and lives with her secretary, who assists her with churning out her books; she is intelligent, feisty and feminist, with a wry sense of humour. Terry Castle describes her as 'tweedy, bookish, and sentimental . . . and one of those mawkish middle-aged English lesbians whose imperfectly suppressed homosexuality is plain to everyone but themselves'.[3] As this implies, Coleman's sexuality is not necessarily explicit, and requires some teasing out by the reader. Writing to Amis in September 1943, Larkin told his friend that 'homosexuality has been completely replaced by lesbianism in my character at the moment – I don't know why'.[4] This was a reference to Coleman, whose lesbian-inflected works Larkin had started writing at Oxford several months earlier, as Finals loomed. He and Amis had already collaborated by correspondence on a number of comical pieces: according to Richard Bradford, in early 1942 they had co-produced what Amis would describe as 'obscene and soft-porn fairy stories', and Booth notes that Amis had invented a 'lesbian alter ego' of his own, Anna Lucasta, 'in parallel with Brunette'.[5]

There were a number of models – both immediate and literary – behind these experiments with alternative modes of authorship. Larkin's friend and fellow St John's undergraduate, Bruce Montgomery, had in the space of ten days during the 1943 Easter vacation written a detective novel, *The Case of the Gilded Fly*. This was published the following year under the pseudonym Edmund Crispin, and became a minor classic. As will be seen, Montgomery's success and personality mightily impressed Larkin. Larkin's own most recent authorial experiment, 'An Incident in the English Camp', had also suggested the potential of inhabiting an alternative writerly identity. As discussed in Chapters 1 and 2, he was also at this time a disciple of Isherwood, especially the thinly disguised autobiographical novel *Lions and Shadows*, recalling the author's collaboration with Edward Upward on a series of surreal stories set in the invented English village of Mortmere. As undergraduates at Cambridge, Isherwood and Upward had already invented a pair of heteronyms called Hynd and Starn – both pornographers – and it was from this that their Mortmere world emerged. As suggested in Chapter 2, Larkin was, during the late 1930s and early 1940s, busy acting out a fantasy of male homosociality and authorship modelled on the Isherwood-Upward-Auden group of the 1920s and 1930s. For reasons set out there, these writers would prove unhelpful to his literary development, but their impish example did stimulate an impulse which gave birth to Brunette Coleman. Katherine Bucknell has described Isherwood and Upward's Mortmere stories as

> an elaborate imaginative game played . . . when they were undergraduates at Cambridge in the 1920s. The stories and poems associated with the invented village of Mortmere are the product of a high-spirited, playful, and obsessively private adolescent friendship that lingered self-consciously in the nursery even

as Isherwood and Upward aspired to launch themselves as serious literary artists.[6]

Disregarding the specific details of names, times and places, this could be an exact description of the game played by Larkin and Amis as they developed their Brunette Coleman/Anna Lucasta characters, respectively. Though private and silly, Bucknell sees the significance of the Mortmere collaboration for Isherwood and Upward's development: 'the literary poise of the stories surpasses their schoolboy purpose, for the authors' intellectual and artistic development had evidently outstripped their emotional maturity.'[7] For Larkin and Amis, their inventions also began as immature fun but, in Larkin's case, ended up becoming something much more serious and consequential. With Amis and a number of other Oxford friends – Montgomery, Diana Gollancz (daughter of Montgomery's publisher, Victor Gollancz) and Miriam Plaut – Larkin shared not only the progress of Coleman's work but also extracts from it. His accounts of this in letters seem proud of the comedic effect: Montgomery and Gollancz would return from evenings in the pub to read Coleman's latest, and Larkin boasts in one letter that a particular scene gave the latter 'quite a "crisis de nerfs" or whatever the French is' (*SL*, 75). In other words, Larkin framed the Coleman heteronym as a joke, designed to tickle a small, like-minded coterie of student friends. But Coleman also stimulated his productivity and originality, and even after leaving Oxford Larkin continued to work on her output for several months.

There are five works by Brunette Coleman in the archive: a schoolgirl novella called *Trouble at Willow Gables*; its unfinished sequel, *Michaelmas Term at St Bride's*; an essay on the girls' school story genre, 'What Are We Writing For?'; a fragment of Coleman's autobiography, *Ante Meridian*; and a sheaf of poems, *Sugar and Spice*.[8] Bradford perceptively notes how these texts, written in different genres, work together to produce a single and coherent authorial identity: Larkin 'maintains throughout an authentic image of a particular woman adapting her own presence of mind to each', and the texts 'disclose via their various flaws and idiosyncrasies further dimensions of the character of Brunette'.[9] Something – though only something – of Larkin's motivation in producing these can be gleaned from assessing their physical forms. *Trouble at Willow Gables* exists as a stapled typescript, complete with title page, contents page and a list of 'Correct nomenclature'. The typescript is contained in a folder, on which the following ink stamp appears twice:

ROCHEFORT PRODUCTIONS
(LITERARY PROPERTY) LTD.

Intriguingly, this tells us that Larkin made at least one serious attempt to publish Coleman's work. Booth notes that the agency was associated with Victor Gollancz, and so it seems Larkin was trying to exploit his connection with the publisher's daughter.[10] The sequel, *Michaelmas Term at St Bride's*, exists mostly in manuscript form, although Larkin did begin to type it out. The work is unfinished, albeit with notes on how it should end; and the manuscript is interrupted on page sixty-three by the beginning of Coleman's autobiography, which is also incomplete. Coleman's essay, 'What Are We Writing For?', is another stapled typescript, and therefore a finished piece. *Sugar and Spice*, discussed in Chapter 6 in relation to Larkin's early poetry, is the most charming object in the Coleman archive. Larkin typed six poems, made three carbon copies and turned these into booklets – 'the most limited of editions', as Booth puts it – which he gave to Amis, Montgomery and Plaut.[11] Larkin's own copy, housed in the Hull archive, has a seventh poem loosely inserted. Improvised poetry collections were something of a hobby for the young Larkin: between 1939 and 1942, he made ten typescript collections of verse, giving them titles such as *Chosen Poems* and *Seven Poems*. As Burnett comments, 'the accoutrements of title pages and prefaces show the young Larkin fantasising about being a published writer' (*TCP*, xxi). What marks out *Sugar and Spice* is the delight it takes in its feminine presentation. The cover is fashioned from black paper, with the title written in a self-consciously girlish cursive hand.

A few weeks before his death in 1985, a letter from Plaut offering to return her copy of *Sugar and Spice* prompted a sentimental reply from Larkin: 'I haven't seen Sugar and Spice for years. If you can bear to part with it, I should love to have it.'[12] But even as he worked on them during 1943, Larkin felt coyly protective about Coleman's works. Telling Amis about *Trouble at Willow Gables*, he wrote, 'Please don't ask me to send it, because I simply daren't let it out of my sight, it's too valuable and incriminating' (*SL*, 75). And Larkin was thrilled by the positive feedback – often genuine – which Coleman's work received: 'One can tell in 2 seconds if one likes a poem or not. I sent a set to Bruce and he likes them a lot: the last one, he says, is the best'; 'I am glad you liked Brunette's poems' (*SL*, 66, 70). Booth is right in considering it 'unfortunate that discussion of the Brunette phase of Larkin's writing has been so much coloured by Kingsley Amis's account of it' (*TWG*, ix). Though Amis had, through Anna Lucasta, engaged in the same activity, his motivation for doing so was not quite the same as Larkin's, and Larkin presumably had to ramp up the comedic, laddish and pornographic value of Coleman's work in order to justify its sustained claim on his time and attention. Clearly, something about Brunette Coleman sufficiently absorbed

Larkin to keep her work going well after their initial, or ostensible function had been served. Chapter 4 explains why the *oeuvre* was eventually abandoned, and subsequent chapters discuss its importance for Larkin's literary development. But the present and following chapters also attempt an experiment of their own: to see what happens if these works are taken more seriously than their framing as an undergraduate joke encourages.

Coleman's critical reception

Such an approach goes largely against the grain of the immediate critical response to their posthumous publication and the modest amount of scholarly attention they have attracted since. When an edition of Coleman's work appeared in 2002, the reaction was largely one of bemusement, even irritation. For Jenny Diski, reading Coleman's writings was 'up there with stuffing mushrooms', an activity which suddenly prompts a 'blinding awareness of the precious hours wasted on Larkin's schoolgirl stories when I might have done something more positive with them such as sleeping or filing my nails'.[13] The headline of Jonathan Bate's review described them as 'Very juvenile, this juvenilia'.[14] The assistant librarian responsible for cataloguing them at Hull's Brynmor Jones Library had already likened them to 'the jokers in a pack of cards', and Richard Palmer gave them no time at all, dismissing them as 'prolix arch nonsense'.[15]

Although Larkin made a few brief references to the Brunette Coleman works in later life (he mentions writing 'an unclassifiable story called *Trouble at Willow Gables*' in his introduction to *Jill*), it was Motion who first brought them to wider public attention (*RW*, 24). In his 1993 biography, he claimed that 'They drove [Larkin] to write more fluently than he had ever done before':

> Within a matter of months he had produced two novels (one of 143 typed pages called *Trouble at Willow Gables* and one of exactly the same number of handwritten pages called *Michaelmas Term at St Bride's*), a 'sheaf' of six poems (*Sugar and Spice*), and a fragment of autobiography. All were finished by the following October [1943], and all written under the pseudonym Brunette Coleman.[16]

Summarizing these works, he describes their diet of 'eroticism', 'voyeurism, sado-masochism, and a pleasure in taking advantage of those who ... cannot easily defend themselves'.[17] A few pages later, Motion also introduces Coleman's essay on the schoolgirl story genre, 'What Are We Writing For?'[18] He describes these works as 'facetious', but goes on to argue that 'facetiousness is also a kind of unguardedness. By turns comic and silly, they allow us to see some aspects of Larkin's mind that he normally kept hidden, and others that he didn't know existed'.[19] These hidden corners of Larkin's mind are, for Motion, psycho-sexual. Seizing on a handful of vague references and Chinese whispers regarding Larkin's apparently nascent homosexuality, Motion constructs the Coleman writings as an unconscious attempt to work through feelings of guilt and repulsion, and to settle the matter of his sexuality: 'With Brunette shielding him and guiding his hand, he could see that his attraction to men was a thing of the past, and that his attraction to women was sincere but severely complicated.'[20]

It took years for the Coleman works to be digested, largely because Booth's edition did not appear for another decade, but Motion's account has set the tone for subsequent discussion. Psychoanalysis has offered the most obvious way in: Larkin was a young undergraduate, with a burgeoning but frustrated sexual consciousness, and the works do contain sexual undertones. Critics like M. W. Rowe and Jin-Sung Choi have produced psycho-sexual profiles of Larkin, presenting him as a pervert and a sexual narcissist, a messed-up child ('They fuck you up, your mum and dad') and a defensive homosexual who therapeutically wrote himself straight (without, it must be said, much explanation of how exactly this works) (*TCP*, 88).[21] But there are problems with such an approach. One of the most inconvenient facts about the unconscious is that it is *unconscious*; even if one accepts the view of professional psychoanalysts that the unconscious produces symptoms, it is surely a little disquieting to think that people with a training in literature should be the ones to pick their way through it. There is also the basic problem of evidence, or lack thereof, for such claims. Scrutinizing the relevant passages of Motion's biography, it becomes clear that his initial account of Larkin's temporary homosexuality relies too heavily on a small number of imprecise sources, such as Philip Brown's slightly embarrassed, slightly defensive perception that Larkin once had a crush on him ('Philip may have been in love with me. . . . I was very keen on a medical girl student, as it happens. But there were a few messy encounters between us, yes. Nothing much.').[22] If only for ethical reasons, critics should avoid making such fundamental pronouncements about a deceased author's identity without firmer evidence; in any case, the question of the young Larkin's sexuality is irrelevant to this chapter's findings.

Some contributions have been more helpful. Booth, whose exemplary editorial scholarship brought these works to publication, has attempted to lend more credence to their literary aspects than their pseudo-psychological ones. He importantly debunks the notion that these are particularly erotic works –

they 'will give thin satisfaction to a reader in search of explicit pornography or sadism', he has written – and has similarly cut through the 'coarse masculine nonchalance' of Larkin's letters to Amis, his literary co-conspirator, affected to 'dispel the embarrassment he feels at having spent so much energy on the *genre*' (*TWG*, xvi, xiii). For Booth, Larkin's

> mixture of dissatisfactions [with the genre] is very revealing. He deplores the shortage of lesbianism but he is just as impatient with purely literary faults: tedious style and lack of humour. The two novels he singles out for approval reinforce this duality. Vicary's [*Niece of the Headmistress*] does indeed have an unusually legible erotic subtext, but Breary's [*Two Thrilling Terms*] is sexually innocuous, being distinguished from similar stories by its sophisticated farce and irony. (*TWG*, xiii–xiv)

Booth perceptively identifies Coleman's essay, 'What Are We Writing For?', as 'Larkin's own key' to the works, pointing out that 'Were it not for his careful preservation of this essay we would be unaware how well-read in girls' fiction Larkin was' (*TWG*, xii). More recently, in his 2014 biography, Booth has described the works as an 'affectionate homage' to the genre, and tentatively suggested that they may be read as *écriture féminine*.[23] All of this is welcome, but Booth is also guilty of second-guessing Larkin's psychological state, telling the *Telegraph*, for instance, that Larkin was 'trying to be a girl in his Brunette Coleman stage. He feminises himself . . . as a kind of strategy because he felt no guilt about not being called up for the war'.[24] The same tendency to fall back on psychological speculation blights the otherwise intriguing accounts by Stephen Cooper and Terry Castle. Cooper describes Coleman's stories as 'a thoughtful probing of conventional opinion on matters such as authority, gender and moral judgement', but also endorses the clichéd orthodoxy that they answered 'a sexual and psychological need'.[25] Castle, an expert on the Western lesbian canon, challenges critics' conflation of male and female homosexuality, and questions the 'cursory and cartoonish' narrative of Larkin's sexual development, which she summarizes with brevity and wit: 'After "Normal" Schoolboy Crushes British Male Writer Goes Straight and Stays Straight (More or Less)'.[26] Instead, she adds Larkin's name to a list of celebrities 'whose sexual proclivities I myself find *inexpressible*', including Virginia Woolf, Greta Garbo, Marlon Brando, and Andy Warhol.[27] This is an intriguing thought, but what about Coleman's role in Larkin's *literary* development? After all, Larkin's writing is the only reason audiences know him well enough to want to speculate about his sexuality. It is a shame, therefore, that Castle's otherwise brilliant essay also resorts to the usual amateur psychology: Larkin, whom she calls a 'peculiar wanker', used these works to '[plumb] his own well of loneliness'; Castle's essay ends with a rather bizarre discussion of whether or not Larkin was 'made for sex'.[28]

There is little doubt that speculating about Larkin's sexuality has a greater magnetism than close reading. This chapter steers clear of the Sirens of psychoanalysis, not just because of the methodological issues already identified, but also because, read together as a package, these works coherently interrogate genre and gender far more than they peddle pornography. To see these aspects as being of secondary importance, or to ignore them altogether, is to miss a crucial stage in Larkin's development as a writer.

'Why are these books so bad?'

The epigraph Coleman chooses for her essay on the genre cites Catherine Durning Whetham's parenting manual, *The Upbringing of Daughters* (1917): 'The chief justification of reading books of any sort is the enlargement of experience that should accrue therefrom' (*TWG*, 253). Books – reading them, discussing them, buying them and hiding them – represent one of the major motifs of the Coleman *oeuvre*. In *Trouble at Willow Gables*, Marie finds herself furiously plotting revenge against the headmistress as she reads *The Merchant of Venice* (*TWG*, 16). In the follow-up novella, *Michaelmas Term at St Bride's*, she purchases a copy of *Lady Chatterley's Lover* 'during a delirious afternoon in Blackwell's' (*TWG*, 141). Hilary, an important character in both novellas, has a second bookshelf in her room at Willow Gables – 'In addition to the regulation bookcase' – and the narrator takes the time to *précis* its contents:

> As well as her school text-books, she possessed many shelves of well-known and classical authors, and had a whole bottom shelf devoted, curiously enough, to popular school-stories for girls, and other, less innocent, productions, often with heavy binding concealing their original continental paper covers. (*TWG*, 16)

One book to which Hilary feels a particularly strong attachment is *Mademoiselle de Maupin*, Théophile Gautier's scandalous 1835 novel. Each of these instances of books-as-rebellion should be sufficient to suggest a wider connection between reading, writing and subversion.

Booth describes Coleman's essay, 'What Are We Writing For?', as 'Larkin's own key' to the *oeuvre*; rightly so, because the essay is also explicitly concerned with the reading and writing of books. The key to the key comes right at the start: Jacinth, Coleman's secretary, mentions over breakfast that she has been reading 'a very interesting essay' by George Orwell on boys' stories, and suggests that Coleman should write her own version on the girls' genre (*TWG*, 255). Coleman's first instinct is to dismiss both Orwell and Jacinth:

> Now, Jacinth, you know I don't like you to read in bed when you ought to be getting your beauty sleep. And in any case, what do I know about girls' stories? Don't splutter in your coffee like that – it's very bad manners. I mean, this Mr Orwell or whatever his name is probably spent two months or more in the British Museum reading up all the stuff – back numbers and obsolete works and so forth. I haven't time to do that – you know we're due to start on *Wenda's Worst Term* this morning. (*TWG*, 255)

The tone is both modest and patronizing, but even by this third paragraph we can recognize Coleman's tongue-in-cheek style: her mild rebuke comes immediately after she has noted what a 'very clever and widely-read girl' Jacinth is, Coleman having found her 'through the Oxford University Appointments Committee' (*TWG*, 255). Although insincere, Coleman's response is telling: unlike 'Mr Orwell or whatever his name is', she does not have the time or resources to conduct research: as a single woman (who would be denied access to many professions), financial necessity implores her to keep churning out books. There is a whiff of Woolf's *A Room of One's Own* (1929) in this passage about the economics of women's writing, and it is precisely Coleman's individual brand of feminism which I want to excavate here.

In fact, Coleman does spend time after breakfast mulling over Jacinth's suggestion, confessing to the reader that she is 'too familiar with Mr Orwell, and others of his kidney' to pay 'any attention to their ephemeral chatter' – another early sign that she is far more intelligent than she cares to show (*TWG*, 256). Perusing her shelves – clearly important markers of identity for Coleman – full of 'books for and about girls', she wonders 'Why are these books so bad?' (*TWG*, 256). What follows is her attempt to answer that question; in the process, Coleman produces an essay similar, in many respects, to Orwell's. If we pay close attention to it, and take seriously its literary and gender politics, it is possible to uncover a hinterland of reading and thinking on the subject of genre – generally, and specifically in relation to the girls' school story. In this essay, Coleman expresses some remarkably progressive ideas which get to the heart of contemporary literary debates and anticipate later feminist attitudes to women's experience and women's writing. By teasing out these values, and considering the issue of genre as it bleeds into the issue of gender, we can see the foundations of Larkin's own literary future being laid.

Connolly and Orwell

I have called Orwell's essay the key to the key, because we can better understand Coleman's project by considering Orwell's own. 'Boys' Weeklies' was published in an early issue of Cyril Connolly's *Horizon* magazine, and its publication history is important: *Horizon* had been founded during the first months of the Second World War, with the explicit aim of unabashedly sustaining cultural continuity at precisely the moment when culture was being so violently contested. 'At the moment civilization is on the operating table and we sit in the waiting room', Connolly wrote in his inaugural editorial; 'Our standards are aesthetic, and our politics are in abeyance'.[29] At the outset, then, Connolly announced his magazine's art-for-art's-sake ethos. Of course, set against the backdrop of a world war, such a stance was political: to privilege aesthetics in a time of conflict is to think about the sort of culture and society one wants to exist at the end of that conflict. 'Boys' Weeklies' was not the de-politicized, aesthetically charged writing Connolly had in mind, but its publication was evidence of Connolly's willingness – eagerness, even – to include the kind of ideological writing which made his own literary temperament shudder. This was one means of enacting the democracy being fought for across the globe.

Connolly is another important figure in Larkin's literary development. Like Larkin, he was born in Coventry and educated at Oxford. According to Motion, the Bodleian's daybooks 'show that of the fifty-one entries relating to Larkin during his time as an undergraduate, the majority have nothing to do with his tutorials' – a number of them being books by Connolly. 'Larkin later admitted that he spent most of his time straying from the path [his tutor] intended him to follow', Motion writes.[30] Once again, books are tools of subversion and rebellion. *Enemies of Promise*, Connolly's 1938 tract on the making of a good book, includes an autobiographical sketch of the author's youth, and would have greatly interested the young Larkin, who would almost certainly have read it by 1943. Years later, at a memorial service for Auden in 1973, Larkin apparently blurted to Connolly, 'Sir, you formed me!'[31] *Horizon*, then, would have been a project close to Larkin's own heart, particularly given his own sitting-out of the war, and one can easily imagine him absorbed by Orwell's take on the boys' stories he had devoured as a child, eventually feeding this into Coleman's essay during his final months at Oxford.

Orwell's essay considers the abiding fascination and shortcomings of the popular boys' school story genre. A major failure is that the stories are 'fantastically unlike life at a real public school' (he would know). The boys are almost exclusively 'the clean-fun, knock-about type', '"good" in the clean-living Englishman tradition'. The stock horde of '"bad" boys' are not that bad: 'no one is ever caught out in any really serious offence' – no stealing, for instance, whilst drinking and smoking are regarded as 'disgraceful'. Most interesting for Coleman would be Orwell's observation that 'Sex is completely taboo'. He considers it 'probable that there was a deliberate intention to get away from the guilty sex-ridden atmosphere that pervaded so much of the earlier literature for boys', since works like *Tom Brown's School Days* were 'heavy with homosexual feeling, though no doubt the authors were not fully aware of it'.[32] Orwell cannot accept that all this good, clean fun is coincidental or simply naïve. Characteristically, he sees a pernicious political ideology at work: 'Naturally the politics of the *Gem* and *Magnet* are Conservative, but in a completely pre-1914 style, with no Fascist tinge', he writes. 'In reality their basic political assumptions are two: nothing ever changes, and foreigners are funny'; he goes on to describe how working-class characters only ever appear as comical or villainous, whilst foreigners are equally ludicrous.[33] This is no laughing matter:

> It is probable that many people who would consider themselves extremely sophisticated and 'advanced' are actually carrying through life an imaginative background which they acquired in childhood from (for instance) Sapper and Ian Hay. If that is so, the boys' twopenny weeklies are of the deepest importance. Here is the stuff that is read somewhere between the ages of twelve and eighteen by a very large proportion, perhaps an actual majority, of English boys, including many who will never read anything else except newspapers; and along with it they are absorbing a set of beliefs which would be regarded as hopelessly out of date in the Central Office of the Conservative Party. All the better because it is done indirectly, there is being pumped into them the conviction that the major problems of our time do not exist, that there is nothing wrong with *laissez-faire* capitalism, that foreigners are unimportant comics and that the British Empire is a sort of charity-concern which will last forever. Considering who owns these papers, it is difficult to believe that this is unintentional.... The *Gem* and *Magnet* ... are closely linked up with the *Daily Telegraph* and the *Financial Times*. This in itself would be enough to rouse certain suspicions, even if it were not obvious that the stories in the boys' weeklies are politically vetted.[34]

In short, Orwell's problem with this genre is not just that it is unrealistic; much worse, it is deliberately, ideologically, unrealistic.

Larkin, who read weeklies like these as a schoolboy, and even produced his own versions, must have read Orwell's analysis with great interest.[35] Orwell's essay asks 'why is there no such thing as a left-wing boys' paper'; it is significant that

Larkin does not respond with the kind of socialist alternative Orwell craves, but chooses instead, via Coleman, to write in the *girls'* genre.[36] In doing so, Coleman bypasses those hidden and pernicious ideological manipulations which Orwell critiques (which is not to say, of course, that her work is ideology-free; merely that it avoids the specific ideological universe described in 'Boys' Weeklies'). This may be one reason why Larkin chose a female heteronym: as Booth argues of girls' school stories, 'They generate little sense that the British Empire was won on the playing-fields of Roedean or Wycombe Abbey', and therefore provide a foil to the boys' genre scrutinized by Orwell (*TWG*, xii). Before exploring Coleman's intervention in the politics of gender and sex, then, it is necessary to explore her literary politics, as set out in 'What Are We Writing For?'

We have already seen Coleman place her cards on the table: she is a popular writer, producing books for a wide audience, that is, girls, in order to make a living. This is in contrast to the kind of work promoted by Connolly: more intellectually and aesthetically ambitious, but with narrower appeal in terms of audience, and therefore a significantly reduced financial return. This dichotomy, however, becomes much less stark in her work. Though Coleman protests that she must crack on with *Wenda's Worst Term*, it is surely significant that she does not do so, choosing to pause work on her latest potboiler in order to contemplate the state of the genre, and eventually issue a literary call to arms. Her actual reason for dismissing Orwell and 'others of his kidney' is her common-sense mentality, which renders it

> a self-evident fact that Art cannot be explained away – or even explained – by foreign policy or trade cycles or youthful traumas, and that these disappointed artists whose soured creative instinct finds an outlet in insisting that it can are better ignored until Time has smoothed away all that they have scribbled on the sand. (*TWG*, 256)

Even if Orwell could have his way, and get British boys reading stories about workers' unity and Empire brutalities, Time would soon see to this, for that is not what Art is for. On the other hand, Coleman seems comfortable with the ephemerality of literature. But is there any reason why an ephemeral work cannot be a good one?

The 'Ideal Book'

After all, even Connolly in *Enemies of Promise* could only attribute a figure of ten years to a great book's longevity. Over the next few pages, Coleman produces a dossier of the girls' genre's failings, some of which align with Orwell's equivalents. Underpinning them all is what she calls 'market-writing': the deliberate dumbing-down of literature for a young audience. Citing Samuel Johnson's childhood reading habits, Coleman administers another dose of her trademark common sense: 'If a child of reasonable intelligence has nothing but Shakespeare to read, it will read Shakespeare – and will benefit, I venture to say, far more than if its parents had supplied it with books from the Christmas catalogues – "suitable for 8-10 years", "girls, aged 14–15"' (*TWG*, 257). This market-driven atomization of children's and young adult literature is still a feature of book retail.

For Coleman, market-writing is responsible for all kinds of flaws in the genre: she criticizes the exclusively virtuous nature of its heroines; the neglect of minor characters; the incursion of other spaces outside the 'private world' of the school; the moralizing, instructional nature of many books; the over-reliance on realism; and the cheap psychoanalysis (*TWG*, 256–7). As she works through each problem, she displays an impressive array of reading and thinking: the essay tours Shakespeare, Milton and the Old Testament. In one intriguing section, she applies Aristotle's theory of 'the Classical Unities' to the genre (*TWG*, 269). She also has a wide frame of reference within the genre. Bradford notes the essay's erudition, speculating that 'If *Essays in Criticism* had been founded in 1940 this paper might well have been taken seriously by its editor F. W. Bateson'.[37] One thing which those who so quickly dismiss Brunette Coleman must account for is precisely *why* Larkin himself read so widely and so critically within the genre of the girls' school story.

Perhaps the essay once again provides the key: 'I have learnt as time goes on to be more tolerant and open-minded on questions of literature . . . . [T]here are many mansions in the house of literature, and . . . the small half-acre of the human spirit I have chosen as my special province deserves as much respect as any' (*TWG*, 263). Coleman's attitude to literature is fundamentally democratic: she feels no contempt for common readers consuming common subjects. In her vocabulary, 'popular' is not a dirty word. At this point, the charge that this is the butt of a Larkin-Amis joke might be made again. But it seems like an odd joke, given the importance of the demotic and the democratic for Larkin's mature poetry, which manifests itself in various ways: the incorporation of everyday speech ('Get stewed'); popular culture (Westerns, photograph albums); ordinary people and their lives ('uncles shouting smut'); not to mention the popularity of that poetry, something Larkin cherished. Larkin's literary constitution was not one that could support the writing of an epic like *Paradise Lost*, the historically charged poetry of Geoffrey Hill, or the deep mythologies of Ted Hughes.

With only a few exceptions, his enduring subject was the lives, emotions and experiences of 'ordinary' people (Coleman's girls, of course, attend public school, and are therefore more privileged than most; but it is fair to say that schoolgirls have not figured prominently in the literary canon). The fact that Coleman shares this value does not make for a particularly hilarious joke.

Coleman's attitude to literature leads her to issue a call to arms, addressed to her sisterhood of fellow genre writers; but first she must pre-empt their inevitable protestations:

> But I hear an objection, the voice of any one of the authors I have named in this short essay. . . . 'We are not Shakespeare or Milton, we are not dealing with the Unities or any other scholastic claptrap, we are hack writers, yes, even the best of us, even you, and we are dependent upon the markets we supply.' (*TWG*, 270)

But Coleman is a woman with vision:

> To which I reply: Yes, I know it. I know that when I've finished *Wenda's Worst Term*, I shall start *Madcap Mona*; and I know too that in all these books I shall be forced to disregard my own rules because of the simple necessities you mention. But nevertheless, I think there is one book that still remains to be written, a book to end all books. . . . But this is merely shooting in the dark. It is not me, in all probability, who will discover it, not me upon whom the task will fall to reveal the statue already potential in the rock. The point is, that the book remains to be written, in which, once and for all, what we are writing for will be fully expressed, fully realised in all its beauty and exciting charm. When that has happened, we can relax: the ideal will be achieved: we can write as badly as we choose. But in the meantime, in every book we produce, we must make an effort to do better. Every story must add just a little to the progress made towards the Ideal Book, until suddenly, one day, one of us will say to herself with a quiet thrill: It's happening. This is the real thing. (*TWG*, 271–3)

Here, Connolly's influence can be detected again, for *Enemies of Promise* was 'a didactic inquiry into the problem of how to write a book which lasts ten years', just as Coleman has written an essay exploring the possibility of the 'Ideal Book'.[38] Indeed, her first-person polemic, which praises and dismisses various literary predecessors in order to arrive at that hypothetical Ideal, seems just as indebted to Connolly's book as it is to Orwell's essay.[39]

Once again, for those disinclined to take these works seriously, this excavation of literary debts must seem far-fetched. But none of it requires much speculation, if any. We know that Larkin devoured Connolly's work; we know he had for years read the boys' stories Orwell critiques, as well as that critique;

we know he had also read extensively across the girls' school story genre. Such a well-balanced literary diet meant Larkin was ideally positioned to take on the girls' genre in a way Orwell could only imagine for boys. Coleman's call to arms may end with a tone of defeatism – 'And now I must ring for Jacinth, and begin *Wenda's Worst Term*' – but in fact there is no *Wenda's Worst Term* for us to read, no *Brenda's Best Friend* and no *Madcap Mona* (*TWG*, 273). What we do have, accompanying the essay, are the two novellas and sheaf of poems. Coleman is, once again, being disingenuously modest: in the hypothetical *Wenda's Worst Term*, she may well have simply reproduced the usual generic conventions with a view to 'market-writing', but in the realized texts, she produces an impressive and intelligent glimpse at the 'Ideal Book' she longs to see. In other words, not only did Coleman care enough about the genre to survey it, she also went some way to revolutionizing it. She was as able a practitioner as she was a theoretician. By logical extension, so was Larkin. Looked at against the backdrop of the period's literary politics, this matters.

Fiction, the reading public and the Leavises

In the context of the 1940s, Coleman's literary politics were remarkably progressive. The importance of Connolly's work, especially *Horizon*, has already been noted. In this period, the other major contender for the attention of literary intellectuals was *Scrutiny*, the quarterly founded in 1932 by L. C. Knights and F. R. Leavis, and dominated by the latter until it folded in 1953. During these years, Leavis was an incredible force in the reshaping of literary values and the canon, acting as a megaphone for modernists like Eliot and Lawrence. Edward Greenwood summarizes the attitude, and reception, of this Cambridge controversialist:

> In view of the not wholly unjustified accusation that *Scrutiny* in its later years was hostile to contemporary literature, it is worth stressing that the young Leavis was in the vanguard in this matter. He incurred the displeasure of the university authorities and the English Faculty by lecturing on *Ulysses* to his classes in the mid 1920s. He recalls 'conventional academics' saying of him at the time of Lawrence's death in 1930, 'We don't like the kind of book he lends undergraduates'. At this time the Faculty Librarian sanctioned the withholding of D. H. Lawrence's and T. F. Powys's works from undergraduates who wanted to borrow them or read them in the library.[40]

In 1943, Larkin was working towards his Finals, immersed in what he knew to be Oxford's conservative English Literature curriculum. He was also busy rebelling against it through a private diet of modern literature. As Chapter 1 showed, Larkin worshipped Lawrence, and he was also a fan of Powys, so he may well have read Leavis with absorption. In a 1941 letter to his sister, Larkin bristles with irritation as he describes an 'unpleasant' assistant refusing to issue him with 'the original "Lady C." and "Paintings" at the Bodleian yesterday' (*LH*, 38–9). The idea of Leavis lecturing on *The Rainbow* at Cambridge whilst Larkin laboured through *The Faerie Queene* at Oxford must have been exciting and infuriating in equal measures. Although Leavis suffered professionally – his applications for promotion beyond probationary lecturer being routinely rejected – he played an enormous role in dragging the academic discipline of English Literature into the twentieth century. In 1932, the year *Scrutiny* was founded, he published *New Bearings in English Poetry*, a radical revision of the poetry canon, and his wife, Q. D. Leavis, published *Fiction and the Reading Public*, a major study of reading habits in contemporary Britain. We know Larkin was aware of this book: he owned a 1939 edition, and later wrote a poem with the same title on the theme of market-writing (discussed in Chapter 7). No doubt Coleman's democratic instincts would be irked by Q. D. Leavis's sometimes condescending elitism:

> [In] general those who are enterprising and affluent enough to subscribe to a circulating library are prepared to have their reading determined for them. And 'reading' in this case means fiction. It is not an exaggeration to say that for most people 'a book' means a novel. This becomes apparent if one watches the process of selection, in which the assistant is generally consulted in some such formula as 'Another book like this one, please', or 'Can you recommend me a nice book?' The assistant glances at the novel held out and produces another novel which is accepted without question. She may ask 'Have you read this?' and the answer will be 'I can't remember, but I'll take it'. Where criticism is offered, it almost invariably betrays a complete ignorance of values, *e.g.* a common complaint: 'I can't read Conrad, sea-stories bore me', or alternatively: 'I like Conrad because I'm so fond of stories about the sea'.[41]

Leavis's 'anthropological' observations led her to pronounce 'the disintegration of the reading public', and to issue her own call to arms: 'If there is to be any hope, it must lie in conscious and directed effort. All that can be done, it must be realized, and take the form of resistance by an armed and conscious minority.'[42] She had in mind academics and highbrow novelists, a small but elite army tasked with reclaiming standards in fiction and therefore society. At its worst, *Fiction and the Reading Public* displays scorn for the pulp, the lowbrow and the middlebrow, and represents the pervasive cynicism of the period's literary elite. Its theme is precisely the one Connolly engaged with six years later in *Enemies of Promise*, where he advocates the 'Mandarin' style (long, complex, erudite) over that of modern journalese.[43]

This context is important, because it places Coleman's critical and creative practice within a contemporary intellectual landscape of debate and pessimism – a landscape familiar to Larkin the reader, student and aspiring writer. What unites Connolly, the Leavises and Orwell is their preoccupation with culture – its past, present and future manifestations. The Leavises and Connolly feared its dilution, its resort to the lowbrow, and their answer was a shameless defence of the highbrow. Although they deserve immense credit for their modernization of that category, its elite status remained unchallenged by their thinking. Coleman's essay shares remarkably similar concerns, but calls for a more progressive response, which Coleman herself produces. She wants to fiercely protect the core of the girls' school story genre: it must always be about English schoolgirls and their mistresses; it must always concern itself with their hopes and desires, their trials and tribulations; it must always delight in their world of ponies, stockings and hockey training. Crucially, however, she sees no reason why this popular, lowbrow subject cannot be presented in more sophisticated ways. The market must remain, but the women behind the stalls should be more literate; their customers will follow suit. This is a financially viable collective ascent, rather than a financially competitive race to the genre's gutter. Her stance is conspicuous in the *Sugar and Spice* poems (discussed in Chapter 6), dedicated 'to all my sister-writers, with the exception of Margaret Kennedy, who wrote in *The Constant Nymph*: "English Schoolgirls are not interesting."' (*TWG*, 243). For Coleman, English schoolgirls *are* interesting, and worthy of occupying one of the many rooms in the expansive house of literature she describes in her essay.

In the first novella, *Trouble at Willow Gables*, Coleman tightly hugs the conventions of the genre she so clearly adores. Following her own advice about protecting the 'Copernican universe' of the girls' school, she refuses to be lured by the superficial glamour of foreign trips (*TWG*, 268). Indeed, Willow Gables feels like a bubble-wrapped world: in the Prologue, the narrator cinematically zooms in to the school grounds, following a postman as he brings perilous evidence of the outside world in the form of letters that will disrupt the established, regimental order. Although the novella was written in 1943, there is almost no sense at all of war, other than the fear of being sent to the Auxiliary Territorial Service for Women which threatens Hilary, though only after she has been expelled from the school (*TWG*, 124). The Aristotelian 'Unity of Place' is maintained by keeping the story within the school grounds, with the exception of a necessary excursion into the local village. The 'Unity of Time' is maintained, with the entire story taking place within one school term. And the 'Unity of Action' is maintained by ensuring that each and every aspect of the plot clearly contributes towards, as Coleman puts it, 'the advancement of the story' (*TWG*, 269). A number of other generic conventions are also maintained: Booth notes the 'two-in-a-bed scene, endemic to the *genre*' (*TWG*, xv), the 'age hierarchy' and the characters' 'innocent pre-adolescent narcissism'.[44] Indeed, in one review of Booth's edition, the editor of *Folly* magazine (an acronym for 'fans of light literature for the young') remarked on how uncannily these pieces resemble the established girls' genre.[45]

That Larkin should produce any of this may be remarkable in itself, but for Coleman – an established author of schoolgirl fiction – her novella would not be so noteworthy were it not for her improvement of the genre. Each chapter contains an epigraph taken (in the majority of cases) from canonical literature: *Paradise Lost, King Lear, The Canterbury Tales, Essay on Man*. There are also allusions throughout to the moderns: Gautier, Eliot, Shaw, Baudelaire, Maupassant and more. These citations match the erudition of her essay. Not only does their inclusion fire the genre into a different kind of intellectual galaxy, it also tells us something about Coleman's intentions. The *Paradise Lost* allusions, for example, draw attention to Milton's Satan – also namechecked in the essay – as a complex portrayal of evil. Given Coleman's dislike of exclusively virtuous heroines, we can see that she wants to shake up the dusty complacency and intellectual laziness of the genre's sickly sweet characterizations. Marie's cross-dressing is surely (though only partially) a nod to Shakespeare's gender-bending plays (*As You Like It, The Merchant of Venice, A Midsummer Night's Dream*), whilst Hilary's romantic and sexual indecisiveness brings to mind the erotic paralysis of J. Alfred Prufrock and, by extension, Hamlet. All this can be said to make the novellas more literary, more intelligent, more sophisticated – in short, better books. And one can easily imagine young readers tracking down the works mentioned and becoming more sophisticated readers, had *Trouble at Willow Gables* been commercially available, with Coleman's name on the cover, during the 1940s.

It must be said, however, that such changes only really represent a kind of exercise in literariness; what is more remarkable about Coleman's improvement is her radical treatment of gender and sexuality, the subject of the following chapter. The two concerns are, of course, closely related, since Coleman reforms the genre by exploding its traditional gender sensibilities. In doing so, she set Larkin's writing on a very different course. We have seen how seriously George Orwell took the boys' school story genre; we have seen how seriously Brunette Coleman takes the girls' equivalent; and if we are willing to take Coleman seriously, then it is possible to detect a distinctly feminist programme within her *oeuvre* and, therefore, within Larkin's.

4

Brunette Coleman

Experiments in gender

An undoing of genre is also an undoing of gender. Typically, popular genres arrive already-gendered: detective novels with their hardboiled male sleuths, pulp romances with their Italian Stallions and thrillers with their ex-military hardmen. These stock characters are evidence of the gendered readerships and ideological hinterlands of popular genre works. This phenomenon begins in childhood: surveying girls' fiction of the early twentieth century, J. S. Bratton argues that 'A century of writing for girls had established the norm of the domestic tale, in which the trials of the heroine were involved with the learning of discipline, the internalization of the feminine values of self-abnegation, obedience and submission'.[1] Mary Cadogan and Patricia Craig make a similar point in their study of girls' fiction:

> Before girls are old enough to go to school they are familiar with Polly Flinders, who is whipped for spoiling her nice, new, feminine clothes, with the other Polly who is encouraged endlessly to put the kettle on and take it off again; they learn that Miss Muffet has an irrational fear of spiders, and see how the little girls who are kissed and reduced to tears by offensive Georgie-Porgie lack the courage to chase him off, and have to wait until the 'boys' come out to rescue them. Popular fiction over the last hundred years has drawn heavily on images which are extensions from these, representing girls essentially as passive, domesticated, brainless and decorative.[2]

The previous chapter explored Coleman's assessment of the girls' school story genre, revealing her progressive literary politics. Her attitude to the genre is intrinsically wedded to her progressive views on gender and sexuality, explored in this chapter. Judy Simons argues that by the immediate post-war era

> so familiar had the features of the girls' school story become . . . that authors such as [Dorita Fairlie] Bruce and [Elinor] Brent-Dyer could modify what had

already become a standard narrative format in order to suggest that their pictures of school life were more authentic than those of their pioneering predecessor [Angela Brazil].[3]

In other words, the genre had, by the mid-1940s, ossified to such an extent that its conventions could be easily recognized and therefore altered and improved. Writing in 1943, Coleman – and, by extension, Larkin – was just as familiar with its formats and orthodoxies as her fellow specialists. By paying attention to the narratological treatment of gender in Coleman's stories, we can see how her own modifications work to enhance the genre; and in doing so, we can see the beginnings of a new approach to writing for Larkin, who would take this up in the two novels published in his name, discussed in Chapter 5.

Characterization

The numerous citations and allusions lifted from canonical literature, discussed in the previous chapter, do more than merely boost the literary credibility of Coleman's novellas: they also signal her subversive intentions. The Prologue to *Trouble at Willow Gables* opens with an epigraph from *Paradise Lost*, with Satan arriving at the borders of Eden, at this point yet to decide whether he will seek redemption or spread corruption (*TWG*, 6). Given that Coleman bemoans the genre's lack of morally complex characters with inner conflicts, this epigraph foreshadows her exploitation of the fuller possibilities of characterization, just as Milton did with Satan.

At this point, it is worth summarizing her characterizations in *Willow Gables*, and relating these to the situation of young women in 1943. Although a woman's public status had been transformed during the first half of the century, not least because of suffrage and the two world wars, she remained squarely within a first-wave feminist context: emancipated to some extent, but also subject to a culture of propriety and protective limitations. Privileged young women, for example, could now aspire to Oxbridge, but only as members of all-women colleges, and Cambridge would not award full degrees to women until 1948 – five years after Coleman sent her fictional girls to university. Literature, and especially children's literature, played its part in this culture; the social linguists Murray Knowles and Kirsten Malmkjaer describe how

> Adults see it as their task to socialise children, that is, to make them behave in ways that are generally acceptable to adults – in ways that will fit the children

to take their place in society, as adults perceive it. Obviously, adults have many means towards this end available to them. . . . However, they . . . inevitably influence children more subtly, often subconsciously, and, many would argue, most effectively, through language. . . . The language of social texts – including those texts which we read to our children or give them to read for themselves – is therefore a particularly effective agent in promoting the acceptance by the child of these customs, institutions and hierarchies.[4]

They discuss how children's literature galvanizes this process of socialization by means of narrative legitimation and normalization. It is within such a context that Coleman's exercises in characterization should be comprehended. A summary of the main characters in *Trouble at Willow Gables* would read something like this: Mary, regarded by her older peers as precocious, receives illicit private tuition, instigated by Philippa, who sees Mary's potential to reach university; but Philippa wants to focus on her own ambitions, and asks Hilary to take over tuition; Hilary, a prefect with a taste for subversive literature, agrees, but is motivated by sexual attraction to Mary; Margaret, always battered and bruised from her energetic exploits, and whose bad language is prolific, constantly looks for ways to make a quick buck, eventually becoming an astute gambler; Marie, a mischievous girl, resolves to spend her pocket money as she wishes, thereby triggering the novella's chief sticky situation; which in turn leads her friend Myfanwy – normally a sweet, gentle girl – to become a kind of detective seeking justice in an unjust world.

When considering the intertwining of genre and gender in Coleman's *oeuvre*, Myfanwy's characterization is particularly interesting. Glenwood Irons, editor of a volume of essays on feminism and detective fiction, notes that 'The popular representation of [the] male detective-as-urban-cowboy who stands out against the rottenness of society has a powerful appeal'.[5] But he also points out that 'since the late 1960s, it can no longer be argued that such an image is the only one informing the popular imagination with respect to the detective. Even those who ignore the plethora of women detectives in popular novels cannot help but recognize the change in TV and cinema depictions of this character'.[6] As early as 1943, more than twenty years before the sea-change identified by Irons, Coleman had already regendered that masculine archetype. Of course, *Trouble at Willow Gables* was never going to achieve the phenomenal popularity and impact of Joan Hickson's Miss Marple or Angela Lansbury's Jessica Fletcher, though Larkin did attempt publication. And some of the popular screen characters Irons mentions were adaptations of earlier fictional ones, such as Agatha Christie's Miss Marple. But without overstating the significance of Coleman's female detective, it is worth noting that by 1943, the Miss Marple character had only appeared in three of Christie's novels: *The Murder at the Vicarage* (1930), *The Body in the Library* (1942) and *The Moving Finger* (1943). Coleman's female sleuth was not the first, but she was novel.

In itself, Coleman's inclusion of multiple significant characters is a modification of the genre, which typically focuses on one heroine; but the impact on gender is the more significant change. Implicitly, this alteration asserts the value of *all girls*, rather than a single and singular girl, by presenting, legitimizing and normalizing a number of different versions of girlhood and femininity, each one with its own set of possibilities and limitations. That implied importance is then reinforced as Coleman follows their lives through school (Willow Gables) and college (St Bride's).

Plot

The brief summary of the girls' personalities is sufficient to suggest Coleman's consistent fashioning of young, female characters as strong and active agents of their own destiny. The title of the first novella's opening chapter, 'Trouble in Envelopes', is a useful place to begin thinking about plot, given the connection between letters and identity, established in Chapter 1. Marie is the recipient, not the author, of a letter delivered in the Prologue, but this letter still has consequences for her identity, prompting her to ask questions about her relationship with authority and the wider community in which she lives. Another letter, intended for Margaret, is 'from one Arthur Waley, Turf Accountant, saying that he would be pleased to oblige Miss Tattenham at any time and odds' (one of many cultural references, Waley being a famous translator of Chinese and Japanese poetry) (*TWG*, 9). It is these events which drive the plot of *Trouble at Willow Gables*; the pornographic elements, which have preoccupied critics, are negligible, though they also relate to the issue of gender, as will be seen. Active, wilful girls are the norm in this novella. From the earliest passages, the narrator is at pains to show their individuality. Although the school corridors flood with girls 'all dressed in maroon tunics, white blouses, and black stockings', we are told that 'The effect, curiously enough, was not one of uniformity':

> [S]o many different faces paraded past, so many colours of hair, complexions, eyes, different hair-styles, contrasts in age, build and height, that an observer would have been dazzled by variety rather than dispirited by any impression of

> mass-production. Girls pushed different ways[;] all had a destination and were impatient to reach it.... All chattered, laughed, and squealed at the tops of their voices, pushing and pinching as the crowd jostled this way and that. Prefects tried vainly to introduce some order into the squabble. (*TWG*, 10)

It is significant that the narrative voice, though an observer, is no voyeur, instead focusing on the dazzling and spirited display of activity and diversity. The description of each girl having 'a destination' and being 'impatient to reach it' is as much a comment on their ambitions and energy as it is a simple narration of their journeys to classrooms and dormitories.

This depiction of headstrong, self-governing girls is persistent. When Hilary confiscates a five-pound note posted to Marie by her aunt, one character asks, 'Can't you *do* anything about it?', and *doing something about it* becomes the central theme of this story. But Margaret's comment – 'One's got to make some sort of a stand against the bitches of this world' – also indicates that the tale will not slide into a realm of idealized sisterly solidarity (*TWG*, 15). Coleman, in her essay, quotes Baudelaire's 'dictum' that 'There are in the young girl all the despicable qualities of the footpad and the schoolboy', exclaiming 'Alas! it is only too true!' (*TWG*, 260). Coleman knows that girls can be 'bitches' as well as sweet little things, and at Willow Gables, the repressive force is not immediately that of the patriarchy but the authoritarian rule of its Headmistress, Miss Holden. Rosemary Auchmuty has argued that the headmistress in schoolgirl fiction 'becomes, in a sense, a surrogate male figure governing her surrogate community', but Coleman considers women characters as women, with just as much capacity for wrongdoing as men.[7] Miss Holden's name suggests she has a 'hold on' the girls' lives, and it is indeed she who holds on to Marie's money, deciding how it will be spent. Similarly, it is a female peer, Hilary, who delights in confiscating the money and delivering it to Miss Holden. Hilary certainly functions as the novella's 'baddie', but she is also the best example of Coleman's Miltonic characterization, by far the most interesting and conflicted character in the *oeuvre*. Once the girls' indignant reaction against Hilary has been described, the focus shifts to her study, where the 'original chaste nudity' has been worked into a luxurious harem of decadence:

> The carpet was soft, the furniture well-sprung, and there was an abundance of silken cushions: a reading lamp trailed a heavy fringe, and there were several unobtrusive and lightly-coloured pictures and engravings on the walls, culminating in a studio-photograph of Hilary herself over the mantelshelf, heavily chiaroscuro'd. In addition to the regulation bookcase, Hilary had supplied a second, for she was a voracious reader. (*TWG*, 16)

The narrator then describes the contents of Hilary's illicit bookcase, cited in the previous chapter. As a prefect, Hilary is the long arm of Miss Holden's law, but this does not stop her from privately undermining the Headmistress's iron rule of austere uniformity. Hilary's most treasured possession is a disguised copy of *Mademoiselle de Maupin*. In this French novel – a literary scandal in its time – the cross-dressing swordswoman Julie d'Aubigny falls into a love triangle involving a man and his mistress. Has this novel perhaps taught Hilary the importance of metaphorically donning a pair of trousers in order to cut through patriarchally imposed limitations on women? And has the novel legitimized, in her mind, a philosophy of free love, including love between women?

She is not the only girl willing to subvert the stringent school regime. Willow Gables is set up to maintain order and uniformity: as the postman approaches its 'grey façade', there is 'complete silence', 'The trees are very tall and shut out the light', and the lawn has a 'Keep Off the Grass' notice – perhaps a nod to Woolf's *A Room of One's Own* (*TWG*, 7). The girls lead a martial life: 'Regularly at a quarter past nine every night the Fourth Form trooped off to bed, up the stairs and along corridors to the long, low dormitory. It was a large room, with a row of washbasins at one end, and beds ran down both walls'. Each night, prefects patrol the dorm, shouting '"Everybody in bed!"', . . . sweeping up and down the lines of beds, flicking the dawdlers . . . with the end of a leather belt' (*TWG*, 22–4). The school's structure is hierarchical and divisive, separating girls not just by age but also pedagogy: Philippa and Hilary, for example, although both prefects, members of the same form, and 'intellectual equals', meet 'very seldom', as their subjects separate them in temporal and spatial terms as much as mental ones (*TWG*, 18–19). But within this environment, Coleman makes sure that every girl displays a personality of her own and pushes against school regulations in small but expressive ways. This can be by means of sartorial choices, or more explicit transgressions like smoking, or poker games for penny stakes after Lights Out; Coleman even takes care to reproduce schoolgirl slang ('Is she getting bunked?', 'Pretty cool of Philippa to split on her'), including Margaret's 'coarse' language, which is not merely dialogic verisimilitude, but also evidence of a school subculture – that is, a vernacular community separate from, and resistant to, the dominant one (*TWG*, 74). Collectively, these features of the narrative build up an atmosphere of low-level resistance and transgression, an important foil to the established and Establishment boys' and girls' genres which Orwell and Coleman critique. That atmosphere provides a platform for the plot's more risqué turns.

These centre on the confiscation of Marie's five-pound note, which she indignantly decides to take back. The subversive power of literature is again registered when Marie resolves to do so whilst studying *The Merchant of Venice*; Shakespeare's complex portrayal of a wronged and revengeful Jew germinates in a hitherto innocent mind thoughts of reprisal. But she is caught, and, as punishment for taking back the money, Miss Holden coerces Marie into donating it to the school's Gymnasium Fund. Once again, Miss Holden has wielded her authority arbitrarily, but given the character of these girls, her decision will spark further transgressions. When the money goes missing again, Marie is wrongly accused and violently searched in Miss Holden's office (in fact, Margaret has stolen it to invest in her budding gambling enterprise). This injustice infuriates Myfanwy, who takes it upon herself to solve the crime. Myfanwy's sections of the narrative then inhabit the language of detective fiction:

> True, the evidence was strong against her, but there was such a difference between the first offence and the second that Myfanwy felt sure that Marie would never have ventured so near a crime not only against Miss Holden, but against the Gymnasium Fund and the whole school. (*TWG*, 49)
>
> Myfanwy briefly retailed the facts of the case as she had learnt them from Philippa Moore. Marie listened intently.
> 'So it must have been taken between prayers and about half-past two,' Myfanwy finished. 'That's quite a long time. Can you prove where you were all that time?' (*TWG*, 50)

True to the genre (and games of *Cluedo*), the solving of the crime hinges on a crowbar. Coleman inhabits a genre-within-a-genre, mimicking the conventions of detective fiction, but crucially inserting a sleuth-hero who is a young girl, spurred simply by her keen sense of (in)justice.

Meanwhile, Marie has been solitarily confined on the top floor of the school as the search for the missing money continues. Once again recalling Shakespeare, she plots her escape with Pat, a servant: '"You must bring me some other clothes – trousers, and a shirt. People might take me for a boy if I tied my hair up," she added, with vague memories of a school production of *As You Like It*' (*TWG*, 78). The symbolism is obvious: Marie must literally pretend to be a male in order to escape; her freedom depends on disguising her femininity. Perhaps this is also a self-referential nod to the Coleman *oeuvre*, a question about the possibilities of cross-dressing, since these works are, after all, a product of Larkin's own transgendered authorship.

Indeed, Marie's realization is echoed elsewhere in the novella, when Myfanwy, a prodigious swimmer, wishes a 'more masculine' costume could be permitted: 'There is something about shoulder-straps that impedes a first-rate crawl. What a nuisance being a girl, she reflected' (*TWG*, 115). Myfanwy is not impeded as a swimmer because she is a girl, but because she has to wear a girl's costume; Marie must dress as a boy in order to escape punishment for a misdemeanour she did not commit; Margaret must conduct her gambling operation covertly; Hilary must disguise the books she loves to read. Throughout the narrative, the girls repeatedly show that a young woman's lot is not a happy one, and consistently strive to push at the limits of their world. Coleman creates great pathos in showing how their vivacity is persistently threatened by an authority modelled on and propping up the patriarchy. Perhaps the most symbolic scene comes when Margaret also decides to escape from the school, this time on the groundsman's horse. Once out of the school grounds, she rides through a river and removes her wet clothes. Hilary and two other girls are sent to find Marie, but the moment they locate her, the noise of 'thundering hooves' is heard; they turn to see it 'bestridden by a hatless, coatless, stockingless, blouseless, saddleless, stirrupless, bridle- and reinless Margaret Tattenham' (*TWG*, 107). The image of an indignant naked woman astride a horse can only bring to mind the story of Lady Godiva, the Anglo-Saxon noblewoman who rode nude through the streets of Coventry in order to protest her husband's repressive taxes (images of her are found throughout Larkin's hometown, including a permanent collection in the Herbert Art Gallery and Museum). Nakedly straddling horses, what Margaret and Godiva have in common is a determination to resist patriarchal authority where it is wielded arbitrarily.

Soon after, the girls are confronted with a crisis, as Myfanwy, who has been swimming in the river in her impeding costume, is swept downstream, and looks set to drown before the girls work together to save her. This is part of the novella's Unity of Action, contributing towards the plot's overall resolution; but it also shows the girls' potential to survive away from the stiflingly protective school regime. We know from 'What Are We Writing For?' that Coleman is eager to protect the core elements of the schoolgirl story, but in her constructions of gender she provides a counter-model to the genre. In her quest to see the Ideal Book realized, Coleman uses a number of strategies to raise the quality of the genre, and the most radical means of doing so is her representation of femininity. At the levels of plot and characterization, both crucial elements of popular fiction, she creates girls who, in minor and major ways, wilfully obliterate the limits imposed on them simply by virtue of having been born girls. This prefigures a key aspect of the mature Larkin's literary practice: Osborne has shown how, in poems like 'This Be The Verse' and 'I Remember, I Remember', Larkin enacts the Derridean paradox of fidelity and betrayal to his literary masters:

> [To] follow in the footsteps of a person one admires for originality is to betray that originality by being a replica rather than a prototype, an emulator where the role model was an instigator. To truly follow an original master one must still commit an act of betrayal, overthrowing his or her example in order to be comparably *sui generis*. Either way, one's pledge of loyalty, one's vow to follow, is simultaneously an act of perjury, a refusal to follow.[8]

This neatly encapsulates Coleman's work as the author of schoolgirl fiction: paying homage to a genre she so dearly loves, she must also be true to that genre by actively improving, rather than merely replicating it. Her affectionate enrichment of the girls' school story is achieved by taking a swing at its gender representations.

Narration

Coleman's literary reworking of gender extends beyond plot and characterization to include the mode of narration, which in the novellas is that of free indirect discourse (FID). This is also the mode of some of the most important women novelists, most notably Austen and Woolf, who both innovated FID with significant consequences for literary history. In this sense, Coleman aligns herself with influential women writers. This could be part of the alleged Larkin-Amis joke, but given Larkin's adoration of Woolf, and her clear influence on *A Girl in Winter* (written within three years of the Coleman *oeuvre*, and discussed in Chapter 5), this is difficult to accept.

Austen's stamp on FID was chiefly her exploitation of its potential for irony, but it later became a tool which enabled novelists like Woolf to explore consciousness and the inner lives of characters. To narrate a character's life in such an intimately interior way was, implicitly, to assert that character's value and potential to fascinate. When Woolf used FID in *Mrs Dalloway* (1925), flowing in and out of major and minor characters' minds on that day in June 1923, the implication was that each and every one of them, from society hostesses and Members of Parliament to abandoned war veterans and passing pedestrians, was somehow interesting and somehow mattered; likewise, when Joyce used FID in *Ulysses* (1922) to narrate Leopold Bloom's bowel movements, the passage (no pun intended) scandalized precisely because it suggested that a Dubliner defecating on the morning of 16 June 1904 mattered enough to be endowed with the permanency of art. We have already seen Coleman fight the corner of English schoolgirls – how silly of Margaret Kennedy to think them uninteresting, she implies in her epigraph to the *Sugar and Spice* poems – so it should come as little surprise that FID might be adopted as yet another way for her to be loud and proud. The Woolf connection becomes clearer if we briefly consider *Ante Meridian*, the autobiographical fragment describing Coleman's childhood, which cites *The Waves* (*TWG*, 235). The influence of Connolly's *Enemies of Promise* has already been noted in the previous chapter, and Booth detects the influence of a different sister-writer, Daphne du Maurier (*TWG*, ix). However, Coleman's coastal Cornish birthplace also echoes *To the Lighthouse* (1927), Woolf's most obviously autobiographical novel. Although *To the Lighthouse* is set in Scotland, Woolf's descriptions of place are based on St Ives, where the Stephen family had a summer home for ten years of her childhood. Coleman's father is certainly as austere and imposing a figure as Woolf's Mr Ramsey, or Leslie Stephen himself. Given that Larkin abandoned Coleman's autobiography after just a few pages, it is difficult to attach much importance to it, but at the very least *Ante Meridian* plays its own small part in the performance of a wider web of gendered literary influences. Since these influences so often align with the early Larkin's own, this makes it harder yet to dismiss Coleman's *oeuvre* as a joke about gender or literature or both.

Sex and sexuality

So far, these two chapters have rejected the critical consensus on Coleman's writings, which focuses on their pornographic elements – what Motion calls their 'diet' of 'voyeurism, sado-masochism, and a pleasure in taking advantage of those who . . . cannot easily defend themselves'.[9] They have instead proposed that the early Larkin found it productive to write genre- and gender-busting girls' school stories using a female heteronym. The next chapter, on Larkin's published fiction, demonstrates the impact of this on his subsequent and more 'serious' prose work. Only Booth has strenuously challenged the critics' preoccupation with sexual content, arguing that *Trouble at Willow Gables* 'will give thin satisfaction to a reader in search of explicit pornography or sadism' (*TWG*, xvi). This is important: to read these works without presupposing the significance of Larkin's sexual biography, and to read them as a coherent *oeuvre* (something Motion does not do), is to witness genre and gender emerge as far more insistent and interesting themes. This is not to say that sex never appears – it does, but its thematic treatment is more intelligent than critics seem to want to allow.

The first passage which can in any way be characterized as erotic comes in the second chapter of *Trouble at Willow Gables*, when Hilary clears out the changing-rooms after cricket:

> She was ... surprised to see, on glancing cursorily into the showers, one girl still splashing about in the wet. She learnt later that it was Mary Beech, but at the time she had merely glanced appreciatively at the strong young body that shuddered under the cold shower, and had told her to clear out and not slack about in the changing-room. As the girl had scurried past her out of the tiled shower-room, Hilary had emphasised this warning by a smart slap on the behind, and the imposition of fifty lines. (*TWG*, 17)

The passage is representative of the novella's soft and scarce eroticism; that it barely provides the mildest of titillation hardly needs stating. Moreover, although sexual in nature, Hilary's interest in Mary has an unusual emphasis:

> Hilary was very conscious of the absurdity of it all, particularly as Mary was not, judged by ordinary standards, beautiful. She was a sturdy girl, with auburn hair and freckles, grey eyes, and a sensible, cool expression that exactly mirrored her character. To Hilary she had the tawny strength of a young lioness .... [W]hen they happened to come face to face Hilary would feel a voice shouting in her head 'strong young lioness! strong, tawny young lioness!' which embarrassed her so much that she had to look away. (*TWG*, 18)

What absorbs Hilary is not conventional feminine beauty – the quality these girls are expected to possess – but precisely the opposite: Mary's strength, sturdiness and coolness, qualities associated with masculinity. (The lioness imagery also mimics Baudelaire's in 'Femmes damnées: Delphine et Hippolyte', discussed in Chapter 6.) Although the encounter is voyeuristic, and therefore one-sided, how many readers today would want to condemn Hilary's burgeoning lesbian consciousness? Coleman's treatment of sex, like her treatments of genre and gender, is more intriguing and intelligent than that managed by her sister-writers, and another important dimension of her game-raising strategy for the genre.

It is also not true that the story is completely devoid of sado-masochism; such moments are rare, but they do occur, and need to be accounted for. Perhaps the most explicit comes in the fifth chapter, when the innocent Marie is violently searched in Miss Holden's office for the missing five-pound note:

> As Pam finally pulled Marie's tunic down over her black-stockinged legs, Miss Holden, pausing only to snatch a cane from the cupboard in the wall, gripped

Marie by the hair, and, with a strength lent by anger, forced down her head till she was bent nearly double. Then she began thrashing her unmercifully, her face a mask of ferocity, caring little where the blows fell as long as they found a mark somewhere on Marie's squirming body. (*TWG*, 43)

The passage is disconcerting, but critics have been reluctant to look beyond the obvious and suggest alternative readings. The fact that the search takes place against the backdrop of an ostentatiously Gothic pathetic fallacy ('Lightning flashed, and the globe reeled upon its pedestal, bouncing heavily as thunder crackled like sheet-metal overhead') renders it kitsch, and therefore difficult to take seriously (*TWG*, 43). But there is a seriousness here. The search, and ensuing violence, is instigated by Miss Holden, the personification of authority against which the girls systematically and idiosyncratically rebel. If there is a sense of delight in the sado-masochism, it is *hers*, but the violent descriptions are undercut by an affecting sadness and overwhelming sense of injustice: Marie's 'little body was shaken with tempestuous sobs, and tears trickled from her tightly-shut eyes' (*TWG*, 43–4). Furthermore, as a development in the novella's plot, it seems more important as the experience of injustice and abusive authority against which Marie and others will now fight (the chapter ends here, with the subsequent one called 'What Is to Be Done?'). Coleman is careful to obey Aristotle's Unity of Action: if the scene only served an erotic purpose, it would fail her own test of good fiction. Motion believes that the novella conveys 'a pleasure in taking advantage of those who (because they are young or servants) cannot easily defend themselves', but Marie's caning is necessary to the plot's emphasis on the girls' development as rebels and dissenters. Marie can only fight Authority because Authority has waged a war on her independence and individuality.

Sex, in other words, is another part of the text's radical gender coup – and, in this sense, plays a role in Coleman's overall project of working towards that Ideal Book. We have seen Orwell complain in his essay on the boys' genre that it is 'fantastically unlike life at a real public school', in part because 'Sex is completely taboo, especially in the form in which it actually arises at public schools. . . . Even the bad boys are presumed to be completely sexless'.[10] He speculates that these sex-free stories perhaps betray a 'deliberate intention to get away from the guilty sex-ridden atmosphere that pervaded so much of the earlier literature for boys'. Sex, then – a reality of life at public schools as much as anywhere else – is repressed in the boys' story genre. In turn, we have seen Coleman criticise the girls' genre's heroines as 'too frequently "good"'; Dorita Fairlie Bruce's Dimsie, for instance, 'repels us by being . . . the little angel of joy that sets everyone's problems right'. According to Coleman, 'by making the heroine unrelievedly "good"... the author almost inevitably fails to make her attractive'. In 'What Are We Writing For?', she introduces the vice of 'greed' as neglected by her fellow authors: 'there is rarely a greedy girl' (*TWG*, 258–61). She cites a rare exception involving food in Nancy Breary's *Two Thrilling Terms* (1943); but one can easily imagine Hilary having been written as an exercise in sexual greed: following her attempts to seduce Mary, she transfers her lusting to Margaret.

Hilary, then, fulfils Coleman's desire for characters who are neither exclusively good nor exclusively bad, and who suffer, like Milton's Satan, from inner conflict – sexual desire being one manifestation of this. And just as Orwell ridicules the idea of schoolboys who never think about (let alone practise) sex, Coleman makes sex conspicuous by its semi-absence. This is a genre which can be twee, sometimes sickeningly so; Cadogan and Craig comment that 'there is nearly almost something flaccid and sentimental about stories which have been described as "much-loved"'.[11] But some critics have pointed to the presence of sex lurking with embarrassment just below the surface of such stories. Even Angela Brazil, whose books sold phenomenally well across the world, and who is generally credited with expressing the schoolgirl mind better than anyone, has been found guilty of accidental innuendo. Gillian Freeman notes that boys never 'stir the girlish breasts. With only a few half-hearted exceptions they remain brothers'.[12] When it comes to relations between girls in Brazil's fiction, Freeman writes: 'of course there are the friendships between the girls (and sometimes between teachers and girls) with passions, jealousies and misunderstandings, demands of loyalty and honesty, and kisses and embraces which today would be interpreted both sexually and psychologically'.[13] Judy Simons describes how

> The passionate relationships which flourish between Brazil's adolescent girls clearly overflow into the sentimental and romantic, yet without the overt eroticism that would make them threatening.... Girls climb into bed together, cuddle and kiss unashamedly and develop ardent friendships that can be interpreted in different ways by different readers.... Inevitably the physical intimacy of the girls and the heady sensationalism of their exploits has encouraged aficionados, detractors and parodists of the school story to insert the sexuality that Brazil left out.[14]

Coleman is cited as an example, though Simons does not specify whether she considers her an aficionado, detractor or parodist. These assessments by Freeman and Simons are interesting: with a disapproving tut, Freeman blames a cruder, corrupt contemporary sensibility, whilst Simons suggests that Brazil deliberately sentimentalized and de-sexualized intimacy in order to protect her readers. Either way, each critic feels sufficiently compelled to deal with the presence of a faint, underlying eroticism in Brazil's fiction. This appears to be characteristic of the wider genre, and something Coleman – an expert – has noticed and addressed. The issue is an occupational hazard for the writer of girls' stories: Cadogan and Craig argue that 'it has been difficult to see beyond the stories' unintentional humour: this becomes more apparent as their literary quality declines'.[15] But Coleman boldly tackles this head on. It is this aspect of Coleman's work which Castle finds particularly notable:

> [In] a genre notorious since the late nineteenth century for its barely sublimated Sapphic inflections . . . what Larkin seems to have prized . . . was not so much any outright kink as an odd, overall, seemingly *unintended* suggestiveness: the comic way that novelists like Vicary and Bruce managed to set up titillating suggestions without ever seeming to be aware that they were doing so.[16]

These 'barely sublimated Sapphic inflections' can be found in Coleman's work, such as when Myfanwy comforts Marie after her caning: 'For a second they clung together, Myfanwy's lips pressed against her chum's hair. Then Marie gave an uneasy wriggle, and slid down onto her side' (*TWG*, 49). But the more explicit passages, which critics have read in terms of Larkin's sexual perversions and dissatisfactions (which, in any case, refuse to pervert or satisfy), seem to be directed more towards the overall improvement of the genre. Coleman recognizes, rather than consciously or subconsciously represses, the fact of adolescent sexuality. It is another example of her undoing of genre and gender: by allowing the repressed and embarrassed theme of sex to surface, Coleman directly represents and legitimizes female sexual expression, countering the de-sexualizing myth and stereotype of feminine modesty and passivity; in doing so, she improves the genre by bringing its representations of girls' lives closer to the inner lives of its actual girl-readers. Inhabited by girls who feel anger at their limitations, who set out to challenge those limitations, who are sometimes good but sometimes bad, who experience sexual desire, or conversely end up on the wrong end of it, Coleman's fictional world is engaged in the undoing of the established genre which is also an undoing of established gender roles and expectations. Behind this endeavour stands a twenty-one-year-old man with serious literary aspirations.

'It's good because it's awful': Coleman's camp

If the Brunette Coleman heteronym is not Larkin's means of working through his own confused sexuality, nor is it the depraved mask of a lustful undergraduate with a penchant for schoolgirls, then what is it? The various attempts to explain this heteronym either get caught up in the clichéd homosexual-turns-straight narrative – in which case, why not simply create a *male* homosexual heteronym? – or fail to answer the question at all. A number of factors help to explain why the heteronym had to be female: Larkin's personal taste for the girls' story genre, his democratic desire to elevate popular genres, and to explore gender in more intelligent and radical ways. But why lesbian? Coleman's lesbianism could, of course, be a form of titillation, but as we have seen, titillation is thin on the ground in these texts, not to mention completely absent from *Ante Meridian*, the only text in which Coleman herself is a character. The reason for Larkin's lesbian female heteronym, I would suggest, is that it allows him to exploit the possibilities of camp.

This decision has far-reaching consequences, entirely in keeping with the experiments in genre and gender explored so far. The various quotations from Coleman's work so far should be sufficient to suggest its main flavour, a kind of delicious campiness. The camp sensibility is notoriously elusive to pin down, though not difficult to detect, and it emanates from page after page of Coleman's writings. Her assertion in *Sugar and Spice* that 'Femmes Damnées' and 'Ballade des Dames du Temps Jadis' are not 'renderings' but 'In my opinion . . . improvements' is a camp one, as is her subsequent put-down of Margaret Kennedy (*TWG*, 243). Her insincere chastizing of Jacinth in the essay ('you know I don't like you to read in bed when you ought to be getting your beauty sleep') is another trace of her camp sensibility, whilst the conclusion to that essay, with its purple prose building to the climactic concept of the 'Ideal Book', is so excessive and exaggerated that it is nothing if not camp (*TWG*, 255, 272–3).

Indeed, much of Coleman's attitude and style tallies with the definition of camp offered by Susan Sontag in her brilliant 1964 essay, 'Notes on "Camp"', the first concerted attempt to define the sensibility. For Sontag, 'All Camp objects, and persons, contain a large element of artifice', and its taste in people 'responds particularly to the markedly attenuated and to the strongly exaggerated'.[17] Coleman, a heteronymous creation, *only* exists as artifice; like a drag queen, she is in her very being a statement of camp intent, and her exaggerated-ness attests to this. Not only that, but Sontag sees camp as a contrary style: 'It is the love of the exaggerated, the "off", of things-being-what-they-are-not', which 'draws on a mostly unacknowledged truth of taste: the most refined form of sexual attractiveness (as well as the most refined form of sexual pleasure) consists in going against the grain of one's own sex'.[18] These descriptions certainly characterize Coleman: on the one hand, the rather quaint and respectable

English author of stories for girls; on the other, a lesbian with a punk ethic, looking to explode the genre. With her razor-sharp sense of humour and her love of exaggeration, Coleman is a beautifully camp creation.

And so is her work. We have seen Coleman endorse the 'many rooms in the house of literature' argument, making the case that her genre deserves a space there as much as any other. Sontag would call this a camp pose, because 'Camp taste turns its back on the good-bad axis of ordinary aesthetic judgment' by acknowledging 'other creative sensibilities besides the seriousness (both tragic and comic) of high culture'.[19] Whilst it is true that Coleman's project seeks to enhance the quality of the schoolgirl genre, there is simultaneously an underlying and persistent sense that the whole thing is really just quite *bad*; one thinks of her poem 'The False Friend', which, in the end, is a poem about one girl's ire with another for buying their teacher a book token, when they had agreed only to buy a card.

Running parallel to the attempted enhancement of this genre, then, is a strong sense of revelling in the 'bad' and the undervalued. Not only does camp 'dethrone the serious', Sontag tells us, and show that 'One can be serious about the frivolous, frivolous about the serious', it also says 'it's good because it's awful'.[20] For Sontag, this is the 'ultimate Camp statement', but it is surely also Coleman's attitude to schoolgirl fiction in a nutshell. In other words, camp reforms one's relationship with 'good' and 'bad' art, unleashing the possibility of seriously appreciating the frivolous. This is important, particularly in relation to the Coleman *oeuvre*, which has been so easily dismissed as nothing more than an extended joke. Sontag argues that 'Camp taste identifies with what it is enjoying. People who share this sensibility are not laughing at the thing they label as "a camp", they're enjoying it. Camp is a tender feeling'.[21] There is plenty to laugh at in this *oeuvre*, but that does not necessarily mean it is a joke. Having invented a camp heteronym who writes camp works, there is every chance that Larkin loves and identifies with that invention. And it is fine for readers to do so too.

For Sontag, 'It goes without saying that the Camp sensibility is ... apolitical' – an uncharacteristic oversight in an otherwise unassailable essay.[22] How can this be, when she herself points to camp's delight in 'going against the grain of one's sex'? Sontag also describes how 'Camp sees everything in quotation marks', so that 'woman' becomes '"woman"'; consequently, 'To perceive Camp in objects and persons is to understand Being-as-Playing-a-Role. . . . Camp is the triumph of the epicene style. (The convertibility of "man" and "woman", "person" and "thing")'.[23] This is where Sontag's essay becomes most relevant to the heteronym, because Coleman is a delightful manifestation of 'Being-as-Playing-a-Role'. In this, camp has deeply political implications, showing as it does the constructed nature of gender.

This impulse is entirely in keeping with the deconstructive Larkin described by Osborne, though he only glances at this aspect of Larkin's career. Osborne places the Coleman *oeuvre* in what he calls the 'first phase' (of three) of Larkin's experiments in gender deconstruction, showing Larkin to be 'thoroughly at odds with the mid-century libidinal economy', when the nation 'witnessed the deepest entrenchment of patriarchal values since the Victorian era'.[24] It is important to remember that these texts were written during the fourth year of the Second World War, when four-and-a-half million British men were risking their lives in combat. In such a context, it would be easy to view the heteronym as straightforward escapism, but that would be intellectually lazy. Coleman's novel approach to gender and identity surely cannot be separated from its historical context, however oblique that context may be. The most explicit reference to the war is found in Coleman's brief introduction to the *Sugar and Spice* poems, where she writes: 'I make no apology for presenting a collection of what may seem "trivia" in these disturbed times. I feel that now more than ever a firm grasp on the essentials of life is needed' (*TWG*, 243). This statement has camp written all over it, especially when one turns the page and reads of how one girl has told her teacher that another girl's 'liking for French prose' is 'nothing but a pose' (*TWG*, 244). But we know from Sontag that camp is a form of seriousness unto itself. In this sense, it is easy to concur with Osborne's characterization of Coleman's words as 'a sturdy defense of the sanity of schoolgirl fiction when compared with the insanity of the actual world of men'.[25] To read Coleman's work as a joke is, to a very large extent, to short-change its radical potential. There are reasons for Larkin's use of a heteronym, and reasons for her to be both a woman and a lesbian – but a homophobic sneer is not one of them.

The end of an *oeuvre*

Rowe is clear that to understand 'the Brunette problem', 'we need to begin with Larkin's sexual history'.[26] But in these chapters, I have declined to build an analysis of the *oeuvre* on the dubious foundations of speculation about which way Larkin swung; instead, I have read these works on their own terms, allowing their preoccupations with genre, gender, sexuality and camp to emerge. Two parts of this *oeuvre*, however, have barely been discussed: Coleman's sheaf of poems, *Sugar and Spice*, which is discussed in Chapter 6 in constellation with

Larkin's early poetry; and the unfinished novella, *Michaelmas Term at St Bride's*, owing to the fact that it is the strangest and slipperiest of Coleman's works. On the one hand, *St Bride's* is simply the logical sequel to *Trouble at Willow Gables*: the girls have left school and gone up to Oxford to study at an all-women's college. But the plots are odder, Coleman's hitherto meticulous adherence to the Unity of Action falters and, as Castle puts it, 'the story breaks off abruptly in a welter of half-hearted "metafictional" incidents'.[27]

Why is this? The few critics sufficiently interested in the *oeuvre* have tried to account for why this story stumbles to a close, never to be revived. For Motion, it is simple: 'The main reason why *St Bride's* fails to reach a conclusion is that it loses its erotic impetus.'[28] But these are not erotic works, and it is difficult to see where the 'erotic impetus' takes off, let alone where it runs out of steam. Choi sticks with her psychoanalytical approach, arguing that 'in *Michaelmas Term at St Bride's* homosexuality becomes a more adult matter and by the end of the novella has faded into normality, which suggests that writing the stories played a therapeutic role.'[29] But this explanation suffers from the same problems as the psychological approach overall, namely its reliance on the clichéd, rather bizarre notion that one can work through one's homosexuality in order to arrive at the 'normative' state of heterosexuality (not to mention the fact that homosexuality was, in 1943, perceived as anything but 'normal'). Even if a particular sexuality can be exorcized through writing – which seems odd – the evidence for Larkin's own sexual preferences at this time is shaky. Cooper offers a different explanation, finding in the novella's closing pages an exploration of Jungian beliefs and practices: 'What the pub scene . . . represents', he argues, 'is the (Jungian) means by which Philippa is to be cured of her belt fetish' (a reference to this character's troubling obsession with belts).[30] Cooper takes his cue on this from Motion's biography, which traces Larkin's burgeoning interest in Jungian analytical psychology: at Oxford, he was stimulated by his contact with John Layard, erstwhile lover of Auden and student of Jung, whose talks at the university encouraged Larkin to practise dream analysis.

However, in making this connection between the biography and the heteronym, Cooper overlooks another, perhaps more integral influence, also discussed by Motion: Bruce Montgomery, who had pseudonymously written *The Case of the Gilded Fly* at the same time Larkin heteronymously wrote the Coleman works. Montgomery's detective novel is referenced in Coleman's second novella, months before its actual publication, and Larkin seems to have been hugely impressed by his friend's success and personality. Motion cites an autobiographical essay Larkin wrote the same year, which praises Montgomery:

'Under his immediate influence I suddenly revolted against all the things I'd previously worshipped – poetry, law, psychoanalysis, seriousness . . . and so forth'.[31]

This revolt fits with the camp ethic and aesthetic identified earlier, chiefly camp's very serious undermining of seriousness. (It also mimics, syntactically and emotionally, Isherwood's description of his relationship with Chalmers/Upward in *Lions and Shadows*: 'Under his influence . . . [t]he icy layers of my puritan priggishness, which were thicker far than he ever suspected, had begun, very slowly, to thaw'.)[32] Although Philippa's belt problem is moving – Booth detects a much more contemporary concern for adolescent anorexia – the response of her sister, Marie, is utterly ludicrous, and sends up the whole world of psychoanalysis and its high-minded seriousness.[33] Indeed, Layard even makes a thinly disguised appearance in the novella as 'Barnyard' (itself a version of 'Barnard', his fictionalized name in *Lions and Shadows*), and his expert guidance is about as reassuring as his name. Having attended Barnyard's talks, Marie decides her sister's belt fetish must be symbolic of something:

> 'Think of them. *Belts*.' She made a suggesting, writhing movement with her right arm, spilling her coffee.
> 'Swimming?' hazarded Myfanwy.
> 'No, silly. *Snakes. Worms. Slugs.* Symbols,' Marie enunciated portentously, 'of immense psychological depth.' (*TWG*, 186)

The answer – obviously – is to fill Philippa's room with worms, for which Philippa punishes Marie by lashing her with – guess what – a belt. This psychoanalytical subplot is patently absurd, and a mock-up of the 'cheap psychology' which Coleman identifies in her essay on the genre. In turn, it implicitly and pre-emptively ridicules the psychoanalytical approaches of those critics who have subsequently interpreted these texts through such a lens.

If not a loss of eroticism, if not a working-through of homosexuality and if not a Jungian resolution, what did happen to Brunette Coleman? Given her brilliance in laying down and following some solid rules of schoolgirl fiction, the biggest obstacle to the second novella's success must surely be her flouting of them. Taking into consideration Larkin's writerly anxieties during this period, discussed in Chapter 1 and elsewhere, an outpouring of highly original and entertaining prose must have been a joy, and the temptation to see it through to the girls' varsity years entirely understandable. But the problem with sending the girls to Oxford is that a sacred rule is instantly violated: Oxford is a university, and a city, but not a school for girls, and although the characters are resident in an all-women's college, the original 'little Copernican universe' of their school has been lost, when the point was to recover it. This violation has various consequences, not least the sudden presence of men, in all their horrid, paternalistic, self-important, sexually desperate and predatory forms. It is not long before men do indeed intrude on the girls' lives, most notably Clive Russell Vick and 'the Creature', neither one a poster boy for masculinity, or even humanity. The subplot involving these two men is humorous: they bond over their girl-troubles, not realizing that they have been chasing the same girl; but it is also clichéd, when much of Coleman's writing is not, and in truth, simply much less fun than the other works. In fact, the waning of fun is palpable. The final scene analysed by Cooper is not so much Jungian analysis as an outright lapse of interest in the narrative: entering a pub and recognizing the barmaids as the servants from Willow Gables, Marie asks why they are no longer at the school:

> 'That story's over now, Miss Marie,' she answered. 'Willow Gables doesn't exist any more.'
> 'Story?'
> 'Yes, Miss Marie. You tied me up, don't you remember?'
> 'Yes, of course, Pat, of course I remember. I'm sorry about that.'
> 'That's all right, Miss Marie. It was in the plot, so of course we had to do it. It wasn't your fault, Miss Marie.'
> 'Then whose fault was it, Pat?' enquired Marie, stumbling over the brass rail at her feet.
> 'The woman who writes all these books. Haven't you ever met her, Miss Marie? I saw her once.' (*TWG*, 228–9)

This is the 'welter of half-hearted "metafictional" incidents' which Castle describes. Confused, Marie continues to ask questions: 'But if this is a story, Pat . . . where's real life? If this is all untrue, where's reality?'; Pat responds that 'There's a good deal of it going on in the Smoke Room, at the moment' (*TWG*, 229). That room happens to be full of drunken, rowdy, immensely unlikeable men: the Creature; a 'weedy, jumpered' specimen; a 'rather aquiline old Malvernian' grinning 'in a ferocious manner', and so on. Members of 'The Seven', Larkin's Oxford gang, would likely recognize themselves in this depiction, but it is a depiction which shows how far Larkin has come from his earlier attempts to fictionalize the group: whereas in the short stories he wrote at Oxford he sought to enshrine the group for posterity in the way Isherwood had done for Auden et al., here it is a much more self-conscious portrayal of their repellent masculinity. This is explicitly rejected by Marie, who shuts the door on the Smoke Room: 'If this was reality, she decided, she would rather keep in the story' (*TWG*, 230). There is something very moving about the idea that Marie would rather remain in a make-believe world than deal with the realities of life as a young woman; this anticipates Katherine's numb refusal to play her gendered role at the end of *A Girl in Winter* (discussed in Chapter 5).

Coleman, too, can no longer feign interest in the story, which fails her own tests. Marie stumbles out of the pub, sees a green light in the darkness, recognizes it as her sister Philippa's torch, 'which Marie remembered had been dimmed with green tissue-paper from round a cracker' – and with this banal detail, the Coleman *oeuvre* ends (*TWG*, 230–1). Having set out with such a strong vision, Coleman has been unable to block out 'reality' – which largely means men – and consequently gives up. The heteronym dies off, never to be revived with the same energy or clarity of purpose. But Coleman's significance for Larkin's career would be momentous, and the following chapters demonstrate why. Chapter 5 traces her influence on the two novels Larkin published within four years of Coleman's retirement. Chapter 6 then reads Coleman's *Sugar and Spice* poems as part of Larkin's poetic development during these years, showing how an otherwise imitative and immature poet learned the lessons of this heteronym to become a great poet.

5

The outward turn
Larkin's novels

This chapter looks at Larkin's two published novels, *Jill* (1946) and *A Girl in Winter* (1947). It reads them as the next stage in his literary development which was, crucially, indebted to the Coleman works of 1943. Though this development would be slower to take hold of his poetry, discussed in Chapter 6, that poetry could not have been written without the outward turn which these novels involved.

Coleman's legacy

At first, *Jill* seems like a regression for Larkin's fiction, returning to a male protagonist and male undergraduate life. But following Coleman's surprisingly productive intervention in Larkin's writer's education, there was no return to the imitative, Isherwoodesque, self-absorbed writing of the earlier short fictions. It is surely significant that Larkin began working on the story that would eventually become *Jill* in autumn 1943, whilst still engaged with Coleman's work. He told Amis that Coleman was 'helping me', although he did not explain how (*SL*, 63). Coleman's influence is clear to see in the letters, stories and diaries which the protagonist John Kemp concocts. These recycle many details and much of the atmosphere of Coleman's genre fiction: Jill, John's fantasy stepsister, attends a girls' boarding school called 'Willow Gables', and she continues the Colemanesque tradition of principled rebellion against authority (*J*, 143–5). But Coleman also helped Larkin in ways he would have been too embarrassed to tell Amis. Although *Jill* would see publication, and therefore finally herald Larkin's arrival as a bona fide novelist – his ambition since the 1930s – the unpublished and in some ways unpublishable works of Brunette Coleman continued to enhance Larkin's writer's education. In *Jill*, however, the surrogate authorship which 'P. A. Larkin' and Brunette Coleman represented is now absorbed into the text: the novel *explores*, rather than enacts, the possibilities and pitfalls of authorship and invention.

Although Motion also reads *Jill* as a stage in Larkin's education, he does so in the same psycho-sexual terms as his analysis of Brunette Coleman: the novel delves into Larkin's unconscious, but keeps this 'strictly monitored, and renders it respectable'; Larkin 'knew that its narrative depended on a secret source: the novel's heterosexually inspired finale was based on an earlier, homosexually inspired story' ('Peter').[1] Motion's account is not alert to the artificially homosexual aesthetic of the earlier story, identified in Chapter 2, but also overestimates the novel's heterosexuality. Whilst it is true that *Jill*'s crisis turns on John's botched attempt to seduce a girl, the events leading up to this are distinctly non-sexual.

This is reflected in the language of the novel: more than once, John's attraction to women is described as 'theoretical'. Standing face-to-face with Elizabeth as she corrects his bow tie, he feels a 'flaring theoretical lust'; later, talking to Gillian, he thinks that 'In theory he wanted to take hold of her' (*J*, 109, 191). This is an intriguing word to repeat, especially in the context of desire, and especially given Larkin's claim that he wrote his novels 'with intense care for detail. If one word was used on page 15 I didn't re-use it on page 115' (*FR*, 24). This is where we can begin to properly detect Coleman's legacy: John's interest in women has little to do with lust and everything to do with their otherness. Just as Hilary in *Trouble at Willow Gables* is drawn to Mary's 'tawny strength', John's attraction to the opposite sex is unconventional. Sitting in a lecture theatre 'full of young women' – the demographic reflecting the wartime context – he does not show the kind of interest which might be expected of a male undergraduate surrounded by female peers; instead, he thinks about Mrs Warner, his roommate's mother, with whom he has just had tea:

> His mind dwelt pleasurably on her uprightness, her precision in handing a cup and saucer, the individuality that caused her to go hatless and show her fine dark hair, that was at once comely and mature. There was something about her that he had never met before, something that made him want to see her again, to live where she lived. She affected him like an invigorating climate. (*J*, 96)

These things do not suggest sexual interest in the older woman; similarly, his 'theoretical lust' for Elizabeth is triggered by thinking about her hair, which 'fascinated John, who imagined her brushing it, beating it up on both sides till it stood up of its own accord like whipped white of egg' (*J*, 107–8). In contrast, sex is an alien, even troubling concept for John. Discovering his roommate's contraceptives, he feels 'as alarmed as if he had found a loaded revolver' (*J*, 38). As in 'An Incident in the English Camp', and Coleman's stories and poems, the world of women and their things – their hairbrushes and hats – provides a particular pleasure. But that pleasure is noticeably non-sexual, and any expectation of a more salacious male gaze does not materialize.

John's otherness

Indeed, John is not merely fascinated by otherness, but is in many ways the embodiment of it. His asexual personality is just one aspect of his characterization as an 'in-between' figure, someone whose identity never quite fits in. Larkin's burgeoning interest in otherness, clearly shown by the work he produced throughout 1943, manifests itself in John in several ways. The most apparent is John's social class, the subject of much discussion in the scholarship on *Jill*. When the novel was reissued by Faber in 1963, Larkin's introduction recalled an American critic who had 'recently suggested that *Jill* contained the first example of that characteristic landmark of the British post-war novel, the displaced working-class hero'. Although willing to acknowledge this as 'fair trend-spotter's comment', Larkin denied that this was his intention: 'In 1940 our impulse was still to minimize social differences rather than exaggerate them. My hero's background, though an integral part of the story, was not what the story was about' (*J*, 11). When asked about this in a 1982 interview, he denied it again: '*Jill* has none of the political overtones of that *genre*. John's being working-class was a kind of equivalent of my stammer, a built-in handicap to put him one down' (*RW*, 63).

Whilst Larkin's assertion that this is 'not what the story was about' is reasonable, his desire to suppress critical interest in social difference is betrayed by his own evocations of it, in the short stories he wrote at Oxford, and in *Jill*. Always a slippery guide to his own work, Larkin is happy to cite his autobiography when it suits: the novel reflects his 'impulse' in 1940 to minimize social differences, and John's class is actually a version of his 'stammer'. But in a different interview, Larkin uses autobiography to distance himself from John: 'I certainly went up to Oxford, I certainly shared a room with a chap, I certainly rushed home to Coventry when it was bombed in my first term; on the other hand, I was not poor, I liked the chap I shared rooms with, and I didn't make up a fantasy about a younger sister' (*FR*, 33). When an American edition of *Jill* appeared in 1976, Larkin reiterated this point in an extended introduction:

> My original purpose in writing an introduction of this kind was to make clear that my own Oxford life was rather different from that of my hero; nevertheless, over the years I can see that I have been to some extent identified with him . . . Perhaps . . . I may receive a few more degrees of imaginative credit for my hero's creation. (*RW*, 25)

With a hint of snobbery, he remarks that 'thanks to my father's generosity, my education was at no time a charge on public or other funds' (*RW*, 25). Which is it to be, then? Should we ignore the class element in *Jill* because Larkin experienced no sense of social difference, or because Larkin *was* socially different to his protagonist? The contradiction should prevent us from accepting Larkin as the interpretive authority.

In fact, Larkin's 'intense care for detail' consistently presents John as a working-class fish out of water. He has grown up in Lancashire in the fictional industrial town of Huddlesford; his father is a retired policeman who supplements his pension by 'job-carpentering', and who needs persuading to let his son apply to Oxford, where John is eventually admitted as a 'poor scholar' (*J*, 73, 26). From this background John finds himself in a university where other students have names like 'the Hon. S. A. A. Ransom' (*J*, 27). In short, class matters in *Jill*. However, Larkin's denial that the novel should be seen as a forerunner to the Angry Young Men movement should be heeded, and for important reasons. Other than a working-class upbringing, John shares nothing in common with a character like Jim Dixon in Amis's *Lucky Jim*. Jim is a boisterous, sexually successful male whose fragile tolerance of the bourgeois academic environment can only last so long. By the end of the novel, he has rejected the conceits and pretensions of middle-class academia and moved with a new girlfriend to London, where, it is implied, he will lead a more cosmopolitan and liberated life. In the novels of the Angry Young Men, working-class protagonists kick out at their constraints and forge more desirable paths for themselves. John is constitutionally incapable of doing this. His attempts to ingratiate himself with Christopher Warner, his loutish, public school-educated roommate, invariably fail. His is *not* the story of a plucky working-class lad determined to punch his way up.

That said, *Jill* is also not the story of a working-class lad who learns to be comfortable travelling between his humble background and his privileged new life. That part is played by Whitbread, who should make a natural choice of companion for John. A fellow northern poor scholar, Whitbread believes that 'you have to choose your friends carefully. No good going about with millionaires'; he takes his studies seriously, and understands the opportunities for self-improvement opened up by an Oxford education (*J*, 52). In contrast, the novel's analepses show John to be just as alienated in Huddlesford as he is in Oxford. To his English teacher he is just 'A pale boy in a corner', a description which echoes the novel's opening, where we find John 'with a pale face and soft pale hair' sitting 'in the corner of an empty compartment in a train'. Although loving, his relationship with his family is awkward, and contrasts with the self-assurance of the two 'Ws', Warner and Whitbread. John is brighter and harder-working than Warner, despite the latter's expensive education, but lacks the determination and confidence of Whitbread.

Consequently, from his first day at Oxford, John feels as though 'he had wandered into a place where he had absolutely no counterpart' (*J*, 33). Without the benefit of the very different kinds of confidence exuded by Warner and Whitbread, he floats through his first term as a nobody. Cooper argues that *Jill* charts John's 'Alienation from bourgeois values', but a major barrier to John's happiness is his alienation from working-class values too.[2] Caught in the no-man's land between an assured working-class identity and an assured middle-class one, if there is an analogue to be found in post-war British literature, it is in the moving poetry of Tony Harrison, rather than the celebrated impudence of novels by Kingsley Amis, John Wain and Alan Sillitoe.

Perhaps because of this nuanced relation to class, a number of critics have questioned John's characterization. Booth, for instance, considers the novel 'confused and incoherent', arguing that this is resolved in *A Girl in Winter*, where the protagonist is a 'foreign woman' whose 'loneliness requires no detailed social explanation'.[3] Whilst Katherine Lind's otherness is more obvious, it seems odd that John's should require explanation. His double alienation – from working-class and middle-class life – is surely recognizable to the many thousands of working-class graduates who have passed through Britain's elite universities in the decades since they began opening up to a wider social pool.

John is also shy – a personality trait shared by millions, regardless of social class. Because he is shy, he cannot embrace or exploit undergraduate life, as Whitbread and Warner do. Instead, he floats through Oxford in a daze, as the other to every potential 'counterpart' he meets. Two early depictions of John's shyness are extraordinarily acute: the train carriage farce, in which John does not dare to eat his own food in front of the other passengers, and ends up having theirs pressed on him; and the encounter with a taxi driver, whom John gives 'half a crown' and then hurries off, because he is 'afraid that the man would try to give him sixpence change' (J, 22–5). When Christopher helps himself to the crockery John's mother has lovingly bought for him, John stares 'at the coffee-strainer that had been used to strain tea, and feeling sorry for it, as if they had suffered in the same way' (J, 33). These are painfully real psychological moments, and they show Larkin exploring the condition of otherness with even greater sensitivity and pathos than in the Coleman works.

In short, then, John represents a logical progression from the experiments Larkin was undertaking in Coleman's name around the same time he began writing *Jill*. Having been drawn away from the artificial autofictions of 'Story I' and 'Peter' by the exercises completed at a distance by 'P. A. Larkin' and Brunette Coleman, Larkin restored a male undergraduate protagonist to his writing, but was now more interested in exploring the awkward and often painful experience of an otherness only superficially related to his own life. If Coleman was the major breakthrough in his writer's education, then *Jill* reaped the rewards by giving Larkin his first 'serious' and published novel.

Jill and the problems and possibilities of authorship

Coleman, of course, influences *Jill* in more apparent ways. Her schoolgirl world is transplanted into the novel within the altered context of John's inventions. The fictions he generates by imagining a younger stepsister transform John into an author-figure, and therefore make it even easier to read *Jill* as another stage in Larkin's writer's education. This aspect has stimulated the most discussion about the novel's objectives. Cooper believes that the novel charts John's 'movement away from fantasy and towards reality, a process accompanied by hard lessons about the social milieu he once courted', whilst Booth tentatively argues that *Jill* 'offers, so it seems, a didactic lesson on reality and illusion', although the novel's poetry shows that 'In the end the author himself prefers dream to reality'.[4] Motion also writes that John's 'attempt to create an independent existence has failed', but qualifies this by drawing attention to John's change of tone at the end: 'Previously he had resigned his ability to make choices; now he is able to concede that control over things – which involves making choices between them – is at least desirable, even if finally impossible.'[5] But these accounts simplify the novel as a didactic narrative about the inevitable slide from comforting fantasy to harsh reality. In fact, John's project has two stages: the first is his artistic creation of a world 'outside himself', to once again borrow this phrase from 'The Eagles Are Gone'; the second stage is his attempt to imagine himself into that world. It is at that point that everything goes wrong and John faces disastrous consequences. But this disaster should not hurry us into an analysis of the novel which soberly rejects invention: the thrill of John's pure artistic creation is palpable, and cannot be suppressed. In other words, John's mistake is not to artistically invent and explore the lives of others, but to try and artistically alter the circumstances of his own life. Given Larkin's transition away from writing fictions that were paradoxically autobiographical *and* efforts to present himself as the kind of writer he was not, this thematic concern in *Jill* clearly represents a working-out of literary principles and practices for the young author. John invents an other so that Larkin can further explore the problems and pitfalls of writing otherness.

John's initial impulse for inventing Jill is to stimulate Christopher's interest and jealousy. The emotions he experiences whilst doing so are likened to music, and therefore align John's tale-telling with the act of artistic creation: 'he was excited, filled with tentative little lyrical thoughts, like the mutterings of the orchestra before the overture to an opera' (J, 119). At this point there is a subtle shift in the narrative perspective: for the first time, Christopher observes John, thereby signalling John's sudden assumption of agency. It does not take long for Christopher to lose interest, but John's only intensifies, and is again associated with music: 'From next door came the sound of a piano . . . Jill came into his mind, as now she would (though he did not know this yet) whenever his emotions were stirred gently. He imagined that it was she playing the piano that he could hear' (J, 120–1). He then begins to write letters ostensibly from Jill. Her schoolgirl slang ('*Give me plenty of details because Maisie Fenton's got a brother at Cambridge and is being just* insufferable *about him*') is something Larkin has picked up from Coleman, but some critics have remarked on the implausibility of John's instant ability to adopt it (J, 122). But John is surrounded by the argot of privileged male and female teenagers fresh from boarding school. Within minutes of entering college for the first time, he is taken aback by Elizabeth's speech, 'never having heard before this self-parodying southern coo' (J, 28). Perhaps it is John's excessive sensitivity and his enforced status as passive observer which enables his mimicry. More importantly, Larkin's treatment of dialogue like this is evidence of the progress he has made since the stories written the previous year: whereas in 'Story I' and 'Peter' the affected manner is something he imitates because he covets it, in *Jill* it is imitated in order to be parodied. No longer trying to mimic the authors he admires, Larkin instead faithfully records the world around him.

John temporarily adopts Christopher's vernacular in his replies to Jill ('*My dear Christopher, you shall have it by ten o'clock*'), but abandons this when his own intentions are suddenly crystallized:

> He found an envelope from the drawer and addressed it to:
>
> *Miss Jill ——*
>
> His pen hung over the word 'Kemp'. He did not like it. He did not, he found, want to connect her with himself in that way. What should he call her? After a moment he finished it:
>
> *Miss Jill Bradley.*
>
> Bradley was a nice name, it was English, it was like saddle-leather and stables. (J, 130–1)

Having initially conceived of Jill as someone intimately connected to him in order to make Christopher jealous, John begins to relish the impersonality of his creation. Dropping the letter into a postbox, he is 'filled with exultation at the idea of thus speaking with nothingness' (J, 131). There are important resonances with Larkin's own development here. Firstly, John's adoption of the letter as a space in which he can construct and rehearse other identities mirrors one of the major functions of Larkin's correspondence with Sutton, discussed in Chapter 1. Secondly, the 'exultation' John feels at having created a character and narrative with an independent existence mirrors Larkin's move towards characters and narratives 'outside himself'. As Booth puts it, 'Larkin succeeds in conveying the exaltation of the artist in the act of selfless creation.'[6] Dialogue with the self – psychologically boundless but an aesthetic dead end – has been replaced by dialogue with an imagined other: 'That Christopher had been the mainspring of the idea had long been obscured', John realizes (J, 133).

It seems logical that John should then exploit this onset of creativity to rewrite his own unhappy existence. In subsequent letters to Jill, he recounts the events of his first four weeks at Oxford, but falsifies them in order to make himself appear interesting and impressive. Much like Larkin's attempts to make The Seven appear significant before any of them were, this has limited potential, and John becomes unable to continue writing to Jill:

> He got up, wandered round the room; stood idly making bread pellets and flicking them at the photograph of Mrs. Warner, then made up the fire. These sudden pauses were quite usual, but this time he felt that he had reached some insuperable barrier that it was unlikely he could remove. . . . The next day he tried again, even starting again on a fresh sheet, but he could manage nothing but a few scanty reminiscences of their holiday in Wales. (J, 135)

His epiphany is a crucial one: 'Suddenly it was she who was important, she who was interesting, she whom he longed to write about; beside her, he and his life seemed dusty and tedious' (*J*, 135). With this in mind, John tries out different ways of writing about Jill: he works on a 'continuous narrative' 'in the third person'; 'It was much easier . . . than continuing to write the letters: he found his invention put out more flowers than he had expected' (*J*, 136). By the end, he has produced 'a kind of short story', and has, therefore, entered the realm of authorship inhabited by Larkin. Reading it back the next day, however, John is disappointed: 'It seemed to present nothing of the Jill he knew; indeed, it blurred her image rather than anything else.' Deciding that 'what it lacked was intimacy', he abandons the third person and instead imagines Jill's diary (*J*, 149). He is soon disappointed again: 'He had not moved one inch nearer creating an independent Jill; all he had done was to model himself on her image' (*J*, 152). John wants to truly permeate the inner life of his invention, but struggles to do so. But the important thing is that he has realized this is what he wants to do. The progression of John's writing from second person, to third person, to first person, broadly replicates Larkin's own efforts before and during 1943 to push further into a world 'outside himself'. In other words, John's struggle to achieve insight into a fictionalized other is a version of the struggle which has, so far, brought Larkin to write *Jill*.

Teasingly, John's blockage is resolved in a vision which comes to him as he eats lunch in Hall: 'The sensation he had was of looking intently into the centre of a pure white light: he seemed to see the essence of Jill, around which all the secondary material things formed and reformed as he wrote them down' (*J*, 152). Rushing to his room, 'eager to get back to pen and paper', he is interrupted by a student who 'began talking persuasively about the activities of some political club'. John's revelation evaporates: 'that extraordinary clarity of perception that had been vouchsafed him for a few moments had gone, utterly gone' (*J*, 154). Intriguingly, the annihilation of John's artistic vision by an interruption concerning current affairs echoes Coleman's disregard of the 'ephemeral chatter' of political writers like Orwell (*TWG*, 256). This is where things start to unravel for John, and where the second stage of his adventures in authorship begins. Moodily skulking around Oxford, he enters a bookshop:

> Then as he was absently fingering the edges of an uncut page with a transient sense of frustration, his glance wandered along the aisle where he was standing and he received a shock that could not have been greater if a brick had been thrown through the plate-glass shop-window.
> He saw Jill. (*J*, 156)

Convinced that this girl is the stepsister he has invented, John strikes up an awkward conversation, but she hurriedly gets away. For days, he stalks the streets of Oxford, searching for her. The thrill John feels at thinking his invention has become reality is a reversal of the thrill he felt at creating something impersonal, since he now tries to imagine himself into that invention: 'If he could make friends with her he must push her back into her own life, where he himself could follow. Never must she be allowed to go outside her own life. And then through her he might enter this life, this other innocent life she led' (J, 170). It is notable that the phrase 'outside her own life' echoes the one in 'The Eagles Are Gone': 'everything outside himself'. It also echoes the phrase Larkin would later use to discuss Hardy's influence – 'relapse back into one's own life' – discussed later in Chapter 6. So soon after discovering it, John vacates the realm of impersonal artistic creation, and enters the realm of self-interested fantasy. He has already tried, more than once, to reconstruct the reality of his life. After meeting Mrs Warner, he fantasized that he was 'her son' (J, 90); later, he tried to embody Christopher: 'John went through all the actions of a rich young man (Christopher), choosing a bow-tie in a shop' (J, 98). In the end, he only felt 'shame' (J, 106). Christopher was also the reason for Jill's invention, but this was soon forgotten when John began to enjoy the experience of artistic creation for its own sake. The bizarre projection of his creation into reality shows John repeating his earlier mistakes. On discovering that the girl – Gillian, not Jill – is Elizabeth's cousin, and that she has visited his rooms, 'he crossed to the sofa and drank the cold dregs from Jill's cup, putting his mouth where hers had been' (J, 177). This is a recurrence of Patrick Rush's act in 'Story I', and whilst this might suggest that homosexuality has been replaced by heterosexuality in Larkin's fiction, John's action comes from a far more complex and non-sexual place. It is another attempt to become part of the world he has invented.

That the novel considers this a mistake is surely shown by subsequent events. John's obsession with Gillian is temporarily forgotten when a German air raid is launched on his home town. He hurries back, conscious that 'he seemed to be leaving a region of unreality and insubstantial pain for the real world where he could really be hurt' (J, 211). As Booth suggests, this should, 'by all normal novelistic criteria, be Kemp's sternest lesson in "reality"'.[7] But his home is undamaged, his parents safe, and John seizes the opportunity to return to his fantasy existence: 'The thought excited him. It was as if he had been told: all the past is cancelled: all the suffering connected with that town, all your childhood, is wiped out. Now there is a fresh start for you: you are no longer governed by what has gone before' (J, 219). There is a quietly hysterical coldness about this too-easy break with the past and with reality. Returning to Oxford, he suffers a breakdown, vandalizing Whitbread's room, burning his own creative writings, getting drunk and making a pass at Gillian. In consequence he is punched by Christopher, manhandled by a crowd of drunks and thrown into the college fountain. Days later, laid up in bed with bronchial pneumonia, John's thoughts about how he should now approach life have something of the tone of Paul Morel's crisis at the end of *Sons and Lovers* – Lawrence's own writer's education novel, worshipped by Larkin. John's dunking in the fountain is a very literal way of extinguishing his fantasies, and inverts a classic staple of the college initiation ceremony. Instead of being initiated into a community, John is expelled from his fantasy world back into the real one. This makes it easy to read *Jill* as a 'back to reality' narrative, as numerous critics have. But the lesson is subtler than that. John's error is to breach the border between creativity and fantasy; it is this mistake for which he pays. One cannot help but wonder how things might have turned out had John stuck with the impersonal model of authorship which he began to practise, nor can one forget the joy he felt whilst doing so.

If *Jill* offers a didactic lesson, it is this: you cannot simply write yourself into different, more desirable circumstances. This is precisely what Larkin had tried to do in his imitations of Lawrence and Isherwood, and which he was still attempting in his Yeatsian poetry, a problem discussed in Chapter 6. Gillian resists the frame within which John tries so hard to enclose her: 'It's not Jill!', she snaps (J, 192). John's mistake is also paralleled elsewhere in the novel by his English teacher, Mr Crouch, a promising young graduate who feels 'his work as a schoolmaster ended at a point below that at which his work as a graduate began' (J, 67). In order to alleviate his discontent – his name suggests inhibited potential – he devises a plan to 'catch a boy in the present fifth form . . . and encourage and develop his talents' (J, 68). John is that boy, and there is no question that his place at Oxford would not have been possible without Crouch's influence, though it is questionable whether this was the right path. Interestingly, this provides another instance of Larkin's undoing of genre conventions. As James Fenton points out, the 'literature of the British school' is full of examples of 'a certain gifted or exceptionally dedicated individual on the staff', someone who 'finds a way of engaging', 'amusing', 'impressing' and getting the pupils to 'work to some purpose'.[8] Crouch fulfils this generic function only to undo it. Importantly, he fails to elicit the satisfaction his scheme was designed to deliver. Had he coached John for selfless reasons, this might not have been the case, but the plot was self-interested from the start: an attempt to improve his own life by playing with someone else's. Wisely, he gives up and focuses on more attainable desires: 'The chief interest of his life was a correspondence he was conducting with the girl he now wanted to marry' (*J*, 85). In other words, Crouch takes the advice of a later Larkin poem about a different kind of parentage and gets out whilst he can. If only John had done the same, the novel suggests.

This is a lesson Larkin was beginning to learn for himself, as Brunette Coleman wooed him away from his doomed attempts to become a latter-day Isherwood. It was also a lesson he was learning in relation to Lawrence, as shown by the correspondence with Sutton, and a lesson yet to be learned in his verse, which Larkin was still using in order to live up to a Yeatsian poetic identity. *Jill* shows the dangers of fantasy and imitation, whilst still celebrating creativity and the imagination. It privileges the impersonal act of creation over the personal. Bruce Montgomery thought it an error to look in *Jill* for 'portents of the notable poet-to-come'.[9] Yet *Jill* was an important stage in the journey Larkin took to become that poet. To systematically read Larkin's fiction from the late 1930s through the 1940s is to witness a writer developing by taking bigger and bigger strides towards an 'interest in everything outside himself'. *Jill* explores this phenomenon in fiction. In Larkin's subsequent novel, *A Girl in Winter*, we find him no longer exploring these ideas, but instead confidently putting them into practice.

Perspective

A Girl in Winter is the peak of Larkin's achievements in fiction; John Bayley has described it as 'one of the finest and best sustained prose poems in the language'.[10] Though Larkin would attempt other novels, in this one he writes with unprecedented sophistication, having absorbed the lessons of his writer's education leading up to and including *Jill*. The plot is much less clunky than in *Jill*, but, more importantly, Larkin moves away from the safety device of surrogate authorship which he had used differently in 'An Incident in the English Camp', the Brunette Coleman *oeuvre*, and *Jill*. Instead of writing *about* writing otherness, or doing it through a mediating authorial figure, Larkin simply *writes* otherness – sensitively and beautifully.

An important strategy is Larkin's exploitation of multiple perspectives. Multiplicity is embedded in the novel's tripartite structure: Part One introduces us to a day in the life of Katherine Lind, a young woman exiled to a provincial English town from an unspecified European country; Part Two comprises one long analepsis to an English summer in her childhood, spent with the Fennel family as part of an exchange scheme with their son, Robin; Part Three returns to the wintery setting of Part One. This structure means that each part of the novel is inflected by the events of the other two: Katherine's memory of a dreamy summer in the English countryside, for example, is challenged by the icier events and urban provinciality of the two sections which flank it.

Tolley describes both novels as 'a straightforward realist narrative by a third person narrator' with 'none of the innovations of modernism'.[11] This is odd, given the number of modernist reverberations found in both. In its examination of authorship, *Jill* participates in the 'myth-kitty' Larkin would later denounce, by referencing a number of artistic mythologies: Crouch's aim to 'mould' John 'Like a sculptor' makes him a Pygmalion who, unlike his forerunner, falls *out* of love with his creation; his later description of John as 'a mechanical man he had painfully constructed . . . suddenly come to life' turns Pygmalion into Victor Frankenstein; John's 'emaciated' reflection after imagining himself as Christopher is a version of Wilde's Dorian Gray; and the interruption of his vision alludes to Coleridge's tale of the Person from Porlock (*RW*, 79; *J*, 72, 83, 97, 154). Larkin described *Jill*'s style as 'double-distilled purity of essence-of-Mansfield', the New Zealand modernist being one of his literary obsessions at this time.[12] In *A Girl in Winter*, he honours her by giving his protagonist the same forename. Other modern influences on his style include Lawrence, George Moore and Henry Green. There are numerous textual echoes of works by Woolf and Joyce: the events of Parts One and Three take place within a single day, a structure borrowed from two monumental works of High Modernism, *Ulysses* (1922) and *Mrs Dalloway* (1925). Importantly, although Katherine provides the novel's centre of consciousness, Larkin adopts the 'tunnelling' technique devised by Woolf for *Mrs Dalloway*. In a 1923 diary entry, she wrote:

> I should say a good deal about *The Hours* [the novel's original title] and my discovery: how I dig out beautiful caves behind my characters: I think that gives exactly what I want; humanity, humour, depth. The idea is that the caves shall connect and each comes to daylight at the present moment.[13]

Larkin's novel certainly contains more 'humanity, humour, depth' than any of his previous fictions; but whilst Katherine sometimes achieves the insight Woolf describes, the process is fraught with difficulties. This is important, because it shows Larkin no longer obsessively examining himself, and instead grappling with the more interesting and fruitful subject of human relations.

Katherine's boss at the library where she works, for example, is the novel's almost vaudevillian hate figure: his name, Mr Anstey, is as close to an anagram of 'nasty' as Larkin can get away with. Katherine's dislike for him, although by no means unjustified, is bitterly unrelenting; even after learning that he lost his wife five years ago, her response shows no sign of warming: "'I'm sorry for her,' said Katherine. "She must have had a dog's life. He's so *stupid*"' (*AGW*, 37). She sees Anstey as 'a thin, wizened man of about forty, with a narrow, lined face and delicate spectacles. His suit was grimy, she disliked his tie, and he wore a pullover whose sleeves came down below his cuffs' (*AGW*, 16). To Katherine, he is 'an insect she would relish treading on' (*AGW*, 19). Later, the novel's plot conspires to make her pick up the wrong handbag, which contains a letter she suspects is written in Anstey's 'mincing hand': 'If it was a private letter, of course, that still did not prevent Anstey's having written it; it was only that she had not imagined him as an individual who had friends like everyone else. The thought was as unfamiliar as meeting him in the street on a Sunday' (*AGW*, 187). Katherine's hatred for Anstey dehumanizes him; to find evidence of his life elsewhere, let alone his inner life, comes as a shock. Reading the letter, written to a woman called Veronica Parbury, whom he wishes to marry, her astonishment is exacerbated:

> It was ridiculous to think of Mr. Anstey marrying anyone, but that was the first thing that would come to anyone's mind if they read the letter. No-one would write so guardedly unless their feelings were involved. But him! Had he any feelings? It was absurd. Yet she was not amused. She read through it again. If only it had been a simple, blurting letter, she might have been scornful easily . . . . But as it was, the figure of him was blurring in her mind, no longer a sharply-cut target for loathing . . . . Her compact hatred dissipated against it, like a herd deprived of its driver, pulled up, beginning to amble in all directions, grown purposeless. (*AGW*, 189)

That Anstey might have a life independent of the library, and a romantic one too, had never crossed Katherine's mind. It is only the chance discovery of the letter which forces her to confront the possibility. Here, two caves are tunnelled out to meet each other. Indeed, when Katherine is invited into Miss Parbury's flat (having returned the handbag), she experiences something of a Woolfian moment of being:

> Katherine looked across the hearthrug to where she sat . . . and at this she happened to see both of them less as people than as the 'other person' who is so necessary. Looking at her . . . she glimpsed the undertow of people's relations, two-thirds of which is without face, with only begging and lonely hands. (*AGW*, 199–200)

Returning to the library, she is summoned to Anstey's office for yet another of his petulant reprimands, but realizes 'with annoyance that she could not hate him as simply as she had done, now that she had come across this part of him that had no bearing on her. For her conception of him as a hostile cartoon she had to substitute a person who had and could evoke feelings' (*AGW*, 204–5). Although Anstey does not reciprocate, Katherine has been forced to confront and realign the limited subjectivity of her perspective on others.

It is surely significant, given Larkin's own conception of letter-writing as an opportunity to model alternative selves, that he should use the device of the found letter to signal the performativity and multiplicity of identity. Katherine herself should not be surprised to discover an unexpected dimension to Anstey, given her own epistolary experiences. The novel's middle section charts her gradual uncovering of a kind of epistolary fraud. The fraught perspective on others which this gives her foreshadows the situation with Anstey. Katherine's initial feeling about the letter exchange scheme proposed by her teacher is one of 'alarm': hearing her classmates read their partners' replies, she feels 'quite incapable of keeping her end up in this kind of exchange' (*AGW*, 67). This shows, as Chapter 1 argued, how much letter-writing is a conscious and laboured act of identity construction. With Robin Fennel's 'very formal' replies, she feels relief, since the pressure to construct a consistently interesting epistolary identity is removed: 'Even her friends were hard put to it to find anything funny or thrilling'; 'The only tangible thing he seemed to do was go [*sic*] bicycle rides, and so they called him "the bicyclist"' (*AGW*, 68).

But Katherine soon resents the girls' verdict that she 'had drawn a blank', and, 'although the exchange affected her no more than an interminable business correspondence', she finds ways to 'draw him out' (*AGW*, 68). Katherine believes she can access Robin's 'real' self, if only she can coax him to write more intimately. This becomes a dispassionate exercise for her, done only because 'she disliked failing in anything she attempted' (*AGW*, 69). Eventually she gives up, sending only perfunctory replies. But then a letter arrives with an invitation for her to stay with the family, which makes her feel as though she was 'holding a live hand-grenade' (*AGW*, 70). The simile reflects the potential for the artificiality of epistolary selves to be exploded by face-to-face contact. As a result, she re-reads their correspondence 'critically': 'The first thing that struck her was that they really said very little about cycling – or cathedrals, for that matter. . . . What was really important, she thought, was that he should have kept on writing, promptly and indefatigably' (*AGW*, 71).

Katherine hopes her stay with Robin will finally reveal his true character, but is again disappointed: 'When was Robin going to start behaving naturally? So far he had stood insipidly upon his party-manners, even when they had been alone, as if playing at grown-ups' (*AGW*, 90). In contrast, she takes an almost instant dislike to Jane, his older sister, mirroring her later dislike of Anstey, and seemingly for similar reasons: 'She was short-mannered and irritable. Her hair was cut rather outmodedly into an Eton crop, and her figure was small, bony and unemphatic' (*AGW*, 94). Annoyingly, Jane goes everywhere with them, and Katherine hopes for some time alone with Robin so that he can drop the act of polite stiffness. The opportunity comes, but results in yet more disappointment: 'Katherine had returned from the walk puzzled. Nothing notable had happened after Jane left them. If she had expected an onset of personalities, she was disappointed' (*AGW*, 135). On a punting trip, she instead engages him in conversation about his sister, but Robin has little to say: 'She is strange, as you say. I don't know much about her. If you watch carefully, we ought to be seeing some of the spires from here' (*AGW*, 138). As in 'The Eagles Are Gone', the favoured and apparently more precocious sibling shows little interest in the sibling who has been written off. And when Jane and Katherine talk privately, Larkin also replays the narrative of 'The Eagles Are Gone' by revealing the written-off sibling to be the more intriguing one: Jane confesses that it was her idea to invite Katherine. This, too, has strong resonances with the epistolary theories discussed in Chapter 1. Katherine feels angry that Jane has read her correspondence with Robin; as Jane points out, 'there was nothing personal in them', but Katherine's emotion is valid, given how letters are tailored specifically for the intended recipient; being read by unintended eyes feels like a violation (*AGW*, 148). Furthermore, Jane's envy of Robin's participation in the letter exchange scheme is explained by her understanding of letter-writing as an activity which makes anything possible:

> It was about the only thing he's done I should have liked to do myself.... I think it would be fascinating to write to somebody who didn't know you, who'd never seen you, even, and who didn't even live in the same country. You could tell them anything, and it wouldn't matter: you could make out you were all sorts of things you weren't, and they wouldn't know any different. Or you could tell them the truth, and see how they took it. (*AGW*, 148)

This, too, is redolent of the Larkin-Sutton correspondence: although the two had known each other since school, the wartime context in which much of their correspondence occurred separated them geographically, and it was that distance which allowed them to collaborate on the construction of their artistic identities.

Indeed, for much of the correspondence, Larkin made himself out to be 'all sorts of things' he was not, most notably the next D. H. Lawrence, whilst also deeming Sutton to be the next generation's great painter. When Larkin's projected artistic identity began to be fulfilled, albeit according to a non-Lawrentian model, and Sutton's did not, the correspondence lacked purpose and dissipated. Whilst different selfhoods may be constructed by the act of letter-writing, then, this can have unintended or unforeseen consequences. Jane envies Robin because she would like the chance to explore different identities; reading Katherine's letters, she thinks this is someone 'I should have liked to know myself'; but having now met her, she tacitly acknowledges this to be a mistake: '"I hoped we should get on well", she ended, raising her eyebrows and looking downwards' (*AGW*, 149). Later, Katherine reflects on how she 'had come expecting to solve a mystery, and had found at the end there was no mystery to solve' (*AGW*, 165). Robin had not somehow withheld his 'natural' self, but simply engaged in a courteous exchange of letters for educational enrichment. The invitation was not a sign of something deeper and more mysterious lurking in him, waiting to be drawn out, but the result of the wrong pair of eyes reading, interpreting, and therefore falsifying a bespoke epistolary identity: 'the nets she had contrived so cunningly to capture Robin had succeeded down to the last syllable in snaring Jane' (*AGW*, 150).

These two significant epistolary episodes in Katherine's life, then, provide a lesson in perspective, subjectivity and difference. Much like John's efforts in *Jill*, the various acts of authorship in *A Girl in Winter* fail to bring about desired changes to the characters' realities, but they do allow the protagonist to glimpse 'the undertow of people's relations, two-thirds of which is without face, with only begging and lonely hands' (*AGW*, 199–200). This awareness of other people's lives creates great pathos: Jane's circumstances, and those of Anstey and Miss Parbury, are quietly sad, and give nuance. The novel's exploration of perspective suggests the impossibility of a universal or final point of view, and this is an important step in Larkin's writer's education, given how many of his great poems switch perspective to poignantly inhabit the lives of others.

Political perspectives

There is also a political dimension to Larkin's exercises in perspective. Because Katherine is foreign, her interwar and wartime experiences in England provide an external perspective on the nation. That Larkin finds much to critique should at least qualify those posthumous interpretations of his work and values as falling somewhere on the spectrum between patriotic nationalism and outright xenophobia. Reading the letters to Sutton, 'An Incident in the English Camp', and the Brunette Coleman works, it becomes clear that Larkin's parodic attitude to Empire and Englishness is not merely a secondary theme in *A Girl in Winter*, but a consistent feature of his writing throughout the 1940s, which reappears in the mature poems.

The hazy English pastoral which Part Two of *A Girl in Winter* paints with impressionistic strokes is challenged by attention to the finer details. Robin is keen for Katherine to experience the beauty of his green and pleasant land, but when he is shown leaning 'against a noticeboard that said "Private. No Landing Allowed"', looking 'across the water at a field scattered with golden-fleeced sheep', this English Arcadia is exposed as the privatized preserve of the middle class (*AGW*, 87). The river running through the Fennels' land is a twentieth-century version of Blake's 'charter'd Thames', and Robin, perfectly at ease in this environment, and with ambitions of working for the Foreign Office, is its inheritor. Robin knows his country's colonial status, and is entirely comfortable with it. He reminds Katherine that 'Britain is a small country, once agricultural but now highly industrialized, relying a great deal for food on a large Empire'. He says this as he stands next to the village pond, throwing bread to the ducks. Jane tells him to direct some towards a duck who 'hasn't had any', but Robin dismisses this sentiment: 'He's not trying . . . He doesn't really want one' (*AGW*, 96–7).

In this juxtaposition of action and words, we see Robin's worldview: the dynamics of the duck pond are essentially the same as those of global geopolitics, in which Britain manfully overcomes its diminutive geographical size to rise to the top. In this, Robin is a recycled version of the earnestly patriotic Robbie in 'An Incident in the English Camp'. Jane, conversely, shows her distaste for Englishness. When Katherine describes the local village gymkhana as 'very English and interesting', Jane retorts: 'It's English all right . . . . But then I am English, more's the pity' (*AGW*, 113). She is critical of glossy clichés – England as 'A maypole, and everyone going hunting and eating roast beef' – and of Robin's 'guide-book style' which tells a very partial tale of 'the birthrate and the standard of living' (*AGW*, 95–6). It is a surprise, then, when she agrees to marry Jack Stormalong, a caricature of tiger-shooting English imperialism, who is 'disconcerted' by Katherine's mere presence (*AGW*, 160). However, a conversation with Katherine reveals that for Jane it is 'marriage or nothing' (*AGW*, 154). As the lesser-valued female sibling in a conservative, middle-class family, her paralysing boredom is palpable, and her acceptance of Stormalong's proposal and a new life in the Empire makes sense: like Pamela in the earlier story, and the girls of Willow Gables, she yearns for something more than the constraints her sex has hitherto afforded her.

Some years later, the adult Katherine finds herself back in England, exiled there for reasons that are not given: 'apparently meaningless disasters that had driven her to England' (*AGW*, 185). In the English psyche and its popular culture, the Second World War occupies a special place, recalling a time when a hardy and virtuous population overcame the cold Teutonic evil of Nazi Germany. In *A Girl in Winter*, however, Katherine is intensely aware of an English capacity for mean-spiritedness and xenophobia. When she urges the dentist treating her colleague's toothache to administer gas, he snaps back with a phrase designed to put her in her place: 'It's the law – the law of *this* country' (*AGW*, 46). At the library, she is given the title 'temporary assistant', which 'marked her off from the permanent staff', and affirms 'what was already sufficiently marked: that she was foreign and had no proper status there' (*AGW*, 25). Anstey seems intent on reminding her of this: his conversations with Katherine invariably throw up self-conscious markers of national difference: 'Now you've started on this job with a very good, valuable education, better by a very long chalk than I ever had, and none the less valuable for being obtained in another country, as human knowledge is the same in England, France, Germany or anywhere on God's earth' (*AGW*, 19). If Anstey considers his nationality evidence of his superiority, however, then his speech often betrays that notion: 'And neither of them, if I may say so, should have been made by anyone with an ounce of what we English call savvy or gumption or . . . *nous*' (*AGW*, 17). His competence for the job is repeatedly called into question: as Osborne puts it, he has been 'over-promoted in accord with a patriarchal culture that would sooner place incompetent men in jobs . . . than call upon the services of talented women', and his character exposes the British 'as unworthy custodians not just of a great empire but also of a great world language'.[14] These experiences teach Katherine that the English are 'characterized in time of war by antagonism to every foreign country, friendly or unfriendly, as a simple matter of instinct' (*AGW*, 22).

In short, then, whilst Larkin's attention to multiple perspectives can bring out the depth and humanity of his characters, it is also used to expose a lack of depth and humanity in the national character. His novel exposes the cloying myth of Britain's 'Keep Calm and Carry On' war. This is consistent with attitudes found elsewhere in his writing. Larkin was working on *A Girl in Winter* on V-E Day, when he wrote the coruscating letter to Sutton describing 'Churchill blathering out of him this afternoon, and the King this evening' (8 May 1945). His disregard for an icon of Britishness is antithetical to the nationalism which

Paulin and others claim to find in Larkin's life and work.[15] The sordid realism of Larkin's presentation of Englishness in *A Girl in Winter* explains the parodic treatment of Empire and nation in 'An Incident in the English Camp', and justifies Coleman's attack on the colonial propaganda of the boys' school story. Significantly, these attitudes are also to be found in Larkin's mature poems: 'I Remember, I Remember' critiques the English sentimentality of Thomas Hood's poem; 'MCMXIV' undermines the mythologizing of the twentieth century's other world war; 'The Importance of Elsewhere' evokes feelings of alienation on home turf; 'Homage to a Government' criticizes a policy of decolonization only introduced 'for lack of money'; 'March Past' attacks military nostalgia (*TCP*, 41–2, 60–1, 64, 87, 277–8). *A Girl in Winter* is, among other things, a political novel, and its politics do not come out of nowhere, but are consistent with Larkin's early and mature work.

Sympathy

Running parallel to this Woolfian novel of perspective, and perhaps offered as an antidote to its political critiques, is a Forsterian novel of sympathy – a word found many times in *A Girl in Winter*. When Katherine is asked to escort home Miss Green, a colleague suffering from toothache, she feels 'some sympathy was called for', but when she is curt, Katherine thinks it 'a relief not to have to pretend sympathy' (*AGW*, 26). Later, she finds herself 'startled to sympathy' (*AGW*, 34). Although Miss Green continues to be rude, and Katherine thinks that 'Pain was so remote from what she herself was feeling that she felt helpless', she nevertheless finds herself imagining Miss Green's pain (*AGW*, 32). Katherine exhibits an intensely physical consciousness which makes her alert to the suffering of others. We get a subtle sense of this as they ride the bus:

> Miss Green was nearest the gang-way, and the bus had become so crowded that a shopping basket swayed above her head, from which hung the end of a leek. At every movement of the owner it tapped Miss Green's hair. But she had looked mutely in front of her and said nothing.
> Now she leaned against Katherine.
> Katherine accordingly gave her more room. (*AGW*, 30–1)

When Miss Green drinks from an ice-cold public fountain, Katherine

> saw as she raised her head afterwards that she was gasping at the chill of the water and half-smiling, the tiny hairs around her mouth wet. . . . Till then she

had seen only her ugliness, her petulance, her young pretensions. Now this faded to unimportance and she grasped for the first time that she really needed care, that she was frail and in a remote way beautiful. (*AGW*, 34)

Despite Miss Green's phobia, Katherine insists on taking her to a dentist. The scene in the dentist's chair is the centrepiece of the novel's presentation of sympathy. The procedure is narrated with exquisite detail, and Katherine's hypersensitivity is such that she could almost be the woman in the chair:

> Miss Green bent over the bowl, a glass of water at her lips, not at all as she had drunk at the fountain. As she spat out the fragments of the filling she slobbered ludicrously, and was instantly self-conscious, trying to break the hanging thread by feeble spitting movements, searching for the handkerchief that was in her bag, and at last clumsily catching it away with her own hand. (*AGW*, 44)

This is an extraordinarily microscopic presentation of human dignity and the vulnerability of Miss Green's frail and distressed body. It shows an immense capacity for sympathy – on Katherine's part, and by extension the author's. When Miss Green whimpers for gas but is refused it, Katherine wants 'desperately to move him, to make some contact'. She calmly argues on Miss Green's behalf, and the dentist reluctantly assents. Katherine cannot stop herself from feeling her way into Miss Green's condition:

> [S]he felt an upswerve of terror lest the girl should still be half-conscious but unable to move or speak. . . . Katherine could almost feel the pain exploding beneath the anaesthetic, and nerved herself against a shriek. It seemed impossible for the girl to feel nothing. . . . Katherine found that step by step she had moved right up to the very arm of the chair. (*AGW*, 48–9)

Moments like these contribute very little to the plot. The almost literally painstaking care with which Larkin narrates the procedure only makes sense if we read the novel as one deeply concerned with sympathy. Indeed, if Katherine experiences persistent, low-level instances of inhumanity as a result of differences in gender, nationality and class – all socially constructed identities – then the novel responds with an intense awareness of pain, which is both natural and something all humans feel and fear. This deeply concentrated inhabitation of otherness is something Larkin would revisit again and again in his mature poetry: whether more benignly in a poem like 'The Trees', which gets as close as possible to occupying the consciousness of the natural world – 'The trees are coming into leaf / Like something almost being said' – or in the devastatingly humane 'Deceptions', discussed in Chapter 7: 'Even so distant, I can taste the grief' (*TCP*, 76–7, 41).

Considering these different perspectives and acts of sympathy, it is worth pausing here to ask an important question: Where is Philip Larkin? This may seem like an odd question, but in many of his earlier stories, Larkin appears either as a named character or a barely disguised one; as a consequence, as Chapter 2 showed, those stories struggle to achieve lift beyond the rather juvenile navel-gazing which appears to be their main objective. Larkin then appears as a more oblique presence in 'An Incident in the English Camp', which self-consciously names 'P. A. Larkin' as its author. In the Coleman works, the invention of a heteronym naturally prompts questions about its relation to the actual author. *Jill* follows on from the Coleman phase with its multiple layers of authorship, but this time within a book that is unambiguously written by Philip Larkin. The same name, of course, also adorns the cover of *A Girl in Winter*, but for the first time authorship does not constitute a major theme.

To put this another way: the more Larkin engages with the difference of his characters and subjects, the more *he* dissolves. His literary journey takes him from being a character in his own fiction to merely the name on the cover. Predictably, a significant swathe of the scholarship on Larkin's fiction has sought to locate him within it. But the lesson of Larkin's writer's education is one which takes him gradually 'outside himself' and into the lives of other people, which surely explains why his work has appealed to so many. This argument is at odds with Larkin's own analysis, which submitted that he was not sufficiently interested in other people to succeed at writing novels (*RW*, 49). It is also at odds with Larkin's dismissal of *A Girl in Winter* in a letter to Sutton: 'It is a pitiless book, and it uses human beings to express an idea, rather than to express the truth about themselves. Lawrence did that I know, but he had far greater natural sympathy for (I won't say "with") people' (*SL*, 134). This debate is taken up again in later chapters on Larkin's poetry; for now, it must suffice to point out how vastly and compassionately interested in others is *A Girl in Winter*.

Gender

So interested in others is this novel that its representation of femininity exceeds even Brunette Coleman's. When Katherine and Miss Green step outside the library into wintery conditions, they feel 'the cold rising up their skirts'; Booth rightly identifies this as a highly perceptive detail for a young male writer, arguing that 'Larkin participates in femaleness' (*AGW*, 27).[16] Like his treatment of Englishness, Larkin declines to present the kind of glossy femininity which he had already parodied in 'An Incident in the English Camp'. Like Coleman, he refuses to idealize female characters, using Miss Green to show women's capacity to be cruel to other women, especially foreign ones. This is another instance of Larkin's genre vandalism; as Osborne points out, *A Girl in Winter* 'forcefully rejects . . . the female friendship novel with its lesbian subtext ("men are the problem, women are the solution")'.[17]

Even more remarkable, though, is the persistent low-level sexual harassment Katherine experiences. Standing on a table in the library to fit a light bulb, for instance, 'old men stared aqueously at her legs' (*AGW*, 25). Walking home with Miss Holloway at the end of the working day, 'two slightly-intoxicated soldiers bumped intentionally into them, and apologized lavishly', grabbing 'theatrically at them for support in the darkness'. The soldiers initially make a show of gallantry – 'Where have you been all my life?' – but when the women walk on, this quickly turns to anger, and the women are called 'Two bags!' (*AGW*, 222–3). At the end of *Jill*, John made an unwanted pass at Gillian; in *A Girl in Winter*, Larkin regenders the point of view and follows Coleman's lead in showing women's day-to-day experience of sexism.

The workplace is one such everyday space where misogyny flourishes. Although Anstey reserves a special sourness for Katherine, the English women who work under him are not exempt from his condescension. Miss Holloway tells Katherine about Anstey's professional history: he has been promoted in the absence of any competent men, who are at war, remarking that 'he just isn't a big enough man for the job' (*AGW*, 222). This explains his blustering displays of patronizing masculinity. Larkin explicitly adopts the language of performance: 'He was giving his usual performance of being too engrossed in matters of importance to notice her entry'; 'He made a theatrical gesture of resignation. This was another of his performances, that of the man forced to spend his time on things that were beneath his intelligence' (*AGW*, 16–17, 20). One colleague meets Anstey's theatre with performances of her own, using a strategy of overt obedience in order to manage him: 'Miss Feather, perhaps alone on the staff, had the knack of keeping Mr. Anstey fairly close to the point: she inserted submissive, insinuating remarks that urged him gently back on the path she wished him to follow' (*AGW*, 20).

These low-level experiences culminate at the end of the novel in Robin's surprise arrival at Katherine's home. Like Robbie in 'An Incident in the English Camp', he is on embarkation leave, but this time the novel inverts, rather than parodies, the trope of the gallant soldier on the doorstep. Whereas Robbie is perfectly content to play squash and have tea – it is Pamela who summons a gently erotic fantasy – Robin is looking for casual sex, and Katherine feels 'nothing but blankness' (*AGW*, 228). Robin has also lied about his leave: a friend is covering for him whilst he tries his luck with Katherine. The earlier parody is an entertaining send-up of decent young Englishmen and women, but *A Girl in Winter* speaks more compellingly to the vulnerability of a young foreign woman in wartime England – 'a foreign girl who could be relied on for a bit of fun' (*AGW*, 238). At first Katherine thinks Robin sounds 'rather drunk', but soon realizes that this is just performative groundwork for the sex: 'not very drunk, she thought, not as much as he pretended' (*AGW*, 225–7). She feels loathe to join in and play the part she has been designated: 'Was she supposed to be flattered, that he had considered it worth while making a special journey on the off-chance of sleeping with her? For he would ask that if she made no protest. Queer, she thought, that he should have turned out like this. Someone must have given him the idea that he fascinated women' (*AGW*, 235). Katherine knows she does not 'care one way or another, being neither insulted or flattered. . . . He could not touch her. It would be no more than doing him an unimportant kindness, that would be overtaken by oblivion in a few days' (*AGW*, 243). Her numbness is a sad testament to her life in England.

However, the novel's language and dialogue at this point become imprecise, leaving wide open the question of whether or not they have sex, though many critics have simply assumed they do: Liz Hedgecock describes Katherine 'lying awake after having sex'; Booth claims 'she submits wearily to his demands'; David Timms writes that 'she does not refuse'.[18] Katherine names 'a condition that he accepted', but it is not clear what: Is it a condition of the sex (such as the use of a contraceptive), or simply a condition that he may stay but not have sex with her? Robin's sudden loss of 'desire', and his gall at the 'lack of enthusiasm', could be the result of either (*AGW*, 243). When he turns out the light, he also casts a kind of textual darkness. Whilst some details suggest that they do have sex, why should the reader seek to iron out deliberate ambiguities? In 'It had snowed in the night', an early prose piece discussed in Chapter 2, Larkin rehearsed his own version of the closing wintery rhythms of Joyce's 'The Dead'. He revives this for the final passage of *A Girl in Winter*. Although the language is somewhat erotic ('mingle', 'heaping up', 'conceptions', 'Unsatisfied dreams rose and fell about them, crying out'), it is also cold, barren and deathly (*AGW*, 248). The novel is careful to leave beautifully unstated the question of whether or not Katherine and Robin have meaningless sex.

This ellipsis is not a flaw but, as Osborne argues, all the more 'extreme' and 'eviscerative' because of its 'application in realist contexts where it is the less expected'. If, as Osborne also contends, the aporia of Katherine's nationality is designed to 'embarrass the reductively patriotic constructions of subjectivity in the name of which contending armies fight and die', then similarly the absence of narrative and coital closure at the end is surely designed to focus readers' minds on the sexism rather than the sex.[19] Larkin's participation in 'femaleness' is too numb to be erotic, and too realist to permit romantic climax. Descriptions like that of the 'cold rising up their skirts' are indeed notable for a young male novelist, but the depiction of a young woman persistently subjected to sexism and harassment is one of this novel's major achievements. It also signals the moment in Larkin's career when he stops writing *about* writing otherness, and simply gets on with writing it – something he would continue to do as a mature poet. The immature habit of self-examination has gone, and Larkin's reward is his most beautiful and sophisticated work of prose.

6

The Coleman effect

Sugar and Spice and Larkin's early poems

Stan Smith has imagined 'a discussion of Larkin between one person who had read nothing of his after 1950 and another who had read nothing before'. He thinks that following

> an initial agreement by adjective – 'Versatile', 'Fluent', 'Too smart sometimes' – a mystifying gap would open between them, as one spoke of a tremendously exciting social poet full of energetic unliterary knock-about and unique lucidity of phrase, and the other of an engaging, bookish talent, too verbose to be memorable and too intellectual to be moving. And not only would they differ about his poetic character: there would be a sharp division of opinion about his poetic stature.[1]

Though Smith confesses that these words are actually a 'near verbatim adaptation of what Larkin wrote' about Auden's career, the point still stands: the poetry Larkin wrote before the century hit its midpoint is unrecognizable when compared to the poetry he wrote afterwards. Naturally, a recurring objective of Larkin scholarship has been to get to grips with this transformation. This chapter presents an original account, building on the previous chapters to argue that the poems Larkin wrote as Brunette Coleman in 1943 were ultimately responsible for the transformation of his verse. Though Coleman's influence on Larkin's poetry took longer to assert itself, her poems undermine Smith's dividing line.

The influence of Yeats

Rather than Smith's 1950, a consensus has settled on the year 1946. This is the result of critics following Larkin's lead. But they should know better; this is, after all, a poet who claimed to be bemused by 'these chaps who go round American universities explaining how they write poems: it's like going round explaining how you sleep with your wife', and who said there was little more to say about how he wrote *The Whitsun Weddings* than the fact that he did so 'with a succession of Royal Sovereign 2B pencils during the years 1955 to 1963' (*RW*, 71, 83). In his resistance to explaining poetic practices, Larkin deployed evasiveness, straightforward misinformation, tricks and traps, and disarming humour. As a rule, scholars of his work are best served by trusting the tale, not the teller. Nonetheless, one account has proved irresistible to those in search of reasons for Larkin's drastic stylistic transformation. When *The North Ship* (1945) was reissued by Faber in 1966, more than twenty years after its first publication, an explanation was required as to why the book was so very different to the two he had written since. Just as with the fiction written before his Coleman phase, Larkin's problem was that he was trying to write like his literary heroes:

> Looking back, I find in the poems not one abandoned self but several – the ex-schoolboy, for whom Auden was the only alternative to 'old-fashioned' poetry; the undergraduate, whose work a friend affably characterized as 'Dylan Thomas, but you've a sentimentality that's all your own'; and the immediately post-Oxford self, isolated in Shropshire with a complete Yeats stolen from the local girls' school. This search for a style was merely one aspect of a general immaturity. (*RW*, 28)

Larkin's candour, and the ease with which the Auden-Thomas-Yeats nexus of influences can be detected in these early poems, make it tempting to accept this account and move on. The 'predominance of Yeats' is further explained when Larkin recalls Vernon Watkins's visit in 1943 to the English Club at Oxford, where he 'swamped us with Yeats' and left the young writer 'tremendously impressed'. As a consequence, Larkin writes,

> I spent the next three years trying to write like Yeats, not because I liked his personality or understood his ideas but out of infatuation with his music . . . .
> In fairness to myself it must be admitted that it is a particularly potent music, pervasive as garlic, and has ruined many a better talent. (*RW*, 29)

In this introduction, Larkin also recalls Bruce Montgomery's intolerance for his Yeatsian conceits (*RW*, 29). This disagreement is recorded in one of their comical collaborations, 'LIFE WITH PHAIRY PHANTASY', a series of sketches subtitled 'A morality in Pictures Drawn by Mr. P. A. L.'[2] In one sketch, Larkin draws himself looking gleeful in a cloak emblazoned with celestial symbols; the drawing is captioned 'DISTRESSING SARTORIAL AFFINITIES WITH MR. W. B. YEATS'. Larkin's 1966 piece recognizes that his younger self had to do more than ditch the sartorial affinities: his poetry, too, had been bewitched by Yeats's magic.

Most of the poems in *The North Ship* confirm this. Throughout the volume there are Yeatsian refrains ('*A drum taps: a wintry drum*'), images of revolution ('Let the wheel spin out'), an abundance of quasi-symbolic moons and stars, ploughmen and horsemen (*TCP*, 5). There are swans, and more than one self-conscious conjuring of poetry: 'Let me become an instrument sharply stringed / For all things to strike music as they please'; 'To write one song, I said, / As sad as the sad wind / That walks around my bed' (*TCP*, 9, 13). The distinctive cadences of Yeats's verse characterize Larkin's prosody:

Shine out, my sudden angel,
Break fear with breast and brow,
I take you now and for always,
For always is always now. (*TCP*, 19–20)

As Timms puts it, 'we can spot Auden and Dylan Thomas', but 'Yeats is everywhere'.[3] Timms's study, the first book-length work on Larkin, contains one of the best and most succinct analyses of the young poet's problems:

These poems are marvellous imitations. Of course, if they were indistinguishable from their originals, they too would be great poems; but they are not. What are their defects, then? It seems to me that their greatest single fault is their lack of particularity, which makes them insubstantial. Too often the young poet sketches a stock poetic landscape in an attempt to evoke a vague mood of ennui or melancholy rather than a feeling of a real object, situation, set of events, or state of mind. The wind is blowing in at least a third of the thirty-one poems . . . . When the time of day is mentioned, it is always day-break, and a cold, often rainy day-break at that. The young poet will never let objects stand as they are – he always romanticises or sentimentalises them. . . . This is self-pity of a kind quite foreign to the mature writer. None of the poems has a recognisable locale, or familiar objects: rooms are lit by candles, not electric lights; when a stranger is set a meal, he is given 'loaves and wine'; when a man is conscripted, horsemen arrive for him, not green army trucks.[4]

There is perhaps a slight mischaracterization here, in that the 'real' which Timms wants and thinks he gets in Larkin's mature poems risks miscasting those poems as straightforwardly realist and autobiographical. This ignores the impressive range of imagined and alien scenarios in Larkin's verse: London's nineteenth-century underclass in 'Deceptions', the New Orleans mindscape of 'For Sidney Bechet' and the Dublin dreamscape of 'Dublinesque', the mystical experience of a chapel-going mining community in 'The Explosion', the historically textured lives of a merchant, a lighthouse-keeper, and a don in 'Livings', and so on.

But Timms's account is useful because it shows Larkin experiencing the same problems he faced in his early prose: a lack of particularity and specificity, and an attempt to find a shortcut to greatness by imitating great writers. Like the short stories he wrote at Oxford, Larkin's early poems attempt to put the cart before the horse: he thinks he can replicate Yeats's achievement by replicating Yeats's verse. David Lodge has argued that the mature Larkin should be regarded as 'a "metonymic" poet'.[5] The metonymic power of Larkin's later poetry is not yet apparent in *The North Ship*, not necessarily because he is a more metaphoric poet, but because the world of *The North Ship* – the loaves and wine and drizzly dawns to which Timms draws attention – instead functions as a metonym for the kind of literary company Larkin wishes to keep.

The influence of Hardy

In Larkin's account, he is rescued from Yeats's Tower by an unlikely knight in shining armour:

> When reaction came, it was undramatic, complete and permanent. In early 1946 I had some new digs in which the bedroom faced east, so that the sun woke me inconveniently early. I used to read. One book I had at my bedside was the little blue *Chosen Poems of Thomas Hardy*: Hardy I knew as a novelist, but as regards his verse I shared Lytton Strachey's verdict that 'the gloom is not even relieved by a little elegance of diction'. This opinion did not last long; if I were asked to date its disappearance, I should guess it was the morning I first read 'Thoughts of Phena At News of Her Death'. (*RW*, 29–30)

Again, the sense that Larkin is candidly revealing something significant is strong. But we should be wary of the identity being constructed by this 1966 piece, which fits more closely with the ordinary, unpretentious public persona Larkin curated throughout the 1960s than with the more cosmopolitan one of his youth. Compared with, say, Ted Hughes's dramatic and disturbing account of a major change in his intellectual and artistic life – the 'burnt fox' dream he experienced at Cambridge – Larkin's epiphany, although 'complete and permanent', is described as 'undramatic', and a mere unintended consequence of certain practical and domestic arrangements.[6] It also plays into his professed investment in a pre-war, pre-modernist tradition of English poetry, something he had been more actively pondering since January of that year, having been invited to take over the editing of a new *Oxford Book of Modern Verse* following

Louis MacNeice's death (the anthology would be published in 1973 as *The Oxford Book of Twentieth Century English Verse*). Writing to Dan Davin at Oxford University Press, Larkin sketched a view of twentieth-century poetry he wanted the anthology to present: that an 'English tradition' had been 'submerged by the double impact of the Great War and the Irish-American-continental properties of Yeats and Eliot' (*SL*, 380). This is very much in sympathy with the narrative Larkin propagates in his introduction to *The North Ship* the same year, where Hardy is the modest English hero who wisely steers him away from Yeats's Celtic frenzy. Perhaps more importantly, however, the account actually tells us very little about the precise nature of Hardy's influence. Two years later, in a radio broadcast, Larkin elaborated:

> When I came to Hardy it was with the sense of relief that I didn't have to try and jack myself up to a concept of poetry that lay outside my own life – this is perhaps what I felt Yeats was trying to make me do. One could simply relapse back into one's own life and write from it. Hardy taught one to feel rather than to write – of course one has to use one's own language and one's own jargon and one's own situations – and he taught one as well to have confidence in what one felt. (*RW*, 175–6)

Given how previous chapters have traced Larkin's increasing interest in writing otherness, at first glance this seems as though Hardy was responsible for destroying that progress, causing Larkin to 'relapse' back into his 'own life'. Certainly, accounts like this have licensed critics to read Larkin as a fundamentally autobiographical poet. And perhaps this is indeed what Larkin meant. But a close reading of Larkin's comments does not necessarily support this. He talks about a '*concept* of poetry' (my emphasis) which exists outside of his own life; one thinks, for example, of Yeats's 'widening gyres'. Crucially, he does not talk of relapsing 'back into one's own life' and writing '*about* it', but '*from* it' (my emphases) – that is, using one's experience as a launchpad for, rather than the subject of, poems. In the same broadcast, Larkin names some 'very dissimilar poets' who have loved Hardy's verse: Auden, Dylan Thomas, Yeats, Betjeman, Day Lewis; 'I rather think that they may have found what I found, that Hardy gave them confidence to feel in their own way', he speculates (*RW*, 175). Paradoxically, then, what these very different poets took from Hardy was permission to write as individuals. Larkin did not need permission to write *about* himself: he had been doing it since the late 1930s, in prose and in poetry, with little satisfaction. It was Coleman who led him away from himself, teaching him that he could write brilliantly on subjects other than himself.

If Hardy taught Larkin anything, then, it was authenticity. This may be a philosophically loaded term, but few would argue that Larkin's early imitations of writers he admired was authentic. In his early prose, and in *The North Ship*, Larkin tried to insert himself into worlds already occupied by those writers. Hardy may well have confirmed to Larkin that he need not do so, but he was by this point already writing differently. As Brunette Coleman, and then as himself in the published novels, Larkin ceased writing narrowly autobiographical literature. Importantly, although his subjects – schoolgirls, or a foreign woman exiled in England – were arguably as other to him as Yeats's universe, Larkin wrote about them compellingly, because of his attention to the way people speak and behave, his acute understanding of their psychologies, and his capacity to evoke the places in which their lives play out. If it was with 'relief' that he found in Hardy's poems what Motion calls 'modest watchfulness' and 'total immersion in everyday things', then it is because he was already becoming that writer.[7] There is no doubt that what would become a lifelong passion for Hardy's poems was for Larkin genuine and deeply felt. But critics have followed him in attributing too much to Hardy. Perhaps Hardy appeared to Larkin as a more respectable literary figure to whom he could credit certain lessons actually learned from Coleman. But that was three years before his rediscovery of Hardy. When critics identify 1946 as the turning point in Larkin's poetic development, they ignore this earlier and radically transformative experiment in authorship.

Sugar and Spice

Critics might feel perfectly comfortable ignoring Coleman. Her work has been met with baffled head-scratching and clichéd psychoanalytical forays into Larkin's sexual psychology, but few critics have been willing to recognize it as a crucially formative influence on Larkin's mature verse. This is, however, precisely what I would argue. Previous chapters have demonstrated Coleman's positive impact on Larkin's fiction, but the consequences of that would be negligible had the impact not extended to the poetry which made Larkin a major figure. Chapters 3 and 4 explored the Coleman works in relation to issues of genre and gender, and the impact of this on Larkin's wider *oeuvre*. Absent from those discussions was an analysis of Coleman's poems, saved back for this chapter, so that they might properly be apprehended within the wider context of Larkin's early poetry.

Put simply, Coleman's poems are nothing like the poems Larkin was otherwise writing during the early 1940s. Yeats and Auden are almost nowhere to be found in *Sugar and Spice*; instead, Coleman's sheaf of seven poems shows the influence of a more eclectic and unexpected range of sources. The first two poems in the sheaf retain much of the spirit and vernacular of her novellas. 'The False Friend' plunges the reader into schoolgirl controversy:

> It's no good standing there and looking haughty:
> ...
>
> It might interest you to know I heard from Audrey
> That Kathleen said that you told Miss LeQuesne
> That my liking for French prose was nothing but a pose –
> Elspeth, I'll never speak to you again. (*TWG*, 244)

In 'Bliss', a young girl excitedly pedals her 'Junior B. S. A.' to 'W. H. Smith & Son', eager to get 'Colonel Stewart's book / Called "Handling Horses"' (*TWG*, 245). Though technically adept, poems like these might safely be described as 'bad'. But they are knowingly bad, in a connoisseuring way; that is to say, their 'badness' gives a kind of subversive pleasure. This way of reading the poems returns us to Sontag's definition of camp, which sees the camp style's dethroning of the serious and the highbrow as political. Sontag's dictum, 'it's good because it's awful', may be applied just as fruitfully to these poems. If 'The False Friend' is *bad* as a poem which is, when all is said and done, about a playground squabble, then it is also *good* insofar as it mocks the pretensions of Poetry (or 'Pwertry', as Amis called it), and unlocks additional rooms in the 'house of literature', Coleman's metaphor, for 'other creative sensibilities besides the seriousness . . . of high culture' (Sontag).[8] In this, Coleman is clearly influenced by the poetry of John Betjeman. In his poem 'Myfanwy', included in the 1940 collection *Old Lights for New Chancels*, there are a number of resonances with Coleman's work:

> Were you a prefect and head of your dormit'ry?
>   Were you a hockey girl, tennis or gym?
> Who was your favourite? Who had a crush on you?
>   Which were the baths where they taught you to swim?
>
> Smooth down the Avenue glitters the bicycle,
>   Black stockinged-legs under navy-blue serge,
> Home and Colonial, Star, International,
>   Balancing bicycle leant on the verge.[9]

Coleman, it will be remembered, used the name Myfanwy for a key character in *Trouble at Willow Gables*, who, like Betjeman's, is a swimmer and a 'tom-boy'. But the influence is also more general and more significant. The world of schoolgirls which Betjeman evokes – a delightful world of hockey games, bicycle rides and tea parties – is presented without embarrassment or irony. In this, he and Coleman sing from the same hymn sheet. This is important: although Betjeman gained a reputation as a quaint and eccentric Englishman, Larkin believed there was more to him than that. In a recently uncovered letter, written after Betjeman's death in 1984, Larkin contends that

> his sense of humour both helped and hindered his work – it was a kind of Trojan horse that sneaked his subversive views into people's minds, yet at the same time it gave them a reason for not taking him seriously. I'm glad to see that much has been written since he died that will help establish him as a serious figure in our literature. In a way he was too clever for us![10]

Back in 1943, Larkin half-joked to Amis about sending Betjeman a copy of *Sugar and Spice*: 'wonder what he'd say?'[11] He would surely approve. What is clear is that Betjeman provided a source for Coleman's expansive and subtly subversive attitude to literature. This is not merely a response to literary snobbery, although that is one of Coleman's pet projects (her poems are dedicated to 'all my sister-writers, with the exception of Margaret Kennedy, who wrote . . . "English Schoolgirls are not interesting"') (*TWG*, 243). There is a bigger political dimension to Coleman's approach to genre, though readers might be forgiven for missing it: in her preface to *Sugar and Spice*, she 'make[s] no apology for presenting a collection of what may seem "trivia" in these disturbed times. I feel now more than ever a firm grasp on the essentials of life is needed' (*TWG*, 243). This is the only reference anywhere in the collection to its wartime context: it is oblique, and Coleman does not elaborate. In seeking a 'firm grasp on the essentials of life', Coleman's objective is aligned with that of Cyril Connolly's *Horizon*, albeit via a very different aesthetic. Written against a backdrop of global bloodletting, it is by no means impossible to feel that these poems about ponies and playground bickering are much less silly than they first appear.

In the poems which follow 'The False Friend' and 'Bliss', however, Coleman's voice takes a surprising turn, one which would have major consequences for Larkin's mature aesthetic. Although 'Holidays' begins jauntily – 'Let's go to Stratford-on-Avon, and see a play!' – by its close the poem charts the seasonal decline of autumn into winter, with a note of distress redolent of Keats or Shelley:

> For winter will come, when the wind endlessly grieves
>   For all it has lost, the youth, the joy, the pain,

> When the last term is over, the theorems forgotten again,
>   And we no more to each other than fallen leaves. (*TWG*, 249–50)

Stripped of its classroom vocabulary, a stanza like this could easily find a home within a number of Larkin's major poems, especially 'Sad Steps', 'Dockery and Son' or 'Aubade'. It is precisely this curiosity I want to address directly, because it is my contention that Larkin's poetic maturity begins here. In 'The School in August', the metonymic tendency identified by Lodge can be seen at work, taking in the empty 'cloakroom pegs' and 'hollow desks ... dim with dust' (*TWG*, 250). Some of the poem's images are genuinely moving: 'slow across the floor / A sunbeam creeps between the chairs'; 'Who practised this piano / Whose notes are now so still?' The final image – 'Games mistresses turn grey' – very delicately straddles the line between absurdity and pathos. In later poems like 'Home is so Sad' and 'Love Songs in Age', readers are made to feel keenly the inherent sadness of rooms and objects brought into focus by the poet's plaintive attention; 'The School in August' establishes this form of elegiac-demotic which Larkin would make his own. 'Fourth Former Loquitur' also contains hallmarks of the later Larkin. Images of solitude are articulated by a voice we associate not with the Larkin of *The North Ship*, published two years later, but with the Larkin of the 1950s onwards:

> And only I remain, now they are gone,
> To notice how the evening sun can show
> The unsuspected hollows in the field,
> When it is all deserted.
>   Here they lay,
> Wenda and Brenda, Kathleen and Elaine,
> And Jill, ...
>   while over all
> The sunlight lay like amber wine, matured
> By every minute. (*TWG*, 251–2)

These poems present a strange experience for readers, who must decide with each line whether to laugh and scoff or to allow themselves to be moved. Readers familiar with Larkin's best-known poems must also negotiate the uncanny experience of recognition. The poem's solitary Fourth Form narrator is an adolescent version of the highly sensitive, semi-anonymous, removed observers of later poems such as 'Reasons for Attendance', 'The Whitsun Weddings' and 'Friday Night in the Royal Station Hotel'. Moreover, the poem's morbid play on 'Here they lay' (a pun on 'here lies') foreshadows not only the girls' inevitable deaths but also Larkin's more well-known meditations on mortality: this is, after all, a verbal conceit which appears in 'Church Going' and 'An Arundel Tomb'. In other words, a recognizably Larkinesque poetics is already present in Coleman's verse.

Coleman's elegiac strain also emerges strongly in 'Ballade des Dames du Temps Jadis' ('The Ballade of the Ladies of Bygone Days'), her rewriting of François Villon's fifteenth-century poem. Villon's *ubi sunt* lyric moves through a succession of famous historical women – Flora, Heloïse, Joan of Arc – each time wistfully asking 'where is . . . ?', 'where is . . .?' Coleman's version is directed towards her overall project, namely the literary elevation of English schoolgirls. In place of Queen Blanche and Beatrix, Coleman asks 'Where is Valerie, who led / Every tom-boy prank and rag – / Is her hair still golden red?', 'And Julia, with violet eyes, / Her cool white skin, and sable hair – / Does she still extemporise / On "The Londonderry Air"?' (*TWG*, 247–8). She too confronts their loss, but replaces Villon's refrain, famously translated by Dante Gabriel Rossetti as 'where are the snows of yesteryear!', with her characteristic schooldays vocabulary: they are 'So many summer terms away'. There are good reasons for Coleman to choose Villon: what unites the women he elegizes is the trouble they caused men; like Margaret and Marie of Willow Gables, they are rebels. Furthermore, Villon was responsible for expanding the content of the courtly lyric to include the lowlife of fifteenth-century France. In doing something similar for schoolgirls, Coleman is self-consciously swimming in the living stream of literary tradition – as is her right. The result is another camp poem which bothers the tonal boundary between the poignant and the ridiculous. Although in many ways comedic, especially with its marginal instructions ('With a trace of sad humour'; 'Rising to, and falling from, an ecstasy of nostalgia'), the poem's central emotion – 'it has all gone too soon' – is a touching one, and capable of moving readers. The emotion is earned by that characteristically Larkinesque accumulation of memories and metonyms: 'The books are changed, beside the bed', 'and in disgust / The diaries have been thrown away'. This is a stylistic deviation from the grander Yeatsian imitations Larkin was otherwise writing. In fact, a reference to Yeats in the margin of the fifth stanza might be seen as evidence of the stylistic transformation underway. Just as Larkin's decreasing dependency on Isherwood was signalled by a shift away from imitating Isherwoodian dialogue towards satirizing it, Yeats's ironic appearance in this poem subtly indicates a change in relationship. When Coleman instructs that the stanza should be read 'With something of "the monstrous crying of wind" – Yeats, of course', she appropriates the elder poet's voice for parodic reasons, not out of infatuation. In the context of

Larkin's infatuation, that 'of course' reads like a dig at the Irishman's all-pervasive presence in his other poems.

'Femmes Damnées'

There is one other poem in *Sugar and Spice* which is by far the collection's *pièce de résistance*. 'Femmes Damnées' ('Condemned Women') is another rewriting from the canon of French literature, this time Baudelaire's 'Femmes damnées: Delphine et Hippolyte'. If the other poems in *Sugar and Spice* confuse the reader's emotions, switching as they do between the sublime and the ridiculous, then 'Femmes Damnées' presents no such difficulty: it is a beautiful poem. Coleman's strategy is still consistent with the other poems: in place of Baudelaire's neoclassical heroines, Delphine and Hippolyte, we have Rosemary and Rachel.[12] And whereas Baudelaire's women dwell 'Within the dwindling glow of light from languid lamps, / Sunk in the softest cushions soaked with heady scent', Coleman's women lead a more demotic, Anglicized existence:

> The milk's been on the step,
> The 'Guardian' in the letter-box, since dawn.
>
> Upstairs, the beds have not been touched, and thence
> Builders' estates, and the main road, are seen,
> With labourers, petrol-pumps, a Green Line 'bus,
> And plots of cabbages set in between. (*TWG*, 246)

This is not nineteenth-century Decadent France, but the contemporary urban and domestic English realism soon to be seen in *A Girl in Winter*, and later in poems like 'Afternoons' and 'Mr Bleaney'. What Coleman preserves is Baudelaire's lyricism, his atmosphere of gorgeous damnation and the theme of impossible love between women. Although other poems in *Sugar and Spice* strike an elegiac tone, none contain the emotional violence of 'Femmes Damnées':

> Stretched out before her, Rachel curls and curves,
> Eyelids and lips apart, her glances filled
> With satisfied ferocity: she smiles,
> As beasts smile on the prey they have just killed.

In the original, Delphine looks at Hippolyte 'Like a strong animal that oversees her prey, / First having taken care to mark it with her teeth'. This textual echo also appears in *Trouble at Willow Gables*, when the voyeuristic Hilary's attraction to

Mary is revealed to be unusually bestial (discussed in Chapter 4). Noting each of these points, we can see how this poem fits with Coleman's wider *oeuvre*, even if it perhaps looks slightly out of place alongside other poems in *Sugar and Spice*. In 'What Are We Writing For?', Coleman stresses that girls are not always sweet little paragons of virtue, however much their characterization in girls' fiction would have us believe. To be authentic, the genre must portray girls with inner conflicts; they should be Aristotelian heroes, neither completely good nor completely bad; some should be downright horrid. This is an important feature of Coleman's feminism, and Rachel's predatory lesbianism in 'Femmes Damnées', like Hilary's in the novellas, protects Coleman's work from sickly sweet sentimentality. Moreover, the clear-sighted Coleman is aware of the unpleasantness of adult life which awaits her girls. In *Michaelmas Term at St Bride's*, it is men who spoil the girls' hitherto sheltered environment; but if some of Coleman's characters seem to affirm the possibility of relationships between women, then her desire for authenticity must also show the possibility of such relationships going wrong. Women, like men, are capable of cruelty, violence and unequal power dynamics. This aspect has piqued the interest of Terry Castle:

> What almost all of the works in the Western lesbian canon share – including even the more worldly or forgiving – is a sense of the *unviability* of female same-sex love. To yearn for a woman, it would seem, is to fall victim to an *amor impossibilis* – to lose oneself in a sterile, unwholesome, usually fatal enterprise. Even the most selfless attachments will be nullified. Passionate Sappho, alas, set the pattern . . . . Yet the logic of the *amor impossibilis* operates just as harshly elsewhere.[13]

Castle thinks Larkin's investment in the '*amor impossibilis*' narrative was 'a doom-laden prediction of what was to become the central and most painful theme of his imaginative and emotional life: *no girls for you*'.[14] Neither Larkin's biography nor his life's work really justify that analysis, and my own reading of the Coleman *oeuvre* resists this kind of clichéd psychoanalytical pronouncement. What is interesting is that Castle should find in Coleman's work a distinctly Sapphic poetics. 'Femmes Damnées' is neither a satirical nor a voyeuristic poem; though its sexual politics are problematic, it movingly presents the tragedy of a same-sex relationship gone sour: 'A vase of flowers has spilt, and soaked away. / The only sound heard is the sound of tears'. In her preface, Coleman describes the versions of Villon and Baudelaire not as 'renderings' but 'improvements' (*TWG*, 243). That is an audacious but also an inspiring claim, given how they consolidate the subversive genre/gender coup begun in the prose works by inserting schoolgirls into established literary genres, not least that of Sapphic poetics. Again, she is following the lead of her source texts: just as Villon brought the lowlife of France into his verse, Baudelaire's *Flowers of Evil* (1857) shocked readers with its depictions of the Parisian underclass. Larkin's mature poetry is alert to the inner lives of 'ordinary' figures like Mr Bleaney and Dockery. Coleman treats schoolgirls with the same lyrical prestige, raising them to the same level as Keats's melancholy, or Tennyson's grief. Once again, an intervention in genre is also an intervention in gender.

As for Larkin, the *almost*-accidental consequence was that he had written one of his best poems of the decade. Many of the poems in *Sugar and Spice* contain early traces of the mature Larkin: his insertion of the demotic into the lyrical; the meeting of the contemporary and the traditional; and the movement from an individual scenario to a more universal theme or emotion. These are accomplished poems, formally elegant and tonally complex. They touch upon emotions more common and more specific than those in Larkin's other 1940s poems, such as 'Conscript' or 'Nursery Tale'. They are also funny. This, too, is important, because Larkin is, among other things, a very funny poet, and whatever the merits of *The North Ship*, humour is not one of them. In short, the poems Larkin wrote as Brunette Coleman are among the best he wrote at any point during the 1940s. I am not the first to contend this, though the list of publicly declared admirers is brief. Castle calls them 'against all expectation . . . spare, elegiac, ominously good', whilst Booth points to their 'assured delicacy of tone far beyond anything in *The North Ship*', and notes that Bruce Montgomery – critical of Larkin's Yeats worship – also saw their worth: 'has it ever occurred to you that quite the best of your earliest poetry is in *Sugar and Spice*?', he wrote in 1964 (*TWG*, xvii).[15] Montgomery is correct: some of the best of the mature Larkin is already there. Whilst Stan Smith's two imaginary readers would indeed be baffled by the difference between early and late Larkin, if we gave them the poems written by Brunette Coleman in 1943, they would find common ground.

Coleman's delayed influence

How might these poems feed into the narrative of Larkin's literary development, then? By accepting 1946 as the turning point for Larkin, critics overlook the pieces written in 1943 which set him on the path to originality. He later told Motion that 'leaving Oxford was like taking a cork out of a bottle. Writing flooded out of me'.[16] Although that flood would produce most of the poems in *The North*

Ship, it also included the *Sugar and Spice* poems, written during the summer and autumn of that year. Given the unoriginal nature of much of Larkin's prose and verse before this point, it must have been an absolute joy to generate work that was spirited and strangely novel. In chronological terms, Coleman's writings occupy the period between Larkin's stilted undergraduate stories and his much more accomplished novels. Either Coleman was just Larkin's way of killing time as he waited for a flash of inspiration, or she actively helped to induce those novels, which seems more likely, given how her work is reappropriated in *Jill*. But if Coleman was the key factor responsible for the radical transformation of Larkin's poetry, why did it take so long for the transformation to cement? The development of Larkin's prose appears more or less cumulative and linear, but it took him until the end of the 1940s to begin to write the poems for which he is famous. That is a gap of seven years. Furthermore, whilst the Coleman project began and ended in 1943, almost all of the poems in *The North Ship* were written in 1943 and 1944. If 1943 was the turning point, why did the turn take so long?

This question can be answered in a number of ways. We might speak generally, and observe that literary development is rarely neat and linear. We might point out that the critical consensus which has settled on 1946 suffers from exactly the same problem of delay, albeit with four years, not seven, unaccounted for. We might also make the point that Hardy's impact has been overstated. In 1947, Larkin assembled a collection of poems with the title *In the Grip of Light*. It was rejected by a series of publishers, and would never itself see light, but the poems he chose for it suggest that Hardy had not really taken hold of his imagination. As Stephen Regan comments: 'Larkin claimed to be reading Hardy with renewed admiration and insight from the early part of 1946 onwards, but there is little indication of Hardy's impact in the poems selected for *In the Grip of Light*. In fact, what is most remarkable is how unlike either Hardy or Yeats they sound.'[17]

But there is more to the story than this. It is important to remember what Larkin was doing in 1943 and 1944. His overwhelming ambition was still to be a great novelist. On 13 August 1943, he informed Amis that *Michaelmas Term at St Bride's* had 'expired'; just a week later, he wrote to Amis again:

> I am writing a story called (provisionally) 'Jill'. It concerns a young man who invents a younger sister, and falls in love with her. It's quite fun, because he writes a lot of imaginary stuff about her – diaries, letters etc. Brunette Coleman, who wrote 'Trouble at Willow Gables', is helping me. (*SL*, 62–3)

By September, the story was being fattened up to novel size. Novels were Larkin's priority, and Coleman held Larkin's hand as he made the jump from writing fiction for himself and a small coterie of friends to writing fiction intended for a bigger and more serious reading public. Whilst his writing underwent changes in authorship and audience, Coleman stuck around to help with the transition – which meant, as we saw in previous chapters, keeping Larkin on the path leading away from narrow self-investigation.

The composition of Coleman's poems also happened to coincide with the first serious opportunities for Larkin to get poems published. In 1943, a chain of events was triggered which would eventually lead two years later to the publication of *The North Ship*, his first full-length collection; but this chain of events would necessarily delay the Coleman effect. It began when Ian Davie, a fellow undergraduate, put together *Oxford Poetry 1942–3* for Blackwell. This would be the only wartime issue of a once-yearly anthology of student verse, and with a publication date of summer 1943, Larkin had to select from what he had, choosing 'I dreamed of an out-thrust arm of land', 'Mythological Introduction' and 'A Stone Church Damaged by a Bomb'. As a possible indication of how rushed Larkin felt, it is interesting to note that only one of these poems was chosen again for *The North Ship*.

Around the same time, plans were afoot for another anthology of student verse, *Poetry from Oxford in Wartime*, edited by William Bell. Containing ten poems by Larkin, this volume was published in 1945 by the Fortune Press.[18] Bradford describes how the Fortune Press published 'proper literature' as a way to give its pornography list 'a shroud of respectability', and as a 'tax dodge' for the owner's 'other role as a landlord of a large number of low-rent, barely habitable properties in Brighton'.[19] That unscrupulous owner, R. A. Caton, had already written to the student contributors with an invitation to submit book-length manuscripts. Larkin at first worried that he 'had not enough poems to make a satisfactory book', but then took up the offer (*SL*, 90). Perhaps he could have held out for a superior selection and better contractual terms (he never received payment for the book), but the desire to be a published poet was strong, and the Fortune Press did have a surprisingly impressive list of contemporary poets, including Wallace Stevens and Dylan Thomas. If Larkin was to be considered a serious poet, this was no time to submit a poem like 'The False Friend' or even 'Femmes Damnées', both of which would be awkwardly out of kilter with the rest of the collection. To take advantage of this opportunity and submit a sufficiently bulky collection, it was perfectly logical for Larkin to fall back on his default mode of writing poems, however unsatisfactory or imitative he found them. Though self-aware enough to know he could do better – his letters from this period are replete with self-criticism, as Chapter 1 showed – Larkin stuck to what was familiar. His two priorities were to write great novels and to get poems published, which meant there was little breathing space for Brunette Coleman in the short term. Her impact would be felt, but for pragmatic reasons the flame burned much slower in verse than it did in prose.

Brunette Coleman and *The North Ship*

This is not to say that Coleman is entirely absent from *The North Ship*. All of the poems in the volume show Larkin's skilful handling of poetic form and his awareness of tradition, but a handful are particularly fascinating and original. These poems tend to be the ones which most reveal Coleman's influence. To put this another way, the most interesting and compelling poems are those which engage with otherness, rather than solipsistically presenting vague emotions like loneliness or Weltschmerz. 'Like the train's beat', for instance, anticipates *A Girl in Winter*'s interest in foreignness: the words of a 'Polish airgirl' in the corner of a train carriage are 'meaningless' to the narrator, but her voice is like 'Watering a stony place' (*TCP*, 11). Hearing it is an aesthetic experience – 'all humanity of interest / Before her angled beauty falls' – but there is also a faint sense of political and cultural weariness here: her difference is contrasted with the 'wilderness' of the English cities the train passes through. The poem's wartime context makes this brief celebration of foreignness all the more meaningful. 'Ugly Sister' is overly essentialist in its gender politics – 'I was not bewitched in adolescence / And brought to love' – but its Cinderella characterization is arguably redeemed by the final image of the narrator attending 'to the trees and their gracious silence, / To winds that move' (*TCP*, 14). The unmarried Coleman liked to do this too: *Ante Meridian* opens with an account of her listening to 'the sibilance of the trees', a soundscape which would appear again in Larkin's 1967 poem 'The Trees' (*TWG*, 235; *TCP*, 76–7). There is consolation in the natural world for those who find human society too restrictive, too repressive.

The most intriguing and enigmatic poem in *The North Ship*, and the one which most reveals Coleman's influence, is 'I see a girl dragged by the wrists', which performs its own act of imaginative transgendering. One line in the penultimate stanza – 'To be that girl!' – has guaranteed this poem more attention than any other in the collection, not least because critics see it as evidence of the young Larkin's transgendered desires; Booth, for example, writes that 'Larkin's desire in the 1940s to *be* a girl was intense' (*TCP*, 15–16; *TWG*, x). The poem is actually more hesitant than that, using gender to negotiate different poetic impulses.

Timms perceptively notes how it seems 'to grow from a close reading of three of Yeats's greatest poems: "Sailing to Byzantium", "The Tower" and "A Dialogue of Self and Soul"'.[20] If in the former we find the narrator preparing to ditch his 'bodily form' and enter into 'the artifice of eternity', we can certainly see the same tension in Larkin's poem between material and ethereal worlds, particularly in the contrasts it paints between the 'dazzling field of snow' and its despoliation, between the girl and the 'two old ragged men' (a more demotic version of Yeats's dignified 'old men'), and between the 'snow-white unicorn' which puts 'into my hand its golden horn' – a sexual image which vulgarizes the beast's pure and mythical status.[21]

Unlike Yeats's narrator, however, there is no reason to believe that Larkin's is 'An aged man': 'weak eyes' can affect even young men, as they did in Larkin's case, precluding his conscription into the Armed Forces, and he seems to have a good 'seventy years' ahead of him. In swapping Yeats's elder for a younger model, the poem prepares itself for the future rather than for the impending end of age, and the contrasting possibilities for that future are figured in aesthetic, or artistic, terms. This is a poem about seeing: the image of the old men stooping and shovelling is beautiful – it 'dries my throat' – in contrast to the image of the 'girl dragged by the wrists', which triggers 'nothing in me that resists'. Two competing aesthetic impulses are at play here: the joyful, self-abandoning otherness of the girl, and the uglier but more 'down to earth' workaday image of the old men labouring. This is not so much Yeats's passage from the earthly to the spiritual as a tussle between them – between different Muses. Of course, the intellectualizing that seems to privilege the latter collapses in the penultimate stanza, with its two sudden apostrophes: 'Damn all explanatory rhymes! / To be that girl!' But the poem recovers its poise, acknowledging the impossibility of that desire, and steadying its grip on the 'explanatory' by arguing that 'everything's remade / With shovel and spade'. There is no shortcut to the other: the narrator, too, 'must stoop, and throw a shovelful'. Self-fashioning, in life as in art, requires hard labour. The poem then seems to change places again in the final stanza:

> If I can keep against all argument
> Such image of a snow-white unicorn,
> Then as I pray it may for sanctuary
> Descend at last to me,
> And put into my hand its golden horn.

This is a more traditional version of, and prayer for, poetic inspiration. Timms summarizes it thus: 'like the "two old ragged men", he must be "content to wear a worn-out coat", until, through his poetry, the horn of plenty comes into his grasp'. In this reading, the poem is a relatively straightforward exploration of the distinction between life and art: its 'central idea' is 'that a poet makes up for the disappointments of his life through his art'.[22] But the poem seems already to know what it wants. Its final act is not one of prayer, of patiently waiting for poetic inspiration, but of subtle despoliation. Whilst the 'golden horn' of the unicorn is like the 'hammered gold and gold enamelling' of Yeats's Byzantium – that is, a traditional mytho-poetic image of something eternally and ethereally beautiful – the underlying sexual vulgarization of the image is an act of self-exclusion from that pure and spiritual realm for which the Yeats poem yearns. The tensions between the worldly and the otherworldly are not resolved in this poem, but left in a state of ambivalence. One exists within the other: the girl is part of the same world as the 'ragged men'. The tension is, by default, a tension between the Yeatsian and what would become the Larkinesque. But if the poem is about competing Muses, it seems to have already made up its mind that one Muse is not going to overwhelm the other.

What is so interesting is that Larkin negotiates these different impulses through the prisms of gender, sexuality and youth. As Osborne points out, the person doing the dragging could be male or female: 'To imagine the girl's captor to be female is to face the dizzying prospect of a work of wartime literature in which a man of military age craves the role of subordinate partner in a lesbian relationship.'[23] Either way, the spirit of Coleman is very much present in this poem about youthful feminine jouissance and its vulnerability in a masculine world. 'I see a girl dragged by the wrists' not only represents a rare instance in *The North Ship* of Larkin beginning to shed his Yeatsian cloak, and therefore approach a poetic more authentic to him, but also shows Coleman helping him do so. Indeed, the poem's imagery of building and labouring is instructive. Like John Kemp, the narrator is excluded from both versions of gender which he sees: from the delightful femininity of the girl and from the rough manliness of the two labourers. He admits defeat, knowing that he can 'Never in seventy years be more of a man / Than now – a sack of meal upon two sticks'. This is the harsh reality of the body: not beautiful like the girl's, not beautiful enough to get the girl, and not even masculine in an honestly ragged way, like the two men. And yet, if the act of shovelling, an essentially menial job, confirms their masculinity (and threatens his), then it at least suggests that identity is achieved by nothing more than a series of acts and behaviours. And if this is true of what might be termed 'the real world', then what might be achieved in the imaginative one? Hence the narrator's resolution at the poem's close:

> For me the task's to learn the many times
> When I must stoop, and throw a shovelful:
> I must repeat until I live the fact
> That everything's remade
> With shovel and spade . . . .

Here, *remaking* is simply a case of *doing* – of intellectual and imaginative labour. After all, Coleman could only exist because of Larkin's literary spadework – because he wrote her into existence. She is no longer the active authorial agent here – Larkin has resumed normal service – but it is not actually normal service at all, in that Larkin is beginning to learn from her by reducing his dependency on the usual sources (Yeats et al.), and by imaginatively transforming the style and subject of his verse. He is still engaged in literary transgendering and othering, but can now do so as Philip Larkin, rather than Brunette Coleman. Although many poems in *The North Ship* are difficult to date precisely – Burnett opts to designate most of them as '[?1943-44]' – this one is confidently dated to 1944, post-Coleman, which at least suggests the kind of development I am tracing here. Larkin also included it in his submission to *Poetry from Oxford in Wartime*. To write a poem in the spirit of Coleman that was also appropriate for publication under his own name must have been one of Larkin's desiderata at this time, and here it was. 'I see a girl dragged by the wrists' is the most compelling piece of evidence to support the claim that the best, most interesting, and most Larkinesque poems in *The North Ship* are those that most clearly show Coleman's influence.

Coleman, 1966

That influence is reinforced by two events in Larkin's publishing history: the first two decades later, the second three decades later. Larkin's slightly embarrassed introduction was not the only addition to the 1966 Faber reissue of *The North Ship*, which also included an extra poem, something he only mentions briskly and obliquely right at the end of his introduction: 'As a coda I have added a poem, written a year or so later, which, though not noticeably better than the rest, shows the Celtic fever abated and the patient sleeping soundly' (*RW*, 30). In what way does poem 'XXXII' ('Waiting for breakfast, while she brushed her hair') represent a 'coda'? It was indeed written later than the other poems in *The North Ship*, which was two years old when Larkin composed this poem in 1947. Interestingly, though, Larkin did not publish it until nearly a decade later, in the July 1956 *Poetry Book Society Bulletin*, perhaps suggesting that he saw it as belonging more to his *Less Deceived* period than his *North Ship* phase, the former volume having been published just a few months earlier in November 1955. In chronological terms, however, the poem's composition is much closer to Larkin's Coleman phase. There need be no contradiction in these statements, given this book's argument that Coleman helped Larkin find the style that would characterize his best work in *The Less Deceived* and beyond. The fact that the poem appears, like 'I see a girl dragged by the wrists', to be another Muse poem reinforces the idea that Larkin was signalling a change of direction. And like the earlier poem, 'Waiting for breakfast' stages its battle of the Muses within the arena of gender:

> Are you jealous of her?
> Will you refuse to come till I have sent
> Her terribly away, importantly live
> Part invalid, part baby, and part saint? (*TCP*, 23-4)

The woman/poetry decision presented here will be familiar to anyone acquainted with the Sutton correspondence. But the poem also tallies with the broader life and art debate voiced by Larkin in that correspondence, where Lawrence's career is appropriated as a version of the artistic life to be accepted, rejected or modified. In other words, the ascetic lifestyle which the poem seems to think necessary for poetic creation – living 'Part invalid, part baby, and part saint' – is in keeping with Larkin's growing realization that some kind of art/life division would be necessary to becoming the writer he wanted to be. There is an irony to that division, in that much of Larkin's greatness stems from his capacity to write with astonishing lyrical power about everyday life – something we see in this poem. Timms comments that the poem has abandoned

> those attitudes towards poetry and what is suitable for inclusion in it that had marred the earlier work. The poeticisms have gone: the rooms in the hotel where it is set are lit by electric light bulbs, not candles, and it has drainpipes and a fire escape. The setting is specific.[24]

This contrasts starkly with the overly romanticized, overly sentimentalized archaisms of the rest of the volume. Now, the narrator looks down 'at the empty hotel yard / Once meant for coaches': had the poem been written two or three years earlier, it is fair to assume he would have seen those coaches. The setting is not just 'specific', then, but contemporary and demotic. There is nothing poetic about 'Drainpipes and fire-escape' – except there can be, if one's idea of poetry is not dominated by 'Celtic fever'. The poem, then, does indeed show 'the Celtic fever abated and the patient sleeping soundly', but what Larkin does not mention is that Coleman has administered the sedative (*RW*, 30). Of course, given Larkin's comments in his introduction about discovering Hardy's poetry the year before, it is understandable that critics should seize upon the English poet as evidence of the Irish poet's declining influence. But Larkin (as Coleman) had already successfully adopted a contemporary-demotic aesthetic in 'Femmes Damnées', where we find a similarly specific English setting of housing estates and main roads. If 'Waiting for breakfast' is 'an address to the Muse', as Thwaite argues, then it is only because the Muse has already asserted herself.[25]

Coleman, 1978

This leads neatly into the second event in Larkin's publishing history: his decision to publish 'Femmes Damnées', under his own name, as a single-poem broadsheet with John Fuller's Sycamore Press, thirty-five years after its composition in Coleman's name. Admittedly, this was a cautious form of publication: Larkin offered Fuller this 'curiosity' in response to a speculative invitation to publish something with the Press, which Fuller ran from his garage in Oxford; Larkin stipulated that production should not exceed 400 copies, and that the poem was 'not on offer for any other form of publication'.[26] (Printing posed a technical challenge for Fuller, who had to improvise an accent for the 'é' in 'Damnées'.)[27] He asked that the date of composition, 1943, appear on the broadsheet, and made a typically Larkinesque joke about it being 'evident [*sic*] that I once read at least one "foreign poem".[28]

There is no mention of Brunette Coleman, or her other work. All this raises some interesting questions. For is it not only intriguing that Larkin wanted the poem to be published under his own name, but that he *could* publish it, and as late as 1978, without it seeming strangely out of place in his mature *oeuvre*? The poem reads like such a characteristically mature Larkin piece that its publication after Larkin had published *The Less Deceived*, *The Whitsun Weddings* and *High Windows* seems entirely natural – as though 'Femmes Damnées' really were a Larkin poem of the late 1970s. It is quite extraordinary, therefore, to remember that it was written in 1943, as part of that package of surrogately authored works by Brunette Coleman. Larkin enclosed a copy of the 1978 publication in a letter to Barbara Pym, very briefly describing it as 'an odd little triptych' (Sycamore Press Broadsheets were folded to make a triptych) (*SL*, 582). This was an astute identification of an ideal reader for the poem: Pym would almost certainly have appreciated the poem's blend of the feminine-domestic and the dramatic; but on the other hand, the poem is not really 'odd' enough to trigger a major rethink of Larkin's late style. Even the poem's French title would not be sufficient cause for alarm, given the publication of 'Sympathy in White Major' in 1967 (and then again in 1974's *High Windows*), a poem containing Gautier's 'Symphonie en blanc majeur' as its subtext, Gautier also being one of the lodestars of *Trouble at Willow Gables* and *Michaelmas Term at St Bride's*.

We can only speculate whether the publication of these poems was later Larkin's quiet tribute to the early Larkin's transformative heteronym. (When Larkin had not heard from Fuller for several months, he sent a playful one-line missive: 'Où sont les Femmes Damnées d'antan?'; Fuller would have got the play on Villon's famous refrain, but would not have been able to understand it as a reference to one of Coleman's other French efforts.)[29] Coleman certainly deserved the tribute, since it was she who unlocked Larkin's distinct mature poetic. Jonathan Bate has called the Coleman works Larkin's 'dirty little secrets', but the 1978 publication of 'Femmes Damnées' suggests pride.[30] Having received the finished product, Larkin told Fuller that 'my opinion of my early talents revives somewhat. A pity I didn't go on writing like this instead of getting tangled up with Yeats!', and asked 'to know how it sells, and to hear any comments that may be made on it'.[31] That this poem could be so easily assimilated into the mature *oeuvre* strengthens the case made here that poetic maturity for Larkin began in 1943, and that although Coleman stopped writing the same year, she hung around Larkin's desk as a spectral presence. Carol Ann Duffy, when compared by an interviewer with Larkin, replied with some irritation that 'As anyone who has the slightest knowledge of my work knows, I have little in common with Larkin', but wryly conceded that 'we are both lesbian poets'.[32] Though mischievous, the comment is revealing: it implicitly recognizes that Brunette Coleman was an integral part of Larkin's poetic identity. Though Coleman will never figure prominently in histories of twentieth-century English Literature, she played a significant role in the development of the major twentieth-century English poet, Philip Larkin.

7

Larkin's first great poems

This chapter traces Larkin's transition from novelist to poet, exploring the changes occurring in his poetry workbooks, and presenting close readings of his first two major poems, 'At Grass' and 'Deceptions', both written in 1950. If, as Stan Smith argues, 1950 was something of a liminal year for Larkin, then one index of this was 'Round the Point: *Débat Inédit*', the soul-searching dramatic piece he wrote that year. In this dialectic, two characters, Geraint and Miller, clash on the question of what makes a good writer. Geraint is struggling to write, and the *débat* opens with him tearing up his latest novel, which he considers 'banal, shapeless, stewed-up, faceless . . . And all overhung by an exhausting pall of apathy, that vitiates style, rhythm, even handwriting' (*TWG*, 471). Since he last wrote a book 'Five years ago', he has suffered from 'A gaping, open-eyed apathy' (*TWG*, 474). Geraint's circumstances match Larkin's own: *The North Ship* had been published five years ago, in 1945, and although 1946 and 1947 had seen the publication of *Jill* and *A Girl in Winter*, it was five years since the latter was completed.

According to Booth, 'even before he had sent off the typescript of *A Girl in Winter*, Larkin was already proliferating detailed ideas for the third novel' (*TWG*, 474n, xxvii). This would be variously titled *The Trap*, *Losing the Music* and *Second Thoughts*, but no drafts survive. Booth's study of Larkin's fiction workbook reveals that every version of the story focused on marriage, a question Larkin was grappling with as his relationship with Ruth Bowman entered a critical point. In 1946, there was also an exchange of letters with Amis, in which Brunette Coleman briefly came out of retirement to collaborate with Anna Lucasta, Amis's heteronym, on their ongoing project 'Iwdafy' (*I Would Do Anything For You*) (see *TWG*, xxvii-xxxi). This, however, was not the brilliant, ambitious, feminist Coleman of 1943, but a cruder, lewder version, perfunctorily co-writing lesbian scenes for Amis's entertainment. Booth notes some brief and mostly uninformative references in letters to yet another fiction project, before work began proper on a new novel in

1948, provisionally titled *No For An Answer*. In 1949, with that novel unfinished, Larkin started yet another one, *A New World Symphony* – also a provisional title – which was seemingly abandoned by the end of the year.[1]

No For An Answer and *A New World Symphony*

Both unfinished novels have autobiographical origins. The protagonist of *No For An Answer*, Sam Wagstaff, finds himself distracted from his girlfriend, Sheila, by another woman. Themes of guilt, choice and entrapment echo the slow breakdown of Larkin's relationship with Ruth Bowman, as he described it in letters to Sutton and others. The story is set in the Midlands, where Larkin grew up and had now returned to work as deputy librarian at University College, Leicester. Despite its ostentatious title, *A New World Symphony* is similarly provincial in its setting and plots. The protagonist, Augusta Bax, is an English lecturer at a university college, and the story charts the often-ridiculous happenings and internal politics of an institution that is decidedly not Oxford. With its female protagonist and provincial setting, *A New World Symphony* may appear to share similarities with *A Girl in Winter*, but in fact the contrast is starkly instructive: whereas Katherine Lind was notable as a sensitively realized character whose circumstances largely stood apart from Larkin's own, Augusta Bax was modelled on his Leicester colleague and new romantic interest, Monica Jones.

This helps to explain why both novels failed. Though Larkin had been steadily engaged with writing fiction since the completion of *A Girl in Winter*, something caused him to give up by the end of the decade. His problem was that he was writing about his own circumstances, emotions and the people in his immediate social circle. This was an approach to fiction that had already proved unproductive, as the stories he wrote before 1943 show. Though his personal experiences may have given him the ideas for these novels, they also ended up being the cause of their suffocation. Both novels are significantly tangled up with real life, and it is perhaps unsurprising that Larkin should choose to simply abandon them rather than try to disentangle them.

But there are also literary reasons behind the novels' failure. Bradford points out that *No For An Answer* involved a new departure for Larkin's writing: 'naturalistic prose fiction which offered an unadorned account of the lives of ordinary people without making any claims upon significance'.[2] Though Larkin's earlier novels were in some respects realist, they also bore some relation to the modernist novel, and both have a poetic, dreamlike quality, Larkin himself thinking of them as 'Long, diffuse poems' (*FR*, 114). For Bradford, Larkin's wholesale embrace of naturalism represents a potentially significant development, and therefore a tantalizingly disappointing failure. He argues that *No For An Answer* 'could have formed the basis for a ground-breaking novel', and explains this by looking to the period's nascent literary landscape:

> The most striking feature of the text is the way in which Larkin creates an atmosphere scrupulously devoid of intellectual or literary issues without implying that the characters are in any way lacking in intelligence or significance. Had the novel been completed and found a publisher ... it might have subtly altered the course of post-war literary history. Braine, Barstow, Sillitoe, Storey and to a lesser degree Amis and Wain dismantled the stereotypes of class determination by showing that good writing could coexist with states of mind that had little time for high culture, but this new wave of writing did not make its presence felt until the late 1950s. Larkin with *No for an Answer* would have set the precedent ten years earlier.[3]

This is an intriguing speculation about the possible course of post-war British literature, but neither of the unfinished novels is a particularly compelling read. As with his early efforts in verse, Larkin shows technical adeptness, especially in the dialogue set pieces and description, but there is something very flat about both novels. This is not because Larkin was unsuited to naturalist or realist writing; after all, his mature poetry is striking for its descriptions of post-war Britain. That is an integral ingredient of Larkin's poetry, but there is also more to it. Amis's *Lucky Jim* is immensely readable and very funny because it perfectly evokes the English middle class of the 1940s and 1950s, and gives that class a good kicking. Larkin was capable of doing this too, but his best writing tends to strike a different note to Amis's, in that it often takes the ordinary and then renders it extraordinary. Major Larkin poems like 'Here' and 'The Whitsun Weddings' may begin by taking the reader through the meticulously described realist setting of a 'large town' with its 'cut-price crowd', or on a train journey passing 'Canals with floatings of industrial froth' and parties of 'fathers with broad belts under their suits', but these poems end up representing their subjects in unexpected ways: 'Here' becomes 'unfenced existence: / Facing the sun, untalkative, out of reach', and the train reaches its destination with 'A sense of falling, like an arrow-shower / Sent out of sight, somewhere becoming rain' (*TCP*, 49, 56–8). Readers value poems like these because Larkin shows them their world, and then shows it to them again, 'in different terms'. He is a different kind of artist to the writers Bradford mentions, and the ground-breaking naturalist novel which he describes would have to wait to be realized by those other figures.

Indeed, it is not just by comparison with Larkin's later poems that we can observe the two novels' flatness, but also by comparison with the Coleman works of 1943. Booth recognizes this, asking: 'Is it that the colourless, omniscient third-person narration precludes the humour, irony and playfulness which give vitality to the Willow Gables works . . .? Was Larkin repeating the same mistake he had made in *The North Ship*, rejecting mixed tones in favour of a consistent seriousness?'[4] In short, although these novels contain some hallmarks of the Larkinesque, other, crucial aspects are missing, and Larkin's return to scenarios and people close to his own life clearly reversed the progress represented by Coleman, *Jill* and *A Girl in Winter*.

'Round the Point'

As the novels floundered, 'Round the Point' provided an outlet for Larkin's frustration (an exercise he must have found useful, following it up in 1951 with 'Round Another Point: *Débat*', this time on women, sex and relationships). Geraint's despair at the wasting of 'Five years' work, five years' hope, five years' ambition' matches Larkin's, and it is easy to imagine the contents of the wastepaper basket which is such a prominent stage prop (*TWG*, 475). What particularly exasperates Geraint is that he has consciously arranged his life in order to enable his writing:

> I don't pickle myself in drink, I don't pelt after women, I don't lie awake sweating about my vocation as a European . . . . I'm not one of the people who 'can't' live in lodgings, and 'can't' eat food out of tins, and 'must get out of England once a year', and 'must' have pretty furniture, and my energies are therefore reasonably free to devote to whatever I want. But NOTHING HAPPENS. (*TWG*, 474)

Like Larkin, Geraint has declined to 'live as an artist'; he has refused many of the pleasures and comforts of the bourgeois, academic-artistic life, keeping himself largely free of the emotional, financial, intellectual and practical worries which might sap the time and energy available for writing. Why, then, in his own words, is his writing so 'banal, shapeless, stewed-up, faceless'? Miller – who is both Geraint's antagonist and supporter, and therefore honest – supplies the answer to this question, and there are two points to note here. The first is that Larkin's best writing was now beginning to appear in the form of poetry, not prose. It is ironic that in the course of airing his literary frustrations in this *débat*, Larkin should include a poem which contains early signs of the 'Larkinesque'. Attempting to cheer up Geraint, Miller recites 'a little song I made up', which is a variant version of 'Fiction and the Reading Public' (*TWG*, 471). This iconoclastic poem, which Larkin would publish four years later in *Essays in Criticism*, is direct in its language, drawing on ordinary speech and common obscenities to make its point. It therefore anticipates later poems such as 'A Study of Reading Habits', 'High Windows' and 'This Be the Verse'. But it also offers a partial diagnosis of Larkin's literary anaemia. The title references the Q. D. Leavis study discussed in relation to Coleman's literary politics in Chapter 3. Though Coleman's attitude differed in many ways from Leavis's, their mutual dislike of degenerate market-writing is reiterated in this poem, which bitterly lampoons the notion of 'writing what you know' and the impulse to satisfy readers' cravings for intimate autobiography:

> Choose something you know all about
> That'll sound like real life:
> Your childhood, your Dad pegging out,
> How you sleep with your wife. (*TWG*, 471–2)

Its cynicism resonates with Geraint, who welcomes Miller's performance with a hearty 'Bravo!' (*TWG*, 472). And yet, as the *débat* continues, we learn how his own writing has been too closely tied to 'real life': 'Now tell me truthfully', Miller says, 'wasn't this novel of yours an attempt to hash up certain events in your own life that you thought you ought to be able to make a novel of?' (*TWG*, 480). Geraint's response, though more moderately phrased, does not deny the charge, and reflects the general impulse behind Larkin's *No For An Answer* and *A New World Symphony*: 'I was trying to write about the people I know, the places I know, the emotions I know' (*TWG*, 481). Miller's analysis is remarkably prescient, and effectively a concise summary of the conclusion this study has been working towards:

> You fancy that a writer is a kind of journalist, working up a story about what happens to have happened to you. Don't you realise that an artist of any depth has his particular grain, his territory, marked out for him long before he's capable of thinking about it? Even his subject? A writer's development is a slow approximation to his fated position. In other words, discovering what one writes about best is a slow business. (*TWG*, 481)

Though there is something dissatisfyingly mystical about the idea of slowly groping towards one's destiny, Miller does elaborate, and in doing so undermines narrow definitions of 'experience':

> To me, 'experience' means a chance to find if you react to something or not, if there's any work for you to do in that field. It's because you are still thinking that

real experience and aesthetic experience are identical. A man may go through air raids, love affairs, changes of fortune, long journeys, and still only be able to write something quite unrelated to them . . . . As far as art goes, life is a process of discovering what stimuli we react to . . . . And once we've discovered what they are, it's nothing but a waste of time trying to get a spark out of the others. (*TWG*, 481)

Miller's analysis is astonishingly acute. If a rather crude theory of literary creation posits that life happens to the writer, who then uses it as raw material for his writing, it would follow that the writer should try to squeeze as much out of life as possible, in order to maximize the available raw material. That might be an effective summary of the career of Lawrence or Isherwood, but it is not the only option available. Miller argues that writing is about discovering what one reacts to. This might also suggest that the writer should try to expose himself to as much life as possible, in order to increase the likelihood of finding his 'stimuli'. But, as Larkin's career would show, that 'stimuli' might be something as mundane as a train journey from Hull to London, or a walk around a Marks and Spencer store, rather than a madly destructive love affair or a bloody battle. If, via Miller, Larkin had come to realize this, it is because of the experience of the preceding decade, during which he had written prose and poetry which slowly came to affirm the theory. How else could one account for the fact that when Larkin writes about his circle at Oxford, or his relationships with women, the texts are interesting chiefly as autobiography, but when he writes about the girls of Willow Gables, or a young woman exiled to wartime England, biography becomes murky, but the work becomes intriguing, moving and compelling?

Miller's advice is sage: 'Drop all this anatomising of your dreary experiences: you'll never make anything of them' (*TWG*, 482). The *débat* ends with him taking a run at Geraint's wastepaper basket and kicking it 'high into the auditorium'; 'During the snowstorm thus created / THE CURTAIN FALLS' (*TWG*, 482). Though Larkin would briefly return to his drafts of *A New World Symphony* in 1953 – *Lucky Jim* having been accepted by Victor Gollancz after considerable editorial interventions by Larkin – there is a sense of finality and liberation in this dramatic act. If Miller's comments seem remarkably shrewd, it is because significant changes were already taking place in Larkin's writing. In a very direct and didactic way, Miller gave voice to these. And though Larkin was clearly still desperate to make his name as a novelist, it is in the poetry workbooks from this period that we can see those changes occurring.

The poetry workbooks

The majority of Larkin's life's work in verse would be drafted in eight manuscript books. Tolley conjectures that Larkin began to use the first workbook at the end of 1943, although the earliest entries are dated October 1944.[5] Despite this being the year after his Brunette Coleman phase, Larkin was still in Yeatsian mode. This is shown not only by the bulk of poems composed there, but also by the shrine to Yeats which Larkin improvised on the inside front cover, where he pasted a photograph of the poet and a typed copy of 'The Collar-bone of a Hare'.[6] The previous chapter suggested possible reasons for the more delayed transformation of Larkin's poetry, following his authorial experiment with Coleman. About two years into the workbook, his poetry does indeed begin to transform – not wholesale, but more gradually. In September 1946, he drafted 'Wedding-Wind', one of the few Larkin poems to be explicitly narrated by a woman, and therefore a clear follow-on from Coleman's work and *A Girl in Winter*.[7] This poem (discussed in Chapter 8) is also notable for making the jump to *The Less Deceived*, published almost a decade later in 1955. Since that was not the case for the majority of poems in this workbook, it is interesting to observe that the 1940s poems most obviously influenced by Coleman are often the ones which find a home in Larkin's mature *oeuvre*, 'Femmes Damnées' being another example of this phenomenon.

More than a year later, in December 1947, Larkin drafted 'Waiting for breakfast, while she brushed her hair' (originally bearing the title 'Sunday Morning'), the poem he would append as a 'coda' to the 1966 reissue of *The North Ship*.[8] Once again, an obvious product of the 1943 experiments is, two decades later, permitted a place in the mature *oeuvre*. A few months after this, in April 1948, the death of Larkin's father prompted the elegy 'An April Sunday brings the snow'.[9] Here, domestic details and a homely vocabulary are used to evoke the poem's central emotions of loss and grief, as the narrator shifts the store

> Of jam you made of fruit from these same trees:
> Five loads – a hundred pounds or more –
> More than enough for all next summer's teas,
>
> Which now you will not sit and eat. (*TCP*, 265)

Such a strategy is a characteristic feature of Larkin's mature verse, but not the early poems – Coleman's excepted.

Sydney Larkin's death seems to have precipitated a long break in his son's writing, but the following year Larkin took up four pages of the workbook trying to get the words right for a poem called 'Modesties', itself a poem about finding the right words.[10] Beginning with the image of 'Hen-birds' wings', Larkin's first attempt undermines his intentions as he contrasts these with 'Emblazoned cocks' – a noisy image – and then describes 'gravid eggs within the nest', 'gravid' being an oddly florid choice of word for a poem about modest words. Having cancelled these lines, he turns to the imagery of coinage, which makes it into the final version's second stanza, though with greater poignancy: the published version's image of coins which 'shuffle . . . / Through each reign' evokes intergenerational loss and change, a superior effort to the draft version's argument that 'Words as smooth as copper pence / Hold no bribe'. Larkin eventually settles on his original image for the poem's first stanza:

> Words as plain as hen-birds' wings
> Do not lie,
> Do not over-broider things –
> Are too shy.

Particularly notable here is Larkin's use of the word 'things': too imprecise to survive redrafting by most poets, and highly unlikely to ever enter into Larkin's Yeatsian imitations. In 'Modesties', the word seems perfectly chosen, and not just because it rhymes with 'wings'. In a much later poem, 'Livings I', Larkin uses the word to evoke the workaday mind of his agricultural salesman narrator: 'I deal with farmers, things like dips and feed' (*TCP*, 77). In 'Modesties', similarly, the context licenses the word. To put this another way, Larkin was beginning to establish an aesthetic for himself in which he could use a word as common, mundane and indistinct as 'things' without writing poetry that was common, mundane or indistinct.

'Modesties' did not make it into *The Less Deceived*, but its ethos is one that characterizes the volume. Though Larkin (via Geraint) was tearing out his hair over the stalling of his prose, prose was beginning to seep into his poetry. A few days after writing 'Modesties', Larkin began work on 'Fiction and the Reading Public' – the disenchanted poem which features in the *débat* – and in between the first draft and a more complete version, tried his hand at a poem called 'To Failure': 'You do not come dramatically, with dragons / That rear up with my life between their paws'; 'It is these sunless afternoons, I find, / Instal you at my elbow like a bore'.[11] Read in conjunction with the *débat*, these poems show Larkin's poetry and his attitude to it in a state of flux. Though he dramatized this as failure

– since at the time writing unsatisfactory fiction *was* failure according to the terms he had set himself – in hindsight we can see that Larkin was undergoing a series of important transitions. The aspiring novelist was becoming a poet; but the poet was disrobing his Yeatsian garb, and instead using the novelist's eye for detail in order to fully engage with the ordinary world around him.

Further evidence of this turn to the world can be detected early in 1950, when Larkin copied into his workbook a list of ex-Forces goods for sale: 'Ex Naval duffle coats', 'Rubber boots', 'Sheepskin flying boots', and so on; and on the opposite page pasted cuttings of newspaper advertisements for Leicester's Millets store and for properties in the city.[12] The next entry in the workbook, an unfinished poem beginning 'Last of all, when a great war has ended', perhaps explains the list of army surplus gear: these were most likely details to be included in the poem.[13] The advertisements are harder to account for: perhaps they were also meant to find their way into the poem, or a different one; or perhaps Larkin placed them there for his personal use, though it would be odd to stick them in a workbook. In any case, we can see the material culture of late 1940s and early 1950s England seeping not only into the workbook but also into the poetry it contains. Though this new attitude to art is attributed to the rediscovery of Hardy in 1946, Larkin had already allowed his verse to be permeated by the period's material culture as early as 1943, when Coleman evoked a world of Junior B. S. A. bicycles, Harrod's, W. H. Smith & Son, *The Guardian*, Green Line buses and modern housing estates. Seven years later, her influence was finally exerting itself on Larkin's poetry.

Larkin's first major poems

The same month he pasted advertisements into his workbook, Larkin also wrote 'At Grass', and copied out a quotation from Henry Mayhew's *London Labour and the London Poor* (1851), which would eventually become the epigraph for 'Deceptions'.[14] Work on 'Deceptions' began the following month, February 1950, and the poem was finally completed towards the end of the year, by which time Larkin had moved onto a second workbook.[15] 'At Grass' and 'Deceptions' can rightfully be described as Larkin's first two major poems. Along with 'Wedding-Wind', they are the only poems drafted (or part-drafted) in the first workbook which made it into *The Less Deceived*. Recalling the importance Larkin placed on the arrangement of collections, these poems also enjoy a special status within that volume, which takes its name from a line in 'Deceptions' and closes with

'At Grass' (*FR*, 55). These two poems also stand out in the workbooks for other reasons. The last poem Larkin worked on before 'At Grass' was 'Do not think to step from art's plain room', in May 1949.[16] This is a gap of seven months; the fact that Larkin chose to return to the workbook a couple of days into the New Year may suggest he considered 'At Grass' a fresh start. Indeed, it was: from this point onward, the poetry comes thick and fast. Whereas the first workbook contains five-and-a-half years of work, the second workbook fits just a year-and-a-half, much of which formed the basis of *The Less Deceived*. 'At Grass' is also notable for its length: the drafts take up an unusually expansive twelve pages of the workbook, which Tolley describes as 'a wholly new approach to composition, undoubtedly associated with the abandonment of the inspiration approach to composition associated with his admiration for Yeats'.[17] Similarly, 'Deceptions' is spread across seven pages of the first two workbooks, and seemingly took several months to complete.

Both poems, then, represent a new, more laboured form of composition for Larkin, but what makes them so different to their precursors, and what makes them 'major'? One answer is that they are no longer exercises in poetic imitation, but in poetic calibration. In each of these poems, Larkin explores the possibilities and the limitations of writing from a distance: 'The eye can hardly pick them out', 'At Grass' begins, whilst 'Deceptions' opens by stating 'Even so distant, I can taste the grief' (*TCP*, 45–6, 41). If Brunette Coleman's work and *A Girl in Winter* showed Larkin the potential of writing about subjects largely unconnected to his own private experience, it is in these poems that Larkin begins to do so seriously in verse. Though Tolley describes how 'At Grass' was 'occasioned by seeing a television documentary', which he takes as evidence of Hardy's influence – 'of the possibility of making poetry out of the things that made up his own life' – the poem erases any biographical origins and focuses solely on its subject, retired racehorses.[18] Similarly, 'Deceptions' takes as its starting point the rape of a woman in Victorian London, documented in Mayhew's 'Cyclopaedia'. In a 1953 letter to Monica Jones, Larkin wrote:

> I do love the past. Anything more than 20 years back begins to breathe a luminous fascination for me: it starts my imagination working. Why? Because it *is* past, I suppose, & leaves my feelings free to get to work on it. Do you think I should trouble my head about a prostitute down in Amelia Street, and not safely tucked away in Mayhew? (*LM*, 109)

Amelia Street was part of Belfast's red-light district, a few minutes' walk from Larkin's Elmwood Avenue flat. This is not to say that Larkin was becoming a fundamentally historical poet, less interested in people and events just streets away than in reviving scenes from centuries past. As readers of the mature poems will attest, Larkin is an excitingly contemporary poet. His imagination, however, was now beginning to turn away from the self. This is in stark contrast to most of the poems drafted in the first workbook, and those included in *The North Ship*, which turn inward, all too consciously, in search of stock emotions that are conventionally and predictably 'poetic' ('How strange it is / For the heart to be loveless', etc.) (*TCP*, 6). Larkin seems to have recognized this himself. When D. J. Enright singled out 'Deceptions' for praise in his review of *XX Poems*, Larkin speculated that it was 'because it showed a bit of interest outside myself – a rare thing' (*LM*, 71). Here is yet another echo of the phrase Larkin used in 'The Eagles Are Gone': 'interest in everything outside himself'.

Of course, it is true that both poems – all poems – have biographical origins. 'At Grass' has a contemporary setting, and was possibly inspired by seeing a film about the famous racehorse Brown Jack.[19] Motion relates its theme of freedom to Larkin's 'feelings about himself, his mother and his fiancée [Ruth Bowman]'.[20] Critics have also worked hard to make 'Deceptions' emerge from the life: Booth, for instance, connects the poem's exploration of violence and culpability to the guilt Larkin expressed for the breakdown of his relationship with Bowman. These interpretations, however, bear little relation to the poems themselves. As well as being about distance, the poems make conscious efforts to respect that distance; and in both cases, the poetry and the pathos emerge beautifully out of the narrators' attempts to calibrate and honour the gap. The arc of this study has been towards showing that Larkin became a great poet by learning to become interested 'in everything outside himself'. The remainder of this chapter takes a closer look at these two poems, Larkin's first masterpieces, in order to demonstrate the significance of their moving negotiations of distance and difference.

'At Grass'

We might be forgiven for thinking that 'At Grass' uses its subject, horses in a field, as a means of exploring the poet's emotions – a conventional way to interpret lyric poetry. The poem is full of emotional language: the horses shelter in 'cold shade'; 'wind distresses tail and mane'; 'Dusk brims the shadows' (*TCP*, 45–6). But metaphors like these are undermined by a series of hesitations and qualifications, as well as another distinct vocabulary signalling the human world's intrusion into the natural. With its definite article, the first line – 'The eye can hardly pick them out' – isolates this organ, making it seem as coldly impersonal as a roving lens. And from the outset, the poem struggles to focalize its subject; the horses resist the human gaze and the poetic impulse behind it. Human ways of seeing are again foregrounded:

> Then one crops grass, and moves about
> – The other seeming to look on –
> And stands anonymous again.

The image of the horse 'look[ing] on' is an astute visual description, but the poem is keen to stress its own projections: the horse only *seems* to do this, with the qualification placed strikingly between hyphens. And what does it mean for a horse to stand 'anonymous'? The word perfectly captures the change from movement to stillness, but it also, of course, means 'nameless', which both horses remain throughout. Human habits, concepts and language press upon, but struggle to fully capture, the scene. The narrator then speculates about the horses' past:

> Yet fifteen years ago, perhaps
> Two dozen distances sufficed
> To fable them: faint afternoons
> Of Cups and Stakes and Handicaps,
> Whereby their names were artificed
> To inlay faded . . . .

The verbal reasoning ('Yet', 'perhaps') reveals a reluctance to force the speculation, whilst the visual language ('faint', 'faded') reaffirms the poem's inability to capture these horses with precision. 'Fable' is another ambiguous word choice: in winning races, the horses were 'fabled' – that is, made famous – but to be fabled also means to be narrativized, and fables typically anthropomorphize animals in order to convey a moral. Is 'At Grass' a fable, then? Given its hesitancy, and the strain felt by language when it seeks to represent these animals, this seems unlikely. Perhaps it would be more accurate to describe it as an 'anti-fable', one which paradoxically uses animals to resist the fabulist tendency. After all, 'artificed' is yet another word of doubleness: etymologically, it comes from the Latin *artificium*, 'ars' meaning art, and 'ficium' making. The poem makes art out of the horses, but artificial also means unnatural; again, human and natural worlds rub up against each other. The middle stanza definitively shifts the focus to the human, imagining the races: 'Numbers and parasols', 'Squadrons of empty cars', 'littered grass'. 'Numbers' has an abstract quality, and 'Squadrons' is an unusual word choice, which again foregrounds human intrusion on the natural world, as does the more obvious image of 'littered grass', a contrast to the grass which now nourishes the horses in their retirement.

By now, the poem's hesitancy has given way to negative capability: 'Do memories plague their ears like flies? / They shake their heads'. The second line seems to answer the first, but it is clear the poem does not believe its own fictions. The simile undermines itself: it is actual flies which make the horses shake their heads. Larkin then deploys another loaded word: 'Summer by summer all stole away'. If 'stole away' represents the horses' receding past – the 'starting-gates, the crowds and cries' – it also has connotations of theft and dishonesty. Does the line mean that with each summer these things feature less in the horses' memory? Or that summer after summer, these things 'stole away' 'all' the horses had – that is, their freedom and independence? The latter becomes more plausible when, returning to the present, the poem describes the horses in their 'unmolesting meadows'. Larkin's use of an 'un-' word inevitably draws attention to what it negates: to think of the meadows as 'unmolesting' is to consider the ways in which the horses have previously been molested. Exploitation by the racing industry may be one such way, and the poem seems to end by emphasizing their newfound freedom: 'Almanacked, their names live; they // Have slipped their names'. Their names exist in the separate, human world of almanacs and racing history; 'slipped' is a curiously proto-Derridean word, dramatizing the arbitrary relation between signifier (the horses' names) and signified (the horses). They have, finally, escaped the imprisonment of the human: of the Word ('they // Have slipped their names'), the Gaze ('not a fieldglass sees them home') and Time ('Or curious stop-watch prophesies'). They can now 'stand at ease, / Or gallop for what must be joy' – but again, these human emotions are a projection.

The poem's ending also refuses sentimentality: 'Only the groom, and the groom's boy, / With bridles in the evening come'. Ending the poem on an eye rhyme feels significant, suggesting there is something to interrogate, and this enigmatic image has indeed been interpreted differently. For some, it is a sinister way to end the poem: the 'bridles' represent another form of human control, and a very physical one at that, and their appearance at the dying of the day has a menacing quality, like the arrival of the Grim Reaper, closing *The Less Deceived* on a cold and deathly note. Conversely, Osborne suggests that 'groom', and the similarity of 'bridles' to 'bride'/'bridal', are marital puns, and the poem's final word, 'come', a play on 'ejaculate', which instead poises the collection on a final note of congress and regeneration.[21] Osborne also draws attention to the title's connotations, arguing that 'At Grass' is not an elegy but a poem about retirement

– written by a young man. As he puts it, other critics 'have exaggerated its morbidity and minimized its originality: elegies are commonplace; meditations upon retirement, rare'.[22] As the volume's final poem, whichever reading we choose has implications for how we interpret *The Less Deceived*: has Larkin chosen to end the volume in elegy, meditation or celebration? My own reading also suggests other fruitful approaches to 'At Grass', which might be read as an animal rights poem and/or through an eco-critical lens. In terms of Larkin's literary development, however, what is significant is that this is a poem of calibration. The poem recognizes various forms of distance and difference: between narrator and subject, human and animal, past and present, youth and old age/retirement. Most important of all is the distance between Larkin and his subject, and the care he takes to respect that distance. In contrast to the majority of poems drafted in the first workbook, 'At Grass' declines to strike a Yeatsian pose – to play the poet – and instead quietly and poignantly explores the possibilities of writing about subjects outside of and separate to the poet's own life. Though it is the last poem in *The Less Deceived*, it represents the first major result of this new approach to poetry, perhaps explaining its privileged position in the book.

'Deceptions'

Like 'At Grass', 'Deceptions' has an enhanced status in *The Less Deceived*, as the poem which provides the volume's title. Larkin pasted the excerpt from *London Labour and the London Poor* into the first workbook in January 1950, the same month he wrote 'At Grass'. Work on the poem itself began the following month, with five pages of drafts; the poem was then abandoned for several months, and completed towards the end of the year, by which point Larkin had broken into his second workbook. That he clearly grappled with this poem over a long period of time may suggest he was personally mixed up in the poem's meaning, finding it difficult to write, or that its sensitive and harrowing subject matter, the rape of a woman in nineteenth-century London, necessitated slow and thoughtful treatment.

The former would seem to support Booth's claim that, having emotionally injured Ruth Bowman, Larkin used the poem and its source material 'as an imaginative vehicle for [his] contradictory feelings of resentment, anger and self-contempt. . . . [The] poet seeks to expiate his sense of guilt through an expression of sympathy with the victim in Mayhew's text'.[23] But the poem's origins in Mayhew might instead suggest this is an impersonal act of imagination and empathy. Was

Larkin so narcissistic that he sought out reflections of his own circumstances in everything he read – and thought that he had found this in a work of Victorian sociology? Or was the poet's mind stirred by reading the historical text, as his letter to Jones explains? Many critics might decide the former, but in trying to establish the poem's proximity to Larkin's life, they fail to observe the ways in which this poem explicitly explores and respects questions of distance and difference. As Christopher Hitchens commented, it expresses 'feeling for the woes of womanhood and the hidden injuries of class'.[24] Although there are issues of representation involved, 'Deceptions' is at heart an ethical poem.

Because it is ethical, it is, like 'At Grass', a cautious poem. The poem's form is one manifestation of the care it takes with its subject. On the page, 'Deceptions' looks like a sonnet: there is a typographical break between its two stanzas, the first of which is slightly longer than the second. Each stanza has its own intricate rhyme scheme, and the poem is broadly written in pentameters. This suggests that the poem contains an argument, since the sonnet, along with the ode, has proved to be one of English poetry's most useful vehicles for such a purpose. In fact, the poem comprises nine and eight lines – seventeen in total – making it a swollen, or failed sonnet. Whereas a Shakespeare, Donne, or Wordsworth sonnet would self-assuredly unfold its argument within the tight constraints of the predetermined form ('"twas pastime to be bound / Within the Sonnet's scanty plot of ground'), this one refuses constraint.[25] In this specific case, the sonnet's rulebook is inimical to what the poem wishes to say; its message must not be upstaged by the formal flourish and technical bravado of how it is delivered.

That said, 'Deceptions' does follow the sonnet's convention of enacting a turn between the first and second stanzas. In the first, the poem focuses intensely on the psychological aftermath of the woman's rape: 'Even so distant, I can taste the grief, / Bitter and sharp with stalks, he made you gulp' (*TCP*, 41). The first three words see this mid-twentieth-century poem cross the distance between itself and the historical event, which is itself mediated through a mid-nineteenth-century text. Distance is compressed by sensory experience, beginning with 'taste', an immediate contrast with what Booth calls Mayhew's 'rigorously objective and sociological' approach.[26] Sound and light evoke the woman's emotional and psychological state. The 'brisk brief / Worry of wheels' is a reminder of the indifferent world outside the room, a world which 'bows the other way'; and 'bridal London' of the matrimonial life a 'ruined' woman in Victorian society will be denied. Though light often appears in Larkin's work as a transcendental, quasi-religious phenomenon ('High Windows', 'Solar'), here it is 'unanswerable',

'Forbids the scar to heal' and 'drives / Shame out of hiding'. The reference to 'Shame' is one measure of the poem's empathic depth, for though the woman has no reason to feel it, Victorian society's double standard essentially demands it, and her words in the epigraph show that this did indeed form part of her emotional response. The enigmatic line, 'Your mind lay open like a drawer of knives', subtly articulates the sharpness of her pain, her vulnerability and a more menacing sense of threat.

The second stanza sees the poem's 'turn' occur. If the first represents an attempt to evoke the complex emotional and psychological condition of the woman in the terrible aftermath of her rape, drawing on the sensory experiences of taste, sound and light, then the second tests and acknowledges the limitations of this empathetic act. Although the poem's opening line contracts distance, the first line of the second stanza grants that 'Slums, years, have buried you'. If 'buried' conveys the cumulative hardships of the woman's subsequent life – a life lived year after year in the poverty of London's slums – it also signals the passing of time between her life and the poem's present. She has become a historical figure, 'buried' deep in the pages of Mayhew. The sensory immediacy of the first part gives way to an acknowledgement of distance, of the pastness of the past. At this point, the poet could easily exit the poem with a vague and facile sentiment, but chooses instead to deliver some of the most devastatingly honest lines anywhere in Larkin's work: 'I would not dare / Console you if I could'. The sentence is simple, monosyllabic, direct, utterly inadequate and true. Temporal distance is breached again, this time by the narrator's compassion, but here the act of compassion is, in part, a refusal to offer emotional falsehood in the form of consolation, since there can really be no consolation. It is a highly moving and mature act of empathy.

The remaining lines, however, have proved highly contentious. Perhaps part of the critical response stems from surprise that the poet should have anything more to add: 'What can be said', the poem asks, before continuing for another six lines. Before it is anything else, 'Deceptions' is a poem about rape, and not rape in some general or metaphorical sense, but the actual rape of an actual woman. It is right, then, that we should expect of it the highest ethical standards. But not every critique has been fair. Three main objections have been made against it. Two involve acts of appropriation: the poet appropriates the woman's story in order to express his feelings about something in his own life; or he appropriates the story in order to express a more 'philosophical' truth about life in general. In either case, the result would be that the reality of the rape itself is diminished, the violent crime transformed into a personal or public trope. The third and more extreme objection is that Larkin's poem appears more concerned to empathize with the rapist than with the survivor.

Booth offers the first reading when he interprets the poem in relation to Larkin's failed relationship with Ruth Bowman:

> If we may short-circuit between biography and art here, it seems that Larkin ... has chosen an extreme metaphor, accusing himself of using Ruth's body, like a rapist. He unhappily acknowledges a sympathy with the man in the poem, who is interpreted as a misguided artist, a voluptuary in search of the ultimate sensual-aesthetic experience. By thus casting his choice of art over life as a rape, Larkin expresses shame for his behaviour.[27]

This leans too heavily on biographicalism. As Booth himself acknowledges, it requires a short-circuiting between life and art, forcing the poem to fit its biographical context rather than reading it on its own terms. Artists may indeed seek 'sensual-aesthetic experience', but there is nothing in the poem to suggest the attacker is some kind of refined but misguided aesthete, nor do the language and imagery invite such a reading.

More troubling is the view that Larkin effectively pardons the rape. For Janice Rossen, 'While not ignoring the aesthetics of the poem, the callousness which it exhibits and the sadism which it in part condones ought at the least to be seen as problematic – and as a limitation in Larkin's art'.[28] Joseph Bristow goes further, describing 'Deceptions' as an 'apology for rape'.[29] But assessments like these seem remote from the poem and what it actually says. Though the poem ends with the rapist's desolation, it also calls him 'deceived', a pretty damning descriptor. This is in contrast to the woman's 'suffering', which is 'exact', and which the poem is at pains to represent. Rossen censures readers who simply accept 'the prose content of the poem', but her rendering of that prose content – 'Is it really worse for the rapist because he is less undeceived than the girl is?' – is not in fact a question the poem asks.[30] It is difficult to find details in the poem which invite us to feel sympathy for the rapist. And it would be an odd reader who, having reached the end of this poem, found their sympathy transferring from the woman to the rapist. In an interview, Larkin offered his own summary: 'As I tried to say in "Deceptions", the inflicter of suffering may be fooled, but the sufferer never is' (*FR*, 52). This is by no means a comprehensive or sophisticated analysis of why men commit sexual violence – and we can criticize the poem for that – but it does very firmly side with the survivor. That Larkin has written a poem which sides with a woman who has suffered from the most extreme symptom of a masculinist and patriarchal society should not appear unusually suspect, if we recall that this is the same author who wrote the Brunette Coleman works and *A Girl in Winter*.

The notion that the poem uses rape in order to make a more universal point about life is articulated by Graham Holderness, who questions its attempt to 'shift the responsibility for this fundamental masculine crime into some abstract power'.[31] This is a more reasonable and judicious objection, given that the poem is framed in a number of ways by the general concept of deception. Because 'Deceptions' supplies the volume's title, it is positioned as that volume's centrepiece, but also as one poem among many exploring a more general theme. The poem's plural title in turn implies that deception exists in various forms. In this sense, rape is one manifestation of a wider issue blighting the human condition. This seems to be a blind spot in Larkin's otherwise humane approach, and it is right to point it out. But it should also be qualified by the poem's own qualifications, since 'Deceptions' is careful to acknowledge that its philosophizing has limits. It takes as its starting point an account 'buried' in a historical text, and sensitively engages with the actuality of the experience. It offers empathy, but is also open about the limits of empathy. It declines to speak for its subject, and refuses to fall back on easy, sentimental platitudes. The poem's compassionate hesitancy arguably represents the most appropriate response to an experience it can never fully understand or represent. As Stan Smith writes, the poem 'makes distance the very ground of our humanity'.[32] Because it is difficult, it is true. 'Deceptions' is painfully honest about what it cannot do. In it, Larkin shows profound respect for the suffering of a mid-nineteenth-century woman, whilst also respecting his distance from her suffering.

'At Grass' and 'Deceptions' are Larkin's first major poems. Written during 1950, they reveal a different approach to composition in comparison to Larkin's *The North Ship* period, but they also reveal a different approach to poetry itself. No longer imitative or self-absorbed, they explore the lives and experiences of other beings, sensitively and without presumption. They form part of Coleman's legacy, in that they explore otherness, but the voice is now entirely his own. These poems are integral to *The Less Deceived*, Larkin's first mature collection; the next and final chapter completes the study of Larkin's early development by reading other significant poems from that collection.

8

The Less Deceived

Towards the end of 1950, Larkin began to assemble poems for a new collection, which he titled *XX Poems*. *In the Grip of Light*, the collection assembled in 1948, had been rejected across the board; 'thank God nobody accepted it', Larkin later told Ian Hamilton (*FR*, 26). Perhaps because of this embarrassing failure, Larkin instead decided to self-publish *XX Poems*. In early 1951, 100 copies were printed by Carswells of Belfast, 'on what I privately called grocer's wrapping paper'. A number of titles had been considered, but in the end Larkin opted for *XX Poems*, which was 'as free from offence as I can manage, & with a slight undercurrent of Guinness double X and Ezra Pound's Cantos'.[1] Such a plain, unpretentious name contrasted with the 'portentous' title of the 1948 collection; individual poems were also stripped of titles and given roman numerals (*FR*, 26). Larkin sent copies to several influential literary figures, including personal heroes like Cyril Connolly. Only one eventual recipient, D. J. Enright, gave *XX Poems* any attention; years later, Larkin characteristically put this down to his having got the postage rate wrong, 'so I suppose all those people were knocked up at about a quarter to eight in the morning and asked for a penny, which may have jaundiced their whole view of the collection'.[2]

In publishing terms, then, *XX Poems* was another flop, but in developmental terms it signalled a major change in Larkin's poetics. One way of perceiving this is to consider the publication history of the poems selected. Six poems from *In the Grip of Light* had already been published in *The North Ship*, but only one would make it into *The Less Deceived*, eventually published in November 1955; conversely, thirteen of the *XX Poems* would be chosen for *The Less Deceived*, thereby making up nearly half of that volume (see *TCP*, xxi–xxiii). To put this another way, Larkin's temperament in 1950 was now much closer to his mature poetic than to his more immature *The North Ship* phase. Given how much of *XX Poems* would also constitute Larkin's masterpiece, *The Less Deceived*, the booklet's almost non-existent reception is perhaps surprising; 'seldom has great poetry been so ignored on its first appearance', writes Booth.[3]

'At Grass' and 'Deceptions', discussed in the previous chapter, were two of the works to make the jump from *XX Poems* to *The Less Deceived*. Following their composition in 1950, Larkin's workbook was populated by a number of other, now-famous poems, which would also find their way into the collection. This final chapter reads a selection of important poems from *The Less Deceived*. Having traced a line of development through Larkin's early writings, this study has highlighted a burgeoning and increasingly productive interest in otherness, sparked by the Brunette Coleman *oeuvre*, and carried through the published novels, certain poems of the 1940s, and those first two great poems written in 1950. In *The Less Deceived*, the collection widely regarded as his first truly mature work, this line of development reaches a zenith, with a series of poems which marked out Larkin as an important voice in contemporary British verse, and which are still read and loved today.

Larkinesque

Osborne summarizes Larkin scholarship's 'theory of the rupture' (discussed in the Introduction) as an attempt to describe the major disparity 'between the prose works of the 1940s (bad) and the poems of the 1950s (good)'. If *The Less Deceived* is seen by critics as Larkin's first mature work, this is because it consistently presents for the first time a recognizably 'Larkinesque' poetics. Previous chapters have sought to demonstrate the shortcomings of this theory, by tracing a line of development from at least 1943, and thereby undermining any notion of a 'rupture'. The disparity between *The Less Deceived* and Larkin's earlier work only really appears so striking if discussion of the earlier work focuses largely or exclusively on *The North Ship*. When situated within the much wider context of Larkin's early writings, in prose as well as verse, it can be seen more clearly how *The Less Deceived* owes much to them – emerging, not rupturing, from the literary experiments discussed in previous chapters.

But *The Less Deceived* also reveals a contradiction in the theory: for whilst critics have praised the collection for its Larkinesque qualities, they have also remarked on its wide range of moods, subjects, genres and personae. The former emphasizes coherency, whilst the latter celebrates variety. Though the term 'Larkinesque' is often invoked to describe a style, which we might summarize as lugubrious, ironic, occasionally transcendental, blending the demotic with traditional forms, it has also come to stand for a particular kind of character found in the poems. The resemblance of this character to Larkin himself is more often than not asserted or simply assumed. The horny voyeur of 'Lines on a Young Lady's Photograph Album', the hesitant loner of 'Reasons for Attendance', the slightly hapless cyclist of 'Church Going', the 'pursed-up' bachelor of 'Spring': these homogeneous figures are read not only as representing Larkin's person and attitudes but also his pivot to an autobiographical mode of writing. But if this is true, how do we account for the sheer variety which gives *The Less Deceived* its strength and interest? For one thing, Larkin arranges poems in ways which suggest counter-readings; individual poems adopt a scrappy attitude, goading others in the collection. This variety is something Larkin acknowledged when he likened his arrangements to a 'music-hall bill', and Osborne has shown how across Larkin's *oeuvre*, poem titles can be paired with their opposites (*FR*, 55).[4] The same phenomenon occurs within individual collections as well as across them. A poem about a newly married woman ('Wedding-Wind') is immediately followed by one which states 'I have never found / . . . that special one' ('Places, Loved Ones'); a poem of total self-annihilation ('Absences') is followed by one in which the narrator confronts his face in the mirror ('Latest Face'); a poem which boasts of how access to 'my head' might 'knock my darling off her unpriceable pivot' ('If, My Darling') is followed by one in which the narrator's outer appearance is 'unfakable' ('Skin') (*TCP*, 28, 29, 42, 43, 43–4, 44). Perhaps, then, the term 'Larkinesque' should be repurposed to reflect not the poet's homogeneity, but heterogeneity.

The emotional range of *The Less Deceived*, and its array of subjects, personae and genres, should come as less of a surprise when placed within the fuller context of Larkin's literary development. For what exactly is it that makes the Coleman pieces so intriguing, if not their unexpected tonal shifts, their careful constructions of personae, their unfixing of genre and, fundamentally, their rich interest in experiences other than Larkin's own? As the previous chapter showed, 'At Grass' and 'Deceptions' draw their pathos from the poet's sensitive negotiations of distance and difference. Understood as a continuation of these impulses, the poems in *The Less Deceived* begin to look like the logical conclusion of Larkin's development, rather than a curious rupturing – though only if we see that development as a gradual movement away from autobiographical introspection and literary imitation, towards a poetics which reveals Larkin's 'interest in everything outside himself', and a more diverse and mature assimilation of influences.

Absences and continuities

One way to register this continuity is to conduct the following thought experiment: to identify poems in the collection which, like 'Femmes Damnées', might just as feasibly have been written under Brunette Coleman's name. 'I Remember, I Remember', for example, would not work, since the narrator's recollection of a dull Coventry childhood does not match Coleman's vivid coastal memories in *Ante Meridian*, nor do the experiences line up with the heroic escapades of her Willow Gables girls. Similarly, 'Dry-Point', with its seminal imagery, does not seem like something Coleman would write. But several other poems in the volume might plausibly have been included in Coleman's *Sugar and Spice* without disrupting its tonal or thematic coherency. Would it be a surprise to find 'Absences', drafted in 1950 and 1951, over the page from 1943's 'Femmes Damnées'? Both poems are drawn from the canon of nineteenth-century French poetry; or, more accurately, both poems assimilate their French intertexts with a kind of wry knowingness, Coleman having described 'Femmes Damnées' as an 'improvement' on Baudelaire. Although 'Absences' has no precise original, various poems may have provided inspiration: Graham Chesters suggests Gautier's 'Terza Rima' (Gautier being an important presence in Coleman's *oeuvre*); Booth points to the 'similar rhetorical climax' of Baudelaire's 'L'Homme et la Mer'; whilst Osborne reminds us that the 'short double exclamation, frequently inaugurated by the word "O"', is a recurring feature of Rimbaud's verse.[5] Larkin may also have had another Gautier work in mind: *Ténèbres*, also in *terza rima*, is a poem about death and nothingness, referencing the three-day Catholic service during which candles are gradually extinguished, casting worshippers into darkness. Booth also notes an intriguing feature in the workbook: having begun to draft 'Absences', Larkin paused, and used the next page to translate Verlaine's bawdy 'À Mademoiselle ***', with its praise of a country beauty's 'swaggering calves' and 'firm fat bum'. Booth observes that 'Larkin's new demotic register, it seems, has French as well as English origins' – something Coleman's work had already made apparent.[6]

Larkin's own comments on 'Absences' adopt precisely the same tone of fondness and mild regret we find in his comments on 'Femmes Damnées'. As discussed in Chapter 6, having allowed John Fuller to publish that poem in 1978, Larkin wrote that it was a 'pity I didn't go on writing like this instead of getting tangled up with Yeats!', and was eager for feedback from readers and sales. Similarly, when asked to pick his favourite poem for the 1962 anthology *Poet's Choice*, Larkin chose 'Absences', explaining that 'I fancy it sounds like a different, better poet rather than myself. The last line, for instance, sounds like a slightly unconvincing translation from a French symbolist. I wish I could write like this more often' (*FR*, 17).

The poem is an exhilarating imagining of absence and self-annihilation. For nine of its ten lines, it plunges into the place of nightmares: far into 'a sea', 'Where there are no ships and no shallows', only towering waves which rise and drop 'like a wall' (*TCP*, 42). It does so in lines of *terza rima*, mimicking the Gautier poems, and generating a dynamic of Dantean descent. The setting is terrifying for its total absence of any human or animal life. Having built up this sublime imagery over nine lines, Larkin suddenly switches in the last: with palpable thrill, he evokes 'Such attics cleared of me! Such absences!' This does indeed sound like 'a slightly unconvincing translation from a French symbolist', but the effect is deliberate; the faintly off-target rendering and the abandonment of the *terza rima* only reinforce the sudden, unchecked excitement which is triggered by the narrator's thoughts of his own extinction. Though the image of 'attics' returns us to a human setting, it is one completely 'cleared of me!' This recalls the ending of 'Deceptions', just two pages before 'Absences' in *The Less Deceived*. There, the rapist bursts into an attic only to find desolation, but here there is not even desolation; just straightforward emptiness, a space cleared of the poet's being – 'absences' in the plural. Larkin's other reason for favouring this poem was 'because of its subject matter – I am always thrilled by the thought of what places look like when I am not there' (*FR*, 17). To Haffenden he remarked that 'One longs for infinity and absence, the beauty of somewhere you're not', and connected 'Absences' and 'Dry-Point' to a semi-political reading of 'High Windows': 'It shows humanity as a series of oppressions, and one wants to be somewhere where there's neither oppressed nor oppressor, just freedom' (*FR*, 59). This concern with freedom, tied to an imaginative attempt to overcome, or at least evade, oppression, is consistent with Larkin's early work, whether the feminist rebellions of Coleman's heroines, or the persistent bullying and harassment of Katherine in *A Girl in Winter* – the ending of which, as Katherine potentially submits to sex she does not want, also imagines an empty environment. One can almost picture Katherine wilfully imagining her own absence at the novel's finale. Likewise, in the premature ending to *Michaelmas Term at St Bride's*, Marie wishes for a kind of self-extinction; dismayed by her early experiences of patriarchy, she attempts metafictional escape: 'If this was reality, she decided, she would rather keep in the story' (*TWG*, 230).

With its French Symbolist intertexts, and its radical imagining of self-annihilation as an escape from worldly oppressions, 'Absences' demonstrates continuities with Larkin's earlier writings. It might also be noted that, for a supposedly autobiographical poet, Larkin has a frequent tendency to imagine his own absence. In *The Less Deceived* alone, numerous poems do just that. 'Dry-Point', ostensibly a poem about sexual reproduction, is in fact preoccupied with 'dying', concluding with the enigmatic image of a 'padlocked cube of light' to which we 'obtain no right of entry' (*TCP*, 31). The following poem, 'Next, Please', also looks to the future, but a future with only one possible event: 'A huge and birdless silence', in whose 'wake / No waters breed or break' (a similarly petrifying marine image to 'Absences', as well as a revival of the central image of 'The North Ship') (*TCP*, 31–2). The poem after that, 'Going', again imagines the narrator's own death, and his removal from the environment: 'Where has the tree gone, that locked / Earth to the sky?', 'What loads my hands down?' (*TCP*, 32). And the poem after that, 'Wants', repeats a frightening mantra: 'Beneath it all, desire of oblivion runs' (*TCP*, 32). Again, the yearning for oblivion is framed as a response to social oppressions: 'the printed directions of sex' (does Larkin mean the sex-drive, or, more intriguingly, the imposed rules of gender?); 'the family... photographed under the flagstaff'; 'the tabled fertility rites'. Gender essentialism, enforced (hetero)sexuality and progenation, nationalism: these aspects of life which the poem seeks to evade return us to the oppressions Larkin variously critiques and satirizes in his early writings, whether the parodic 'An Incident in the English Camp' or the curious transgendering of 'I see a girl dragged by the wrists'. Scattered throughout *The Less Deceived* are poems which not only challenge Larkin's status as an autobiographical poet but go further, radically imagining the poet out of the picture – an impulse he allowed to roam freely as Brunette Coleman, and which now underpins many of his mature poems.

Gender

If 'Absences' could have been penned by Brunette Coleman, so too could several other poems in *The Less Deceived*, especially those which, like the most Colemanesque poems in *The North Ship*, grapple with gender and sexuality. The most obvious examples are 'Lines on a Young Lady's Photograph Album', 'Wedding-Wind', 'Maiden Name' and 'Born Yesterday'. In each of these, Larkin either invests the poem with a woman narrator, or explores aspects of femininity with the same sensitivity and complexity as his earlier feminist writings in poetry and prose.

'Lines on a Young Lady's Photograph Album' (hereafter 'Lines') is the first poem in *The Less Deceived*, and its varied moods and registers set the tone for the collection. Like Coleman's work, the poem contains an eclectic range of intertextual references. Its title evokes the high art of eighteenth-/nineteenth-century verse ('Lines written a few miles above Tintern Abbey', 'On First Looking into Chapman's Homer'), as does the poem's form, with its regular five-line stanzas, *abbab* rhyme scheme and rough pentameters. But, as Osborne has discussed, the photograph album is a twentieth-century cultural phenomenon, and a democratic one, enabling 'the emergence of ordinary people as producers of art, both as wielders of hand-held cameras and as editors of their own histories . . ., selecting and arranging some images while suppressing others so as to construct the desired narrative'.[7] Also, if read literally, the 'lines' on the album may suggest damage; perhaps accidental, perhaps deliberate – perhaps even seminal. This blending of the high and low, elite and demo(cra)tic, is typical of Coleman's work, 'Femmes Damnées' being the most outstanding example of such a tendency. 'Lines' is also, on one level, a rewriting of Cecil Day Lewis's 'The Album', which Larkin included in his *Oxford Book of Twentieth Century English Verse*. Although both poems use the occasion of leafing through a woman's photograph album to mourn the past, a crucial difference emerges which in turn reflects very different sexual politics. The narrator of Day Lewis's poem may yearn for the past and for the younger woman who inhabited it, but his possession of that woman is affirmed: 'all that you missed there / Has grown to be yours', she reminds him (*OBTCEV*, 354–5). No such possession is afforded to the narrator of Larkin's poem; in fact, the language of resistance and frustration recurs throughout.

'At last you yielded up the album', it begins, 'yielded' connoting both economic production and sexual surrender; 'At last' the narrator's excited relief (*TCP*, 27–8). The album sends him 'distracted', and the poem's vocabulary of hunger and gluttony establishes him as a comical pervert: 'I choke on such nutritious images. // My swivel eye hungers from pose to pose'. This is a comically exaggerated figure of masculinity, rather than a precise rendering of the poet himself, and in this sense the narrator is another version of the unsavoury men who interact and interfere with the girls and women of Larkin's earlier writings, most notably in *Michaelmas Term at St Bride's* and *A Girl in Winter*. An important distinction with those works, of course, is that the male now enjoys the narrative point-of-view; the woman is no longer the centre of consciousness, and is exposed to the leering male gaze. But this gaze is repeatedly frustrated, and, much like John in *Jill*, or Hilary in *Trouble at Willow Gables*, what it seems to notice is the woman's less conventional femininity. Astute critics have spotted the literary and cultural models for Larkin's young lady. Cooper notes that the phrase 'sweet-girl graduate' is from Tennyson's *The Princess* (1847), 'where it is applied patronisingly to the feminist character, Lilia', who, as Osborne tells us, 'longs for the day when Oxford University will have a college for women to rival the exclusively male colleges of that era' – a sentiment Coleman would support wholeheartedly.[8] Cooper also notes Diccon Rogers's suggestion that Larkin may have read L. T. Meade's 1894 novel, *A Sweet Girl Graduate*, a citation which situates his poem in the world and politics of the New Woman – a figure often represented, like Larkin's young lady, on a bicycle.[9] Finally, Osborne suggests Lady Brett Ashley, the charismatic and independent heroine of Hemingway's *The Sun Also Rises* (1926), as a source for the rather masculine photograph of the young lady in a 'trilby hat'. As he writes, this makes the young lady 'an alloy of 1890s bluestocking and 1920s barfly'.[10] In other words, what the poem stresses is the woman's independence and mobility; though the narrator might prefer to ogle at the picture 'of you bathing', he confesses that 'From every side you strike at my control'.

The poem also stages a mini-meditation on photography, again mixing high and low registers: 'But o, photography! as no art is, / Faithful and disappointing!' The apostrophe and archaic syntax elevate photography to the arena of high art, but this is quickly deflated by the wry line break. But does the poem really consider photography's faithfulness 'disappointing'? It may not 'censor blemishes / Like washing-lines, and Hall's-Distemper boards', and it may insist on showing 'A chin as doubled when it is', but in Larkin's new aesthetic, these things have become the stuff of poetry. The description of 'washing-lines, and Hall's-Distemper boards' incorporates the material culture of 1940s/1950s Britain, just as Coleman did in her verse, and the photograph's presentation of 'a real girl in a real place, // In every sense empirically true!' seems also to appeal, both to the narrator and to the poet whose aesthetic has undergone a significant shift from the Romantic to the real. The double chin is another image which upsets the male gaze, but once again we should recall the ways in which Larkin's early writings consistently present and celebrate a wide range of femininities. The 'gap from eye to page' is indeed significant, and although the voyeuristic narrator is 'left / To mourn' his unfulfilled and unfulfillable fantasies, and to consider thieving the bathing picture, he also, at the poem's end, contemplates how all this faithful reality actually makes the young lady 'Unvariably lovely'. She is affirmed by her realness, and her persistent but subtle frustration of the male gaze. To read the poem in this way is to perceive more clearly how 'Lines' emerges, not departs, from the work of the 1940s: the Coleman writings, Larkin's published novels and those feminine-preoccupied poems in *The North Ship*. Although women narrators have been replaced by a leering male, his gaze and his desires, and the sexual politics behind them, are undone by this poem. That said, there is no conclusive evidence that the narrator is male, and were one to imagine them as female, this would recall the voyeuristic Hilary of Willow Gables, or the predatory Rachel of 'Femmes Damnées'. Whether male or female, however, the poem continues, not disrupts, a distinct political and thematic strand of Larkin's early writings, and reminds us that Brunette Coleman bears much responsibility for this turn in Larkin's poetic.

In 'Wedding-Wind', Larkin returns to a woman's centre of consciousness. As discussed in Chapter 7, this is one of only three poems in *The Less Deceived* drafted in the transitional first workbook, the others being 'At Grass' and 'Deceptions'. In fact, 'Wedding-Wind' was written much earlier than those poems, in September 1946, almost a decade before *The Less Deceived*'s publication, making it a truly early poem. It is also one of the poems Larkin refers to in his 'Statement': 'I can imagine ... the emotions of a bride without ever having been a woman or married' (*RW*, 79). And like 'Absences', it is another poem about which Larkin expressed pride and regret: to Monica Jones, he wrote: 'I wish I could write more like that, fuller, richer in reference: I am quite pleased with the to-me successful use of the floods & the wind as fulfilment & joy' (*LM*, 25). The poem's rich imagery reveals a sensitive and moving exploration of the woman's complex state of mind. The wind that blows 'all my wedding-day, / And my wedding-night' is a powerful elemental force – the title makes 'Wedding-Wind' a compound noun, combining nature with the act of union – and the stable door 'banging' in the night evokes the passion of the newly-weds' sexual consummation (*TCP*, 28). But there is also a faint sense that all is not right; the wind represents disturbance, and when the husband attends to the door, he leaves his bride 'Stupid in candlelight' – alone, vulnerable, estranged. Seeing her face reflected in 'the twisted candlestick', she sees 'nothing', suggesting a mind ill at ease. Given that this is her wedding night, what are we to make of this sudden loss of identity? The horses, too, are 'restless', and yet the narrator expresses her sadness 'That any man or beast that night should lack / The happiness I had'. She seems confused by her mixed and contradictory emotions.

The next day – the first full day of married life – further complicates the poem's emotional impact. The newly-weds return immediately to a workaday life, and again the woman is left alone. The wind continues to thrash, and she stands by the 'chicken-run, / ... and stare[s]'. Critics have noted the poem's Lawrentian setting and mood; one of the most subtle borrowings from Lawrence is the poem's barely nascent consciousness of pregnancy, redolent of Gertrude Morel in *Sons and Lovers*. As Palmer argues, 'pails and buckets are standard metaphors for the womb'; 'aprons are associated with pregnancy, hiding and protecting the burgeoning child'.[11] Perhaps it is the woman, not the poem, who is beginning to turn her thoughts to the possibility of conception. She again mentions her 'joy', wondering 'Can it be borne', and will she be 'let to sleep / Now that this perpetual morning shares my bed?' But what is the cause of her sleeplessness? The noisy wind? Sexual frenzy? Too much happiness? Or the faint sense of sadness which reverberates through this poem? 'Borne', of course, suggests its homonym, 'born'; but is there not also a more typically Larkinesque pun in 'perpetual morning' – perpetual *mourning* – which further evinces the woman's melancholy, despite her assertions of gladness?

The poem's conclusion is really no conclusion at all. The image of cattle 'kneeling . . . by all-generous waters' suggests religiosity, calling to mind Hardy's 'The Oxen' (another intertext represented in Larkin's *Oxford* anthology); but the narrator asks whether 'These new delighted lakes' could be dried up by 'death'. As Cooper points out, kneeling may also hint 'that marriage can subjugate and oppress', further reinforcing the woman's sense of having lost her identity.[12] In short, the poem ends on a question; and although that question may be paraphrased as 'Can even death spoil the intense joy I feel right now?', the poem itself appears to ask whether this newly-wed bride truly is happy, and to ask what may have been lost as well as gained in marriage. 'Wedding-Wind' is an extraordinary poem, full of ecstasy – elemental, sexual, religious; pregnant with life and with the raw emotions of a woman just-married; but a close reading suggests an even more complex blend of emotions which includes uncertainty, vulnerability, alienation, grief. Part of its sensitivity derives from the fact that no answers are proffered, no possibilities proscribed. Though the poem quietly contains a sexual politics critical of marriage as a patriarchal institution that is bad for women, it also keeps open the possibility that the narrator is, without complexity, 'Stupid' with happiness for her new life as a wife and soon-to-be mother. It is one of the most beautiful and suggestive poems in *The Less Deceived*, and owes much to Larkin's decision to spend the 1940s exploring femininity in his writings. Even more so than 'Lines', 'Wedding-Wind', with its complex feminism and its openness to the plurality of femininity, could easily have been written by Brunette Coleman.

In 'Wedding-Wind', the woman looks at her reflection but sees 'nothing'; in 'Maiden Name', this theme of marriage-as-estrangement is treated more explicitly. In the Haffenden interview, Larkin remarked on the poem's originality, explaining that 'I often wonder how women survive the transition [to marriage]: if you're called something, you can't be called something else' (*FR*, 55). Certain internal details reveal, as numerous critics have discussed, that the poem's logic is bound up with Larkin's feelings about the marriage of Winifred Arnott, who became Winifred Bradshaw (and later, Dawson) around the time of its composition: the name of this colleague and flirtatious friend from the library at Queen's University Belfast supplies the 'five light sounds' of the second line (she is also the owner of the photograph album which inspired 'Lines') (*TCP*, 33). Knowing this, it is possible to detect some sullenness, and one might therefore question the self-interested motive behind the narrator's attempt to maintain a hold over the woman's past; but the biographical context is not needed to perceive this as another poem concerned with patriarchy and its impact on women.

Marrying means the woman is 'so thankfully confused / By law with someone else'; but 'thankfully' sounds unconvincing, a hollow concession, especially when succeeded by 'confused', which suggests an infelicitous merging of persons and identities – 'By law' only serving to make the entanglement seem threatening. 'Semantically', then, she is not 'the same'; her maiden name has become 'a phrase applicable to no one, / Lying just where you left it'. 'Lying' is a common pun in Larkin's work: the name lies there because it is inactive, or rather extinct, but it also lies because no longer true – though the narrator asks whether it is 'wholly / Untruthful?' At this point, the conversation between narrator and narratee becomes most intimate: 'Try whispering it slowly'. She is urged to see how she feels when she reverts to her former name. But 'No', the narrator concludes, 'it means you', immediately modifying this to mean 'what we feel now about you then'. Her maiden name, then, has become a holding place for memory; it 'shelters' the past, 'Instead of losing shape and meaning less / With your depreciating luggage laden'. Of course, that final image of 'depreciating luggage' is not a flattering one, and may well have played its role in prompting 'Photograph Albums Revisited', Winifred Dawson's poetic rebuff to 'Lines': 'For you my past is over, but for me the future waits'.[13] But does the poem's biographical and emotional messiness mean we should reject its fundamental argument that, as Osborne summarizes it, 'the bride's replacement of her father's surname with that of her husband is . . . a species of mendacity'?[14] After all, it is increasingly common for married women to decline the custom, resisting the idea of marriage-as-possession. More overtly and more brashly than 'Wedding-Wind', 'Maiden Name' critiques marriage for its subordination of women, equating it, on the woman's part, with loss and depreciation. Though personal feelings may have contributed, it is worth recalling that Larkin had written empathetically, before he even knew Winifred Arnott, about the threats and restrictions endured by young women in a patriarchal society. The lawful confusion which marriage represents in this poem, and the estrangement from the self which it represents here and in 'Wedding-Wind', are versions of the patriarchal injury which the girls and young women of Willow Gables and St Bride's wish, but finally fail, to avoid.

In 'Born Yesterday', conversely, the theme of marriage is arguably conspicuous by its absence. The poem was written for Kingsley and Hilly Amis's daughter, Sally, born in January 1954. Larkin told Robert Conquest that he had become 'a little weary of poems "for" other people's nippers or wives or husbands or weddings, and felt the convention "dated"' (*SL*, 250). His own poem seeks to avoid convention by wishing 'something / None of the others would' (*TCP*, 33–4). Most will wish 'the usual stuff' – beauty, and love, and so on – but if these should not prove possible, then 'May you be ordinary', or even 'dull', though this is conditional:

> If that is what a skilled,
> Vigilant, flexible,
> Unemphasised, enthralled
> Catching of happiness is called.

Larkin explained to Conquest that he chose the word 'Catching' because it suggested 'something continuous through life, not just one isolated instance' (*SL*, 250).

As numerous critics have noted, 'Born Yesterday' rewrites Yeats's 'A Prayer for My Daughter', another source text included in Larkin's *Oxford* anthology (*OBTCEV*, 80–2). Larkin's defence of ordinariness and dullness contrasts with Yeats's more conventional wish for 'beauty', but it also erases some of the more sexist aspects of Yeats's poem, such as the desire for his daughter to 'think opinions are accursed', since he has known the 'loveliest' women ruined by an 'opinionated mind'. That Larkin is now rewriting, rather than passively imitating, the Irish poet is further evidence of his development. Other sexist tropes are also studiously avoided: Osborne points to a very different intertext, the 1950 hit film *Born Yesterday*, which made 'the curtailed title ["I was not born yesterday"] world famous'. As he argues, 'By deftly alluding to this story of a "dumb blonde" outwitting manipulative men and captivating the cinema audience, Larkin underwrites his theme that those taken for "dull" sometimes lead triumphant lives.'[15] But what also distinguishes Larkin's poem is its neglect of the marriage theme and plot. Although *Born Yesterday* concludes with Billie marrying the 'right' guy, such an ending is still conservative: marriage, after all, restores order to the plots of countless eighteenth- and nineteenth-century novels. In Yeats's poem, marriage is simply a foregone conclusion: his desire that 'her bridegroom bring her to a house / Where all's accustomed, ceremonious' may express hope for a particular kind of husband, but does not consider the possibility of no husband.

No such assumption of a heteronormative future exists in Larkin's poem; indeed, part of the significance of 'dullness' may be that it will afford the woman a greater degree of freedom and independence from men, and therefore secure her 'happiness'. Some readers might not appreciate the poem's mention of 'other women' with an 'average of talents', but this does follow Brunette Coleman, and an idea present in 'Lines', in acknowledging not only that infinite versions of femininity exist but also that not every version must be somehow extraordinary to be valid or valuable. In contrast to 'Maiden Name', the poem which immediately precedes this one, and unlike its poetic and filmic sources, 'Born Yesterday' declines to enclose the young female subject within an inevitable future involving marriage. Marriage is not actively resisted or critiqued by the poem, but remains unmentioned, irrelevant, so as to allow for a plurality of alternative possibilities in a life which has only just begun.

In these four poems – 'Lines', 'Wedding-Wind', 'Maiden Name' and 'Born Yesterday' – Larkin continues to explore the experiences of women, as he had first begun to do in 'Incident in the English Camp', followed by the Coleman *oeuvre*, *A Girl in Winter* and a series of early poems including 'I see a girl dragged by the wrist' and 'Deceptions'. These poems, which make up so much of the *The Less Deceived*'s character, stem directly from his early writings; almost as though Coleman herself had written them, they show that the Larkin of the 1950s remained as absorbed in the lives of others as the Larkin of the 1940s.

Genre and persona

Though not especially difficult to imagine Coleman as the author of those four poems, the same could not easily be said of the majority of poems in *The Less Deceived*. But then the sensitive exploration of gender and sexuality was not Coleman's only legacy: her undoing of gender was also, as discussed in previous chapters, an undoing of genre; and she also taught Larkin the possibilities of adopting personae. Both of these legacies feature prominently in *The Less Deceived*, where strongly persona-driven poems upturn and attack orthodoxies and clichés, including, but not limited to, gender roles. If earlier, experimental texts such as 'What Are We Writing For?' and 'Round the Point' are fundamentally argumentative, then so too are a number of poems in *The Less Deceived*. 'Reasons for Attendance' is one such poem: its title literally implies that 'reasons' will be put forward, and this formality is further reinforced by the fact that, as Osborne notes, '"Reasons for Attendance" is standard phraseology on official documents such as those issued by the medical profession'.[16] It is also one of the many poems which readers closely associate with Larkin's own personality. In this case the assumption is not unreasonable, given how Larkin sought to protect his identity as a writer from multiple assaults by the social world. Indeed, this was precisely the theme he addressed in 'Round the Point', and in his intense correspondence with Sutton. Two of the most involved and fraught questions of Larkin's early development were why and how he should maintain a degree of isolation and independence in order to fulfil his destiny as a writer. As discussed previously, a number of practical arrangements answered the question of how: working a regular and extra-literary job; never marrying or having children; keeping even his most intimate companion, Monica Jones, at arm's length. But why? 'Reasons for Attendance' sets out to answer this question. However, we should be wary of too easily conflating this poem's narrator with the poet. As Andrew Swarbrick has perceptively written: 'many of the poems in *The Less Deceived* are provisional: Larkin uses a speaker to dramatize an internal conflict and then pulls the rug from under the speaker's feet or in some way reveals the speaker as flawed or partisan.'[17]

In 'Reasons for Attendance', the narrator is suddenly drawn to 'the lighted glass' of a dance hall by 'The trumpet's voice, loud and authoritative' (*TCP*, 30). From the other side of the glass, he watches the dancers, all of them young, moving about with 'flushed' faces, 'Solemnly on the beat of happiness'. Imagining the 'wonderful feel of girls', he asks himself 'Why be out here?', but immediately counters this with another question: 'why be in there?' 'Sex, yes', he thinks, 'but what / Is sex?' – a curiously uncompelling and academic question. Without answering it, he scoffs at the idea that couples enjoy the 'lion's share' of happiness. For he, the narrator, derives his joy and self-worth not from coupling-up, but from being an individual; and it is 'that lifted, rough-tongued bell / (Art, if you like)' which affirms his individuality. But here the poem's argument begins to falter. The parenthetical 'Art, if you like' is affectedly hesitant: the narrator wants to announce his commitment to art, but does not want to appear pompous or pretentious. More significantly, there is an odd but revealing contradiction in his choice of imagery. The 'rough-tongued bell', his metaphor for art, is the bell of the trumpet. This is what 'calls' him – a curiously vocational choice of verb – and affirms his individuality, but it is an actual 'trumpet's voice' which has caught his attention. That voice is described as 'loud and authoritative'; the fact that its player is 'in there', among the 'smoke and sweat' and the shuffling couples, does not seem to compromise *his* voice or art. Much has been made of the poem's conclusion, which asserts the distinction between the narrator who stays outside and the couples inside only to then undermine it; but this undermining is anticipated by Larkin's trumpet metaphor. The narrator stays put; the couples, blithely ignorant of his presence, enjoy the dance; and all are 'satisfied'. But finally the narrator considers the possibility that someone may have 'misjudged himself' or 'lied'. Who? Is there perhaps a frustrated artist in there, kidding themselves that they would rather be courting guys or girls than attending to their submerged artistic impulse? Or is it the narrator who, finding himself without a girl, must falsely console himself with the assertion that he is, unlike them, an artist and an individual?

The poem does not answer this question, and readers are left to speculate not only on the question of who has lied but where they would rather be. But the central image of the trumpet, both in its literal and metaphorical form, surely confuses this simple binary. If the trumpet artist can be in there, giving and partaking in the pleasure of the dance, but still maintaining his artistic integrity, 'loud and authoritative', why can't the narrator? Is the choice between life and art really so straightforward? The question becomes not so much 'what is sex?', but 'what is individuality?' And this blurring of the terms of the debate becomes even more complex and fascinating when one considers the full resonance of the word 'attendance', suggesting presence, perhaps mandatory, yes, but also (with its French origins) attending to, giving attention to, and so on. In the latter sense, although the narrator remains outside, a non-participant in the dance and the coupling, he attends to it with his artistic impulse. In this way, the poem enacts the tension it reveals: because the narrator opts to stay outside (however fallacious his reasoning), he is able to attend to the dance, dancers and the questions they raise, whilst they – being swept up in the event – cannot. 'Art' is not the reason for staying outside but the outcome. Ultimately, the poem does not give reasons for attending the dance (and the social world which it represents), but reasons for attending *to* it in art. Like the trumpet player, the narrator's individuality is not asserted or confirmed by some abstract decision to separate himself from other people, but through observation of them, and the artistic creation which follows. 'Reasons for Attendance' is, like 'At Grass' and 'Deceptions', another poem which negotiates and calibrates distance and difference in Larkin's art; what Larkin carries over from his earlier writings, particularly those by Brunette Coleman, is the usefulness of creating and exploring personae who embody complex debates and tensions. What he has also learned is to reject cliché and orthodoxy, something 'Reasons for Attendance' does brilliantly.

So too does 'Toads', one of Larkin's most famous poems, and again one in which readers perceive the man himself. But like 'Reasons for Attendance', the poem works by establishing a persona, who tussles with two contrasting thoughts and feelings, before finally settling on both/neither. In this case, the contest is between 'the toad *work*', which 'Squat[s] on my life', and the narrator's desire to 'drive the brute off' – a modified version of the art/life debate conducted in 'Reasons for Attendance', but this time focusing on the traditionally unpoetic theme of work – that is, contracted labour, rather than the vocational exertions of the artist (*TCP*, 38–9). By the time of this poem's composition, Larkin was established in his library career, and so once again a biographical reading seems to invite itself. But once again the poem's narrator is really an exaggeration, a vehicle for the poem's dialectic. He may consider the time spent at work 'out of proportion', but so too is his language: 'it soils / With its sickening poison', he says with dramatic flair. In fact, the argument never really gets off the ground, though it does – importantly – entertain. The list of folks who manage to 'live on their wits' is mostly unappealing (the inclusion of 'Lecturers' is deeply unjust) but linguistically brilliant. Few would actively choose to join the ranks of 'lispers, / Losels, loblolly-men, louts', but the alliterative performance is delightful: the *OED* defines a 'losel' as 'A worthless person; a profligate, rake, scoundrel; in weaker sense, a ragamuffin, ne'er-do-well'; a 'loblolly-man' is a ship surgeon's mate, but 'loblolly' can also refer to 'A bumpkin, rustic, peasant' and 'Thick gruel or spoon-meat'.[18] 'Lots of folk live up lanes / With fires in a bucket', eating 'tinned sardines', we are told; 'They seem to like it' (do they?). 'No one actually *starves*', the narrator claims – prompting us to respond that yes, they do, and besides, if the choice is between a nine-to-five routine and near-starvation, then it is a pretty easy choice.

The narrator's presentation of a life divorced from work, routine and order fails to persuade, then, but he is also aware that he lacks the courage to say '*Stuff your pension!*', and his nod to *The Tempest* – 'that's the stuff / That dreams are made on' – suggests that his argument is mere fantasy, melting into thin air like the spirits at the close of Prospero's entertainment. It is not, however, just a matter of cowardice: for although the toad work squats *on* the narrator's life, 'something sufficiently toad-like / Squats *in* me, too' (my emphasis), and it is this other toad which keeps him at it. The final stanza is more syntactically complex than a typical Larkin poem (or, more accurately, is more obviously complex than a typical Larkin poem): 'I don't say, one bodies the other / One's spiritual truth' is as difficult to disentangle as the two toads themselves. As Palmer explains, 'the antecedents for the pronouns "one", "either" and "both" are located eight stanzas away in the poem's opening two lines – "*work*" and "life"'.[19] And that is the point the poem makes: although the narrator resists the notion that his working life is the manifestation of a 'spiritual truth' residing in him, he acknowledges the difficulty of 'los[ing] either / When you have both' – hence the poem's plural title, 'Toads'. Nine stanzas in, the narrator resolves to do nothing – or, rather, to carry on as he is – much like the non-decision reached at the end of 'Reasons for Attendance'. As Swarbrick puts it, the '"argument" is settled in advance'.[20] This might render the poem futile, were it not for the fact that its virtuoso performance is really the point. Composed in tight quatrains with unsatisfying half-rhymes ('*work*'/'pitchfork', 'soils'/'bills', 'pension'/'made on'), the poem superbly and comically stages its debate, voiced by a witty, exaggerated persona who, after all that, arrives at no conclusion whatsoever. Though it bears few overt traces of Coleman's influence, the influence is there: the use of a droll, charismatic persona; the cumulative process of argumentation; the refusal of cliché; the lively linguistic performance. These are her traits, largely absent from *The North Ship*, but making *The Less Deceived* what it is.

'Poetry of Departures', the poem immediately following 'Toads', also follows its main theme, the tussle between seemingly authentic and inauthentic ways of living. It is another poem which derives part of its effect from a slant approach to French verse: Swarbrick points out that 'the title is a comically literal translation of a phrase used to describe a style of nineteenth-century French poem which imagines romantic escape from the everyday world'; as Barbara Everett also comments, this 'refers to a whole phase of French Symbolist verse with the kind of ironic casualness that is liable in Larkin's case to be the detritus of more knowledge than he cares to display'.[21] The deliberate bungling of translation reflects not just linguistic differences but also cultural and moral ones. The narrator confesses to being excited by the kind of story you sometimes hear, 'fifth-hand', about people who '*chucked up everything / And just cleared off*, which has the same thrilling effect as '*Then she undid her dress / Or Take that you bastard*' (*TCP*, 39). But if here the poem draws on the tropes and language of post-war movies and pulp fiction, this is because the poem wishes to show that the comparison is apt: such radical moves are fictions, sentimental Hollywood claptrap. The narrator calls it out: it is 'artificial', a 'deliberate step backwards / To create an object', a 'life / Reprehensibly perfect'. The 'perfect order' which conformists seek, with their 'good books' and 'good bed', finds its equivalent in the reprehensible perfection which non-conformists are really seeking – reprehensible because just as false, just as performative. Osborne, reading this poem as an assault on Existentialist philosophy, comments: 'The authentic and inauthentic have thus been equalized, like the chequered pattern on a chessboard; . . . they are relational terms that need each other in order to signify at all.'[22]

As with other poems discussed here, then, 'Poetry of Departures' explores both sides of a debate, but ultimately neutralizes it, exposing both sides as flawed, and deciding nothing. Interestingly, the poem's rejection of the departure-fetish is also a rejection of a particular type of masculinity, for the 'he' – and it almost always is a he – who chucks up everything is a potent figure in popular culture. As Cooper argues, 'In turning down his part of being "stubbly with goodness" the speaker is rejecting the image of an unshaven man as symbolising a form of "goodness" in post-war popular culture (i.e., the unshaven Allied soldier returning victorious from the battlefield)'.[23] This recalls one of the chief strategies of Coleman's work, which is the simultaneous undoing of genre and gender; she, and by extension Larkin, spent the war writing about schoolgirls. As Terry Whalen comments, 'machismo is evoked as an entertainment, but is cast ultimately as narrow and beside the point. . . . Larkin's speakers are self-conscious and uncertain of themselves, given to an unmale habit of confessing their failures, their impotence and/or their sense of defeat'.[24] The hero who casts off the social world and lives life on his own terms, like the books and films in which he appears, gives us pleasure, but he is also a fake, a fiction. Larkin, writing in the wake of Brunette Coleman, prefers more self-conscious, thinking, hesitant versions of masculinity.

Such versions of masculinity recur throughout *The Less Deceived*. In 'Spring', a 'pursed-up' figure of 'indigestible sterility' makes his way across a park, where children, families and their dogs frolic on the 'awakened grass' (*TCP*, 40). This sterile narrator is an unusual choice of celebrant for Spring, and although the sonnet is a common vehicle for such a purpose, Larkin's approach to the form is likewise unusual, its sestet rhyme scheme providing neither the forward motion of a Petrarchan sonnet, nor the witty closure of the Shakespearean kind. But the poem celebrates Spring nonetheless: birdsong, greenery, the play of light are all praised, and the season described as 'earth's most multiple, excited daughter'. It is not, *pace* Eliot, the cruellest season, but 'of all seasons most gratuitous'. Though 'gratuitous' implies pointless and unwarranted, it also means gifted freely, without obligation or expectation of return – a more joyful and appreciative take. And for this 'indigestible sterility' – who might counter the poem's celebration of fertility – Spring is even more meaningful: 'those she has least use for see her best'. Similarly to 'Reasons for Attendance', it is precisely because the narrator is not caught up in family life that he is better able to notice and appreciate Spring's myriad pleasures. This is a touching sentiment, and even more so if one distances narrator from author. Because Larkin remained childless and a semi-bachelor, 'Spring' is another poem which seems to invite the comparison, as do the pronouns: 'and *me*, / Threading *my* pursed-up way across the park' (my emphases). In a letter to Patsy Strang, Larkin tells a revealing anecdote about his Belfast friends, Ansell and Judy Egerton, whom he recalls 'muttering archly "I don't know why you call yourself an indigestible sterility"' (*SL*, 231). It seems not everyone who knew Larkin found the image apt.

But one does not need to be personally acquainted with this poet to sense dissimilarities between him and his narrator. It is surely pertinent to note that Larkin was only twenty-seven when he composed this poem – not exactly past his reproductive prime. Moreover, internal evidence might lead readers with no biographical knowledge to assume the narrator is an elderly woman: 'pursed-up' perhaps has feminine connotations, and 'sterility' has, historically, been associated with the female. The poem's preoccupation with fertility and children might further suggest the narrator is a childless and ageing woman – perhaps Brunette Coleman herself? Even if the narrator is male, he presents an intriguing version of masculinity: single, childless, solitary, sterile, but keenly observant and celebratory of the blossoming of new life, human and non-human. Whatever the narrator's age or sex, we have yet another poem which takes an interest in those who find themselves othered by a normative society, a recurring preoccupation of Larkin's early work. Movingly, this figure is not written off but afforded a taste of life's pleasures in this short and beautiful celebration of Spring.

If 'Spring' upends some of the orthodoxies of traditional nature poetry, so too does 'Myxomatosis', a poem which refuses metaphor in its literal presentation of an animal's suffering and death. 'Myxomatosis' is an unusual title to find in a volume of poetry, and one might therefore expect the poet to dazzle with some clever metaphorical discourse on human suffering, or disease in the abstract. The poem does no such thing, and, as Lodge observes, is one of several Larkin poems which contains 'no metaphors at all'.[25] Like 'At Grass' and 'Deceptions' (which use figurative language, but with much hesitance), there is a sense in which too much metaphor might betray the fact of a subject's existence and pain. Since, like 'Deceptions' and to some extent 'At Grass', the poem is about suffering, this moral question becomes more acute. The poem responds to a massive outbreak of myxomatosis in 1953, an event which polarized attitudes between largely rural groups, who welcomed a reduction in what they perceived to be pests, and those who found the millions of rabbit deaths a tragedy. A national debate about whether the disease should be adopted as official policy for controlling the rabbit population ensued.

Larkin, who fondly anthropomorphized rabbits in some of his personal writings, most notably in letters to Monica Jones, was deeply upset and angry about the disease and certain reactions to it. To more than one correspondent he denounced 'filthy Ronald Duncan', the writer whose 'countryside articles in Punch at the time of myxomatosis were full of caddish glee at this novel solution to the rabbit problem' (*LM*, 117; *SL*, 288). Composing his own response, Larkin knew that this was no moment for anthropomorphism or even metaphor. Some critics have nevertheless read the poem biographically and philosophically: Swarbrick considers it 'an existentialist statement about life as meaningless endurance', whilst Steve Clark sees the wounded animal as representing women's entrapment of men (despite the fact that it is emphatically not a trap which has harmed this animal).[26] In fact, Larkin fretted over the poem's representation: to Jones, his 'Dearest Bun', he described how he 'strove (queer word) to give the essential pathos of the situation without getting involved in argument. . . . Is this "using" the rabbits? Honestly, my motives are really good – better than the poem, I'm afraid' (*LM*, 128). The dead rabbit is centred by the poem, and when we hear a human voice, it is brief and disembodied; narrative explication is likewise kept to a minimum. The disease is treated as a biological and physical actuality: 'suppurate', meaning the formation or discharge of pus, represents literally the rabbit's condition and suffering (*TCP*, 37). Although the narrator tries to imagine his way into the animal's consciousness – this being a form of human projection – he assumes, as Booth puts it, 'no more than shared animal sentience'.[27] That the animal suffered is not contentious; that it 'may have thought things would come right again / If you could only keep quite still and wait' is also perhaps not much of a stretch. That is all the poem does: the dead rabbit is discovered; the narrator's companion wonders about the cause of death; the narrator understands what has happened, and empathetically feels his way into the rabbit's consciousness as it lay dying. 'Myxomatosis' is not an ostentatious poem, linguistically or philosophically. Instead, with quiet horror and immense poignancy, it describes in very real terms the horrid death of one of millions of rabbits. Though this animal poem may seem far removed from the schoolgirl writings of 1943, it was Coleman's stimulation of Larkin's empathetic and ethical interest in otherness which enabled him to write it. The poem shares with other early writings, like John Kemp's shyness and class anxiety, or the dentist scene in *A Girl in Winter*, an extraordinarily painstaking attention to the lives of others.

'I Remember, I Remember' is one of Larkin's most famous poems, and represents one of the most overt assaults on genre in *The Less Deceived*. It contains most of the ingredients of a typical Larkin poem: a strongly delineated persona; a conscious and witty rejection of cliché; acute social-realist attentiveness to contemporary material culture and ordinary speech; and a complex, intricate, yet seemingly effortless formal structure. From the outset, the poem announces its intention to participate in a poetic conversation: for many readers of *The Less Deceived* in 1955, 'I Remember, I Remember' would instantly evoke the popular and much-anthologized Thomas Hood poem no doubt recited in their schooldays: 'I remember, I remember, / The house where I was born, / The little window where the sun / Came peeping in at morn'.[28] An equally sentimental contender for readers' recognition would be Winthrop Mackworth Praed's poem of the same name; and, as Osborne points out, 'In a more general sense, Hood and Praed carry into the Victorian era a Romantic ideology such as one finds in Blake, Coleridge, Lamb, Shelley and . . . Wordsworth'.[29] In short, Larkin's poem refers to an entire package of Romantic poetry and philosophy which celebrates the innocence and idyll of an English childhood.

But it also, as signalled by its opening, 'Com[es] up England by a different line' (*TCP*, 41–2). Although the narrator's train pulls in at Coventry, his birthplace, it does so from a different route than the one he is used to, taking him by surprise, and forcing him to readjust to a setting which should be familiar. This geographical disorientation presages the poem's unsettling of literary familiarities. The narrator struggles to find 'a sign / That this was still the town that had been "mine"', but the train leaves, and his travelling companion asks if Coventry is 'where you "have your roots"?' (Osborne detects a characteristic pun on 'Rootes', the local car manufacturer).[30] 'No, only where my childhood was unspent', the narrator thinks. Bradford comments that this 'other person in the carriage is a fiction, a conceit'; Larkin has 'invented an interrogator'.[31] This is another technique carried over from Larkin's earlier writings: the companion is the Miller to Larkin's Geraint, the Jacinth to his Brunette Coleman – a way of approaching an idea from different angles and thereby getting to the heart of things.

There follows a succession of tropes of the romanticized and aestheticized childhood, each one negated. The narrator recalls his childhood garden, 'where I did not invent / Blinding theologies of flowers and fruits, / And wasn't spoken to by an old hat'; the 'splendid family // I never ran to when I got depressed, / The boys all biceps and the girls all chest'. With its mocking depiction of the perfect English family – their perfection manifested as muscular and bosomy bodies – the poem reinforces the critique of normative, homogeneous identities found elsewhere in *The Less Deceived*, like the 'family . . . under the flagstaff' in 'Wants', suggesting that such wholesome images are largely fictitious inventions we project to the world and measure in others. The narrator imagines the 'bracken' where he did not lose his virginity with a girl. In this notably Lawrentian passage

– 'all became a burning mist' – Larkin brings his hero into the cell of literary ancestors he intends to cull, or at least maim; as with Yeats in 'Born Yesterday', aspects of the writer's aesthetic are exposed as falsely sentimental. As Osborne notes, the language is not just Lawrentian: '"All became a burning mist" was a comedy catchphrase from the 1950s radio programme *Bedtime With Braden*'; this parodic strain recalls Larkin's statement that 'I had grown up to regard sexual recreation as a socially remote thing, like baccarat or clog dancing' (*FR*, 9).[32]

Running through these negations in his mind, he is interrupted by the companion who suggests 'You look as if you wished the place in Hell'. The narrator supposes that 'it's not the place's fault', closing the poem with its final and perplexing statement, 'Nothing, like something, happens anywhere'. Because of the complex interplay between rhyme scheme and stanza units (a nine-line rhyme scheme laid across five-line stanzas), this final line, in order to complete the scheme, is isolated. Consequently, it assumes the appearance of a pithy philosophical statement or aphorism, and its meaning does indeed take some working out. How exactly does nothing 'happen'? And how can nothing happen 'anywhere'? Osborne argues that 'any place, London as much as Coventry, can as readily be a site of emptiness as plenitude'; Rossen proposes that if we accept the logic of Larkin's line, 'then Coventry is merely incidental and not specially to blame for the crushing disappointment of childhood'.[33] Is the narrator's disappointment 'crushing', though? Rather than express sorrow for what did not happen, he seems instead to pour scorn on those writers who falsely depict childhood as like that. Furthermore, as Osborne goes on to argue, Coventry is by no means an incidental setting: for the city is a 'close contender for the title of omphalos of England. To claim to be born there is not just to establish a geographical point of origin but an umbilical relation to Englishness'.[34] When Larkin attacks an entire subset of English literary tradition, he does so from Coventry, thereby negating a whole way of thinking about childhood and Englishness, and making a more positive case for a new poetry. As with 'Reasons for Attendance', the poem enacts the tension it reveals: for if a particularly influential and popular strand of English literary history is rubbished – Larkin's Coventry childhood being the counter-example – then implicitly the unromantic, unpoetic subject of a Coventry childhood (and those like it) is shoved into the limelight, held up as a legitimate subject for poetry – legitimate because it is true; true because it is not beautiful, but beautiful because it is true.

We can perceive this more clearly if we observe the philosophical closeness of Larkin's final line to the famous section of Auden's elegy for Yeats. There, Auden claims that 'poetry makes nothing happen', but complicates this by calling poetry

'A way of happening'.³⁵ Poetry may not make anything happen in a literal sense – it cannot change the weather or the government – but it can give voice to thoughts and feelings which, without it, do not yet exist in the world. This is how poetry 'makes nothing *happen*' (my emphasis): it takes the barely articulated, and gives it 'a mouth'. When we apply a similar logic to Larkin's poem, we can see how Larkin, too, is able to make 'Nothing' happen 'anywhere' – even in Coventry. His unpoetic childhood and its unpoetic setting become the very stuff of poetry.

'I Remember, I Remember' is, then, more than an easy shot at some of the big names of Romantic literature; like so many other poems in *The Less Deceived*, it extends the borders of contemporary British verse to make room for those who historically have only peered across them ('Most people ignore most poetry / because / Most poetry ignores most people', as Adrian Mitchell memorably put it).³⁶ How many of the thousands of schoolchildren who studied and recited Hood's poem in fact had childhoods more like the one Larkin's poem describes? For such readers, Larkin's version is revelation and affirmation rather than negation. Nowhere in the poem does the narrator suggest he had an unhappy childhood, merely an ordinary one, like the life wished for in 'Born Yesterday'. Where Brunette Coleman sought to smuggle her extraordinary English schoolgirls into the territory of English Literature, Larkin here asserts the right to participate of all those who had undistinguished, unheroic, unliterary childhoods. The narrator, the setting, the literary targets and the new subjects ushered in are all different, but in spirit 'I Remember, I Remember' is very much the legacy of Coleman.

'Church Going': Tradition and community

If 'At Grass' and 'Deceptions' are Larkin's first major poems, the latter giving *The Less Deceived* its title and the former its finale, then 'Church Going' is the collection's centrepiece – almost literally, as the fifteenth poem of the book's twenty-nine. It also inaugurates a mini-tradition for Larkin's mature volumes, which is the inclusion of a longer, more serious, more meditative ode at the heart of each one: in *The Whitsun Weddings* (1964), it is the titular poem, and in *High Windows* (1974), 'The Building'. 'Church Going' also represents a kind of centrepiece because it is the apotheosis of Larkin's now-developed voice. If two of early Larkin's problems were his over-reliance on a personally curated canon of influences and his narrow preoccupation with self-examination, then 'Church Going' shows the poet having overcome these deficiencies. This is not because the poem is a particularly impersonal effort, or because it washes its hands of tradition – far from it. What makes 'Church Going' such an outstanding poem in Larkin's *oeuvre* is the way it participates in a tradition which it then updates. Rather than imitate or pastiche, Larkin quietly but surely assimilates his sources and influences into a voice that is entirely his own, in a poem which looks outwards to consider its society and communities.

The narrator who diffidently walks into an empty church, taking off his cycle-clips 'in awkward reverence', is yet another of the figures in *The Less Deceived* associated with the poet (*TCP*, 35–7). However, both the poem and its narrator are entities constructed from multiple and diverse intertextual citations and allusions. Burnett's commentary in *The Complete Poems* helpfully lists most of these: the Church of England prayer book ('Here endeth'); Orwell's *Coming Up for Air* and MacNeice's 'In the Cathedral' (the donation of a 'sixpence'); Hardy's 'The Lost Pyx' ('pyx'); Keats's *The Eve of St Agnes* (the syntactical inversion of 'A serious house on serious earth it is'); Frost's 'Directive' ('house', 'destinies'); George Eliot, Keats, Hardy, Yeats and MacNeice ('blent') (*TCP*, 372–3). Burnett and other critics have found a number of echoes of T. S. Eliot, ranging from more general influences – John Wain, for instance, has likened the narrator to Prufrock – to the specifically syntactical.[37] Raphaël Ingelbien compares the line 'Wondering what to look for' with 'not knowing what you came for' (*Little Gidding*), and notes that 'serious earth' 'could easily turn into Eliot's "significant soil"' (*The Dry Salvages*); Burnett compares 'A purpose more obscure' to lines elsewhere in *Little Gidding*: 'Either you had no purpose / Or the purpose is beyond the end you figured' (*TCP*, 372).[38] The narrator's imaginative description of a ruined church – 'Grass, weedy pavement, brambles, buttress, sky' – is surely also redolent of *The Waste Land*. But if there is a work by Eliot with which the poem engages more than any other, it is surely his 1935 verse drama *Murder in the Cathedral*.[39] Larkin publicly admitted to reading this for pleasure, and excerpted two passages in his *Oxford* anthology (*RW*, 66; *OBTCEV*, 247–9). He also made at least two attempts to write verse dramas in the 1930s and 1940s, at least one of which, *Behind the Facade*, imitates Eliot's style of blending formal, archaic language with contemporary themes and settings.[40]

Murder in the Cathedral and 'Church Going' are both about the Church in crisis, though the nature of the crisis differs in each. For Eliot, the crisis was both historical and immediate: the subject of his play, the assassination of Archbishop Thomas Becket, speaks to what is arguably his real subject, the role of the Church in the early twentieth century. Larkin's interest is the post-war decline of the Church, in both a spiritual and a material sense: his poem is as much about the church going as it is about a decline in church-going. This was partly prompted after reading a later Archbishop of Canterbury's appeal to save the nation's churches from decay. Setting their works within the physical space of a church, whether Canterbury Cathedral or the imagined one of Larkin's poem, both writers pose a question: Why come here? Indeed, 'here' is a significant verbal and theatrical device in *Murder in the Cathedral*, recurring throughout the play; the first line spoken is 'Here let us stand, close by the cathedral'.[41] Similarly, Larkin's narrator pronounces '"Here endeth" much more loudly than I'd meant' in his mock reading from the prayer book, accidentally but portentously announcing the place's demise. 'Are we drawn by danger? Is it the knowledge of safety, that draws / our feet / Towards the Cathedral?' asks the Chorus at the opening of Eliot's play, whilst the narrator of 'Church Going' concludes his visit 'much at a loss', 'Wondering what to look for' – 'Yet stop I did: in fact I often do'.[42] By recognizing how each writer answers these questions, we can better understand the significance of Larkin's poem. In one passage from *Murder in the Cathedral* – the first of the two selected by Larkin for his anthology – the church-setting is celebrated as a space in which the landmark moments of human existence are unified: 'We have seen births, deaths and marriages', pronounces the Chorus. But with the Archbishop in grave danger, 'a great fear is upon us', and this fear is described as 'A fear like birth and death, when we see birth and death alone / In a void apart'.[43] Anxiety about the threat posed to faith, sanctity and stability is, therefore, imagined as a fragmentation of the major events of the life course, normally marked in this one space. In 'Church Going', Larkin merely rearranges Eliot's list of rituals: the church is acknowledged as a place which 'held unspoilt / So long and equably what since is found / Only in separation – marriage, and birth, / And death'; like Eliot, he uses a line break to drive the point home. For both Eliot and Larkin, then, the declining status of the Church in the twentieth century has the serious consequence of sundering social rites, splintering the most important moments in our time on earth. At the end of Eliot's play, the Chorus once again praises the sacred space which the cathedral represents:

> For wherever a saint has dwelt, wherever a martyr has given his
>   blood for the blood of Christ,
> There is holy ground, and the sanctity shall not depart from it
> Though armies trample over it, though sightseers come with
>   guide-books looking over it . . .[44]

In Larkin's poem, one can detect a strong myrrhic whiff of these lines. Eliot's sightseers, clutching their guidebooks, are akin to Larkin's 'crew / That tap and jot and know what rood-lofts were', his 'ruin-bibber, randy for antique', and his 'Christmas addict'. More generally, Larkin's poem shares with Eliot's play a similar accumulation of clauses, the same blend of anachronistic syntax and vocabulary with contemporary and demotic speech, and the use of the historical present.

Of course, Larkin's treatment of the church, whether celebratory or elegiac, is more secular than Eliot's, the elder poet having converted to Anglicanism in 1927. But where these two writers do meet is on the 'serious earth', Larkin's phrase, which the Church represents. Whatever the status of Christianity in the twentieth century, each writer finds a social and cultural significance haunting this holy ground. To understand this connection is to inflect the meaning of 'Church Going', emphasizing the value the poem places on community and tradition. This defence of tradition, however, puts the poem on a collision course with Larkin's 'Statement', published just one year after 'Church Going' first appeared in the *Spectator*:

> As a guiding principle I believe that every poem must be its own sole freshly created universe, and therefore have no belief in 'tradition' or a common myth-kitty or casual allusions in poems to other poems or poets, which last I find unpleasantly like the talk of literary understrappers letting you see they know the right people. (*RW*, 79)

Of course, it is possible to distinguish the kind of tradition which baptism and marriage ceremonies represent from the literary kind which Larkin lambasts. But here we have a poem, written around the same time, which not only places great value on tradition, but expresses this value within a framework of literary allusions, of which Eliot plays the major role. Nowhere in the 'Statement' is Eliot named, but any reader with a rudimentary knowledge of 'Lit Crit. and Theory' will recognize 'tradition' – with its sardonic quotation marks – as a dig at the author of 'Tradition and the Individual Talent'. And there is a potential allusion to that essay in 'Church Going', an allusion which aligns, rather than collides, the two poets' ideas. In a famous passage, Eliot writes:

> No poet, no artist of any art, has his complete meaning alone. His significance, his appreciation is the appreciation of his relation to *the dead* poets and artists. You cannot value him alone; you must set him, for contrast and comparison, among *the dead*.[45] (My emphases)

For Larkin's narrator, who seemingly has no theological reason to visit the church, its space is 'proper to grow wise in, / If only that *so many dead* lie round' (my emphasis). This verbal echo may be a coincidence, but the ideas explored and enacted by 'Church Going' are not; this is a poem which not only alludes to several of Eliot's works, as well as those by many other writers, but also echoes and explores Eliot's essay on the poet's relation to tradition. It is an example of Larkin's hidden depth: 'Church Going' is simultaneously a poem about the consequences of the Church in decline, and an exercise in intertextuality and literary tradition. If the narrator begins in a state of ignorance about church symbolism, feigned or not, but then finds himself growing in metaphysical stature, the same transition can be detected in a poem which begins as concrete nouns and demotic speech before finding its feet – electrified, not stifled, by the literary tradition it engages.

This aspect of the poem has not been to every reader's taste. Kingsley Amis, asked by Larkin to look over the poem, criticized the archaic poeticisms of its closing stages:

> I think the last stanza isn't right yet; not because of the punctuation – couldn't see anything wrong with that – but because of one or two highly poetical words and constructions: the inversion in the first line, for instance, which makes me think of 'A casement high and triple arched there was' and such bits of flannel. I'd say you've got to be extra careful, at the point when you ease your foot gently down on the accelerator, to avoid reminding the reader that 'this is poetry'. See what I mean? 'Blent', too, seems a bit 18th-c. to me.[46]

Larkin, thankfully, chose not to act on Amis's advice. As Michael O'Neill has commented, 'One may feel that it is by no means undesirable that, as Larkin eases his foot gently down on the accelerator, what comes to mind is a Romantic poem'.[47] This is, after all, a poem which tentatively but searchingly steps into the realm of the unknown, asking questions about the nature of belief, superstition, the strange gravity of particular spaces and the human hunger for seriousness – all Romantic concerns. O'Neill's view that 'the poetic diction flirts with archaism but earns its keep' is apt, given how gradually and subtly this poem grows into its own seriousness. Precisely because the modulation is so effective, O'Neill is right to argue that Larkin has found 'an idiom that is at once of its time and in contact with a poetic tradition that includes the Romantics'.[48] This 'contact with a poetic tradition that includes the Romantics' is one of the ways in which 'Church Going' negotiates Eliot's theory of tradition. The 'dead' who 'lie round' are at once the bodies of parishioners buried in the graveyard over the centuries, and Eliot's 'dead poets and artists', woven by Larkin into the fabric of his poem. Of course, to 'lie' is a favoured Larkin pun, one we find in Coleman's 'Fourth Former Loquitur' and in a later poem, 'An Arundel Tomb'. Like the earl and countess who 'lie in stone', it may be that the bodies expose the Christian 'lie' of an afterlife; but given the polyvalence of Larkin's verse, the presence of such a pun does not preclude any of the alternative readings offered here (*TCP*, 71–2).

'Church Going' shows Larkin writing at the height of his poetic maturity and in full command of his capacities. So much of what readers appreciate about the Larkinesque is there: the modulation from the demotic and the here and now towards something more transcendental and sublime; the complex, deeply satisfying formal intricacies; colloquial speech mixed with gorgeous poetry; humour and humility; a subject that speaks to Larkin's post-war society and to humans in all times and places. It is a long way from the staple poems of *The North Ship*. But the success of this poem, and others discussed here, is not predicated on Larkin's abandoning of his influences in favour of a more straightforward and autobiographical mode of writing. Rather, the poem enters into negotiation with a wider tradition that contains but does not engulf it. Beginning in the first-person singular ('Once I am sure there's nothing going on'), it quietly adopts the first-person plural, considering 'our compulsions' and the 'many dead' who came before us. In doing so, the poem looks outward, not inward, valuing community and tradition with its dual impulse of celebration and elegy. As the central poem in *The Less Deceived*, 'Church Going' rightly deserves its place at the heart of Larkin's first truly mature book – a masterpiece within a masterpiece.

Conclusion

Attempting to account for his curtailed career as a novelist, Larkin suggested that 'novels are about other people, and poems are about yourself. I think that was the trouble, really. I didn't know enough about other people, I didn't like them enough' (*RW*, 49). Even ignoring the crudeness of this distinction, Larkin's career does not bear it out. In another interview, he argued that 'The more sensitive you are to suffering the nicer person you are and the more accurate notion of life you have' (*FR*, 52). Again, the language is simplistic, but this time it speaks to the way Larkin's writing is humanely attuned to the lives of others. This book has argued that Larkin became a true artist and a great poet by turning outwards, not inwards. One of the consequences of turning outwards, of writing beyond his own autobiography, was a new and productive interest in other subjectivities and experiences.

Larkin became a great artist in the 1940s. His writings from the beginning of that decade reveal an immobilizing contradiction, in that he wanted to write about himself (and did), but in doing so only imitated his literary heroes. An unusual experiment in authorship, conducted using the Brunette Coleman heteronym, set his writing on a very different path. Whilst the orthodoxy in Larkin Studies is that his rediscovery of Hardy in 1946 taught him to write on his own terms, the fact is that by then Larkin was already producing original work. Its originality depended on his outward turn – a turn to the contemporary world in which he lived, yes, but also to the lives and inner lives of subjects who were not Philip Larkin. Though this change occurred in prose before it occurred in poetry, by the turn of the decade Larkin was writing the poems that would make him famous and secure his place in literary history. 'At Grass' and 'Deceptions' were the first major poems to reflect this transformation, and Larkin would never again abandon his interest in that which lay outside his own subjectivity. In his notorious but slippery 'Statement', Larkin commented that 'Generally my poems are related . . . to my own personal life, but by no means always, since I can imagine horses I have never seen or the emotions of a bride without ever having been a woman or married' (*RW*, 79). Critics have too easily accepted the first part of that statement and neglected the second. *The Less Deceived*, even when it appears to be autobiographical, shows immense range and responsiveness to external experience; and the great poems of Larkin's subsequent collections, *The Whitsun Weddings* and *High Windows*, are so moving and popular precisely because of their openness to the lives of others: 'Mr Bleaney', 'Love Songs in Age', 'Faith Healing', 'For Sidney Bechet', 'The Whitsun Weddings', 'Afternoons', 'An Arundel Tomb', 'The Trees', 'Livings', 'Friday Night in the Royal Station Hotel', 'The Explosion'. Even in the last years of his life, as the ability to write deserted him, Larkin managed a quiet masterpiece, 'The Mower', which takes the death of a hedgehog to stage a deeply moving elegy. The 'we' of its final message does not discriminate between people, or even between people and small creatures: 'we should be careful // Of each other, we should be kind / While there is still time' (*TCP*, 118).

In a review of the 1988 *Collected Poems*, an edition notable for its presentation of Larkin's poems in order of composition rather than the poet's chosen arrangements, Clive James made an astute prediction and compelling counterargument:

> The process of explaining him will be hard to stop now that this book is available. . . . [D]espite all the candour it apparently offers, the mystery will be preserved for any reader acute enough to sense the depth under the clarity. Pushkin said that everything was on his agenda, even the disasters. Larkin knew about himself. In private hours of anguish, he commiserated with himself. But he was an artist, and that meant he was everyone; and what made him a genius was the effort and resource he brought to bear in order to meet his superior responsibility.[1]

James recognizes that great artists are not just exceptional individuals but also 'everyone'. He sees in Larkin's work an artistic impulse which ran far deeper than self-examination or commiseration. But that was something Larkin had to learn. This book has traced the story of Larkin's early literary development, charting the surprising and often unexplored journey this writer undertook in order to fulfil his 'superior responsibility'.

Notes

Introduction

1 John Osborne, *Radical Larkin: Seven Types of Technical Mastery* (Basingstoke: Palgrave Macmillan, 2014), 21.
2 Adam Kirsch, 'Green Selfconscious Spurts', *Times Literary Supplement*, 13 May 2005.
3 Richard Palmer, *Such Deliberate Disguises: The Art of Philip Larkin* (London: Continuum, 2008), 71.
4 Larkin, ts. short story, 'The Eagles Are Gone', c.1935, U DPL2/1/1/4.
5 Palmer, *Such Deliberate Disguises*, 71.
6 Ibid., xxi, 72.
7 Kingsley Amis, *Lucky Jim* (Harmondsworth: Penguin, 1977), 15.
8 Peter Levi, 'The English Wisdom of A Master Poet', in *An Enormous Yes: In Memoriam Philip Larkin 1922–1985*, ed. Harry Chambers (Calstock: Peterloo Poets, 1986), 33–5.
9 Geoffrey Hill, 'I Know Thee Not, Old Man, Fall to Thy Prayers', Professor of Poetry Lecture, University of Oxford, 5 May 2015. Available online: http://media.podcasts.ox.ac.uk/engfac/poetry/2015-05-05_engfac_hill.mp3.
10 Geoffrey Hill, *Style and Faith* (New York: Counterpoint, 2003), 204.
11 Martin Amis, 'Philip Larkin, His Work and Life', in *Philip Larkin: Poems Selected by Martin Amis* (London: Faber and Faber, 2011), xvi, xix.
12 Ibid., xvi.
13 Ibid., xvi–xvii.
14 Morten Høi Jensen, 'Larkin's Way', *Idiom*, 3 April 2012. Available online: http://idiommag.com/2012/04/larkins-way/; Blake Morrison, '*Philip Larkin: Life, Art and Love* by James Booth – Review', *The Guardian*, 22 August 2014. Available online: http://www.theguardian.com/books/2014/aug/22/philip-larkin-james-booth-review.
15 Sean O'Brien, '*Philip Larkin: Poems Selected by Martin Amis* – Review', *The Guardian*, 16 September 2011. Available online: http://www.theguardian.com/books/2011/sep/16/philip-larkin-poems-review.
16 Amis, 'Philip Larkin, His Work and Life', xvii–xviii.
17 John Osborne, *Larkin, Ideology and Critical Violence: A Case of Wrongful Conviction* (Basingstoke: Palgrave Macmillan, 2008), 24–5.
18 Peter Ackroyd, 'Poet Hands on Misery to Man', *The Times*, 1 April 1993, 35.

19 Ian Hamilton, 'Phil the Lark', *London Review of Books*, 13 October 1988, 3.
20 Clive James, 'Larkin Treads the Boards', in *The Meaning of Recognition: New Essays 2001–2005* (London: Picador, 2006), 97.
21 Tom Paulin, letter, *Times Literary Supplement*, 6 November 1992, 15; Lisa Jardine, 'Saxon Violence', *The Guardian*, 8 December 1992, 4.
22 See James Underwood, '"A Kind of Homosexual Relation, Disguised": Larkin's Letters to Monica Jones', *English* 65, no. 248 (2016): 38–57.
23 Osborne, *Larkin, Ideology and Critical Violence*, 19.
24 Ibid., 33.
25 Ibid., 21.
26 Ibid., 196.

Chapter 1

1 In researching this chapter, I have explored the entire extant correspondence in the archive, rather than relying on the *Selected Letters*. This has provided a wider and deeper perspective, allowing me to properly perceive the correspondence's development, its rhythms and repetitions. Readers of the *Selected Letters* will, therefore, be familiar with some material cited here; the rest is being cited and/or discussed for the first time.
2 Andrew Motion, *Philip Larkin: A Writer's Life* (London: Faber and Faber, 1993), 39.
3 Letters from Philip Arthur Larkin to James Ballard Sutton, U DP174. All letters to Sutton cited in this chapter come from this collection; individual letters are hereafter referenced with in-text date citations.
4 Hermione Lee, 'Dangerous Letters: A Biographer's Perspective', in *Letter Writing Among Poets from William Wordsworth to Elizabeth Bishop*, ed. Jonathan Ellis (Edinburgh: Edinburgh University Press, 2015), 19.
5 Rebecca Earle, ed. and introd., *Epistolary Selves: Letters and Letter-Writers 1600–1945* (Aldershot: Ashgate, 1999), 4–5.
6 Amanda Gilroy and W. M. Verhoeven, 'Editorial', *Correspondences*, special issue of *Prose Studies* 19, no. 2 (August 1996): 121.
7 Hugh Haughton, 'Just Letters: Corresponding Poets', in *Letter Writing Among Poets*, ed. Ellis, 70.
8 Jenny Hartley, '"Letters Are *Everything* These Days": Mothers and Letters in the Second World War', in *Epistolary Selves*, ed. Earle, 183.
9 Ibid., 186–7.
10 Julie Maylon, 'The Other Side of a Friendship: Letters from James Sutton to Philip Larkin', *About Larkin* 7 (April 1999): 16–17.
11 Christopher Isherwood, *Goodbye to Berlin* (London: Vintage, 1998), 9.

12 Christopher Isherwood, *Lions and Shadows: An Education in the Twenties* (London: Vintage, 2013), xv.
13 Ibid., 55.
14 Quoted in Michael Black, 'Leavis on Lawrence', in *F. R. Leavis: Essays and Documents*, ed. Ian MacKillop and Richard Storer (London: Continuum, 2005), 213; quoted in Keith Sagar, *The Art of D. H. Lawrence* (Cambridge: Cambridge University Press, 1966), 2.
15 Edna Longley, 'Larkin, Decadence and the Lyric Poem', in *New Larkins for Old: Critical Essays*, ed. James Booth (Basingstoke: Macmillan, 2000), 30.
16 James Longenbach, 'An Imperfect Life: On George and W. B. Yeats', *Nation*, 18 May 2011. Available online: https://www.thenation.com/article/imperfect-life-george-and-wb-yeats/.
17 Denis Donoghue, 'The Hard Case of Yeats', *New York Review of Books*, 26 May 1977. Available online: https://www.nybooks.com/articles/1977/05/26/the-hard-case-of-yeats/.
18 Seamus Heaney, 'The Journey Back', in *Seeing Things* (London: Faber and Faber, 1991), 7.
19 Quoted in James Booth, *Philip Larkin: Writer* (Hemel Hempstead: Harvester Wheatsheaf, 1992), 18.
20 James Booth, 'The Turf Cutter and the Nine-to-Five Man: Heaney, Larkin, and "The Spiritual Intellect's Great Work"', *Twentieth Century Literature* 43, no. 4 (Winter 1997): 374.
21 Cyril Connolly, *Enemies of Promise* (Chicago: University of Chicago Press, 2008), 116.
22 Larkin, ts. essay, 'A note on the freedom of D. H. Lawrence', July 1950, U DPL2/1/4/23.
23 D. H. Lawrence, *The Collected Letters of D. H. Lawrence: Volume II*, ed. Harry T. Moore (New York: Viking Press, 1962), 719.

Chapter 2

1 Larkin, manuscript book used as a diary and notebook for selected and annotated juvenilia, 1938–1940, U DPL2/1/1/10.
2 Larkin, ms. page torn from English exercise book, 1938, U DPL2/1/4/7.
3 Larkin, ms. short story, 'Vampire Island', 1930s, U DPL2/1/1/8.
4 Larkin, ts. short story, 'Incidents from Phippy's Schooldays', c.1935, U DPL2/1/1/2.
5 Larkin, ts. short story, 'Last Man In (or "How Allan Saved His Side")', 1938, U DPL2/1/1/9.
6 Larkin, ts. prose piece, presented as an extract from a larger work, 'A Portrait of the Artist as a Young Frog', 1930s, U DPL2/1/2/1.

7   Larkin, ts. prose piece, 'Letter to Myself', 1940, U DPL2/1/2/8.
8   Larkin, ms. short story, untitled, beginning 'The small, cross-channel steamer, packed with humanity rose high', 1930s, U DPL2/1/1/5.
9   Larkin, ts. short story, untitled, beginning 'It had snowed in the night', 1930s, U DPL2/1/1/5.
10 Larkin, ts. short story, 'Maurice', 1939, U DPL2/1/1/6.
11 The catalogue dates 'The Eagles Are Gone' to '*c*.1935', whereas Booth dates it (along with 'Story I', 'Peter' and 'Maurice') to 1941–2. However, Larkin's manuscript book dates 'Maurice' to 1939. The other two stories which Booth accurately dates ('Story I' and 'Peter') reflect Larkin's Oxford friendship group, known as 'The Seven', in 1941–2. In 'The Eagles Are Gone', a character called 'Philip Larkin' visits an Oxford friend, but there is little, if any, trace of 'The Seven' in this story; instead, the friend's family seems to be a version of Larkin's own. Internal details such as these suggest that the story was not quite written at the same time as the other two. But 'The Eagles Are Gone' is a much more sophisticated work than 'Vampire Island', which the catalogue dates to '*c*.1936'; it seems unlikely that Larkin could have written the former before the latter. I would suggest, therefore, that 'The Eagles Are Gone' was written sometime between 'Vampire Island' and the two Oxford stories, and probably around the same time as 'Maurice' – perhaps in 1939 or 1940, but before Larkin became a member of 'The Seven'.
12 Larkin, ts. short story, 'The Eagles Are Gone', *c*.1935, U DPL2/1/1/4.
13 Larkin, ms. autobiographical prose piece, *c*.1953, Workbook 5, 1953–1960, U DPL/1/5/1.
14 See Booth's account of the Larkin family dynamic (*LH*, xxv–xxvi).
15 Whilst 'Story I' survives in typescript and is carefully dated and titled, 'Peter' is an untitled and unfinished holograph. 'Peter' is the title given by Booth, who edited and published both stories in *About Larkin*; I adopt his title here.
16 Isherwood, *Lions and Shadows*, xv.
17 Quoted in Motion, *A Writer's Life*, 69. Along with Larkin, The Seven comprised Kingsley Amis, Jimmy Willcox, Philip Brown, Nick Russel, Normal Iles and David Williams. Larkin explains that after just one meeting their 'ideas and ideals degenerated into one big supper party per week'.
18 Ibid., 65.
19 James Booth, *Philip Larkin: Life, Art and Love* (London: Bloomsbury, 2014), 38.
20 Larkin, 'Story I', *About Larkin* 10 (October 2000): 9.
21 Ibid., 4.
22 Larkin, 'Peter', *About Larkin* 11 (April 2001): 16.
23 Ibid., 16–17.
24 Larkin, 'Story I', 19.
25 Booth, *Life, Art and Love*, 39.

26 Larkin, 'Story I', 6.
27 Ibid., 20.
28 Ibid., 6.
29 Ibid., 11.
30 Ibid., 7.
31 Ibid.
32 Ibid., 9.
33 Ibid., 8.
34 Larkin, 'Peter', 13.
35 Ibid., 16.
36 Ibid., 13.
37 Larkin, 'Story I', 20.
38 Larkin, 'Peter', 19.
39 Ibid., 19–20.
40 Ibid.
41 James Booth, 'Editorial', *About Larkin* 11 (April 2001): 2.
42 Booth, *Life, Art and Love*, 60.
43 Larkin, 'An Incident in the English Camp: A Thoroughly Unhealthy Story by P. A. Larkin', *About Larkin* 12 (October 2001): 6.
44 Ibid.
45 Booth, *Life, Art and Love*, 61.
46 Larkin, 'An Incident in the English Camp', 7.
47 Ibid., 8.
48 Ibid., 9–10.
49 Ibid., 9.
50 Ibid., 10.
51 Ibid.
52 Booth, *Life, Art and Love*, 60.

Chapter 3

1 Given that Brunette Coleman has her own back story and independent identity, I concur with Osborne's categorization of her as a heteronym, rather than pseudonym, which merely refers to an author's fictitious name; see *Larkin, Ideology and Critical Violence*, 165.
2 Quoted in Booth, *Life, Art and Love*, 63.
3 Terry Castle, 'The Lesbianism of Philip Larkin', in *The Movement Reconsidered: Essays on Larkin, Amis, Gunn, Davie and Their Contemporaries*, ed. Zachary Leader (Oxford: Oxford University Press, 2011), 81.

4   Quoted in Booth, *Life, Art and Love*, 69.
5   Quoted in Richard Bradford, *The Odd Couple: The Curious Friendship Between Kingsley Amis and Philip Larkin* (London: The Robson Press, 2012), 35; Booth, *Life, Art and Love*, 70.
6   Katherine Bucknell, ed. and introd., *Christopher Isherwood and Edward Upward: The Mortmere Stories* (London: Enitharmon Press, 1994), 9.
7   Ibid., 14.
8   Larkin, ts. draft novel, *Trouble at Willow Gables*, 1943, U DPL2/1/12; manuscript book containing ms. and ts. draft novel, *Michaelmas Term at St Bride's*, and ms. prose piece, presented as an extract from a larger work, *Ante Meridian: The Autobiography of Brunette Coleman*, 1943, U DPL2/1/13; ts. pamphlet, 'What Are We Writing For?', 1943, U DPL2/1/1/13; hand-sewn booklet of ts. poems, *Sugar and Spice*, 1943, U DPL2/1/11.
9   Richard Bradford, *First Boredom, Then Fear: The Life of Philip Larkin* (London: Peter Owen, 2005), 52.
10 Booth, *Life, Art and Love*, 70.
11 Ibid., 73.
12 Larkin, unpublished ms. letter to Miriam Plaut, 7 August 1985, U DPL2/2/25/80.
13 Jenny Diski, 'Damp-Lipped Hilary', *London Review of Books*, 23 May 2002, 22.
14 Jonathan Bate, 'Very Juvenile, this Juvenilia', *Daily Telegraph*, 28 April 2002. Available online: http://www.telegraph.co.uk/culture/4727749/Very-juvenile-this-juvenilia.html.
15 Rebecca Johnson, 'Philip Larkin as Brunette Coleman', *About Larkin* 2 (October 1996): 10; Palmer, *Such Deliberate Disguises*, xxi.
16 Motion, *A Writer's Life*, 86. Because Motion consulted Montgomery's copy of the poems in the Bodleian, he was unaware of the seventh *Sugar and Spice* poem, 'Fourth Former Loquitur', which Larkin slipped into his own copy, now housed in the Hull archive.
17 Ibid., 92.
18 Motion erroneously calls this essay 'What We Are Writing For'.
19 Ibid., 89.
20 Ibid., 96.
21 M. W. Rowe, 'Unreal Girls: Lesbian Fantasy in Early Larkin', in *New Larkins for Old*, ed. Booth, 79–96; M. W. Rowe, 'On Being Brunette: Larkin's Schoolgirl Fiction', *Critical Quarterly* 43, no. 4 (December 2001): 42–58; Jin-Sung Choi, 'Defensive Homosexuality and Lesbianism in Philip Larkin's Two Girls' School Stories', *Philip Larkin/British Studies*, special issue of *Hungarian Journal of English and American Studies* 9, no. 1 (Fall 2003): 105–17.
22 Quoted in Motion, *A Writer's Life*, 65.
23 Booth, *Life, Art and Love*, 64, 72.
24 Quoted in Nicola Woolcock, 'Poet Larkin's Lesbian Tales "Reveal Desire to Be Female"', *Telegraph*, 23 April 2001. Available online: http://www.telegraph.co.uk

/news/uknews/1317050/Poet-Larkins-lesbian-tales-reveal-desire-to-be-female.html.
25. Stephen Cooper, *Philip Larkin: Subversive Writer* (Brighton: Sussex Academic Press, 2004), 7, 18.
26. Castle, 'The Lesbianism of Philip Larkin', 84.
27. Ibid., 79–80.
28. Ibid., 82–3, 105.
29. Cyril Connolly, 'Comment', *Horizon: A Review of Literature and Art* 1, no. 1 (January 1940): 5.
30. Motion, *A Writer's Life*, 42–3.
31. Ibid., 438.
32. George Orwell, 'Boys' Weeklies', in *Selected Essays* (Harmondsworth: Penguin, 1957), 179–81.
33. Ibid., 187.
34. Ibid., 200.
35. See Booth, *Life, Art and Love*, 20.
36. Orwell, 'Boys' Weeklies', 201.
37. Bradford, *First Boredom, Then Fear*, 52.
38. Connolly, *Enemies of Promise*, xix.
39. Coleman's autobiographical fragment, *Ante Meridian*, is also seemingly influenced by 'A Georgian Boyhood', the final, autobiographical third of *Enemies of Promise*. Both adopt the convention of describing childhood as a fantastical, mystical, formative time – the very convention Larkin would later negate in 'I Remember, I Remember'.
40. Edward Greenwood, *F. R. Leavis* (Harlow: Longman, 1978), 9.
41. Q. D. Leavis, *Fiction and the Reading Public* (London: Chatto and Windus, 1932), 6.
42. Ibid., xv, 270.
43. Connolly, *Enemies of Promise*, 17–18.
44. Booth, *Life, Art and Love*, 64.
45. Sue Sims, review of *Trouble at Willow Gables and Other Fictions* by Philip Larkin, *About Larkin* 14 (October 2002): 38.

Chapter 4

1. J. S. Bratton, 'Girls' Fiction 1900–1930', in *Imperialism and Juvenile Literature*, ed. Jeffrey Richards (Manchester: Manchester University Press, 1989), 197.
2. Mary Cadogan and Patricia Craig, *'You're a Brick, Angela!': A New Look at Girls' Fiction from 1839 to 1975* (London: Gollancz, 1976), 10.
3. Judy Simons, 'Angela Brazil and the Making of the Girls' School Story', in *Popular Children's Literature in Britain*, ed. Julia Briggs, Dennis Butts and M. O. Grenby (Aldershot: Ashgate, 2008), 174–5.

4   Murray Knowles and Kirsten Malmkjaer, *Language and Control in Children's Literature* (London: Routledge, 1996), 43–4.
5   Glenwood Irons, ed. and introd., *Feminism in Women's Detective Fiction* (Toronto: University of Toronto Press, 1995), x–xi.
6   Ibid., xi.
7   Rosemary Auchmuty, *A World of Women* (London: The Women's Press, 1999), 110.
8   Osborne, *Radical Larkin*, 152.
9   Motion, *A Writer's Life*, 92.
10 Orwell, 'Boys' Weeklies', 180.
11 Cadogan and Craig, *A New Look at Girls' Fiction*, 10.
12 Gillian Freeman, *The Schoolgirl Ethic: The Life and Work of Angela Brazil* (London: Allen Lane, 1976), 74.
13 Ibid., 19.
14 Simons, 'Angela Brazil and the Making of the Girls' School Story', 173.
15 Cadogan and Craig, *A New Look at Girls' Fiction*, 10.
16 Castle, 'The Lesbianism of Philip Larkin', 85–8.
17 Susan Sontag, 'Notes on "Camp"', in *Against Interpretation and Other Essays* (London: Eyre and Spottiswoode, 1967), 279–80.
18 Ibid.
19 Ibid., 286–7.
20 Ibid., 288, 292.
21 Ibid., 291–2.
22 Ibid., 277.
23 Ibid., 280.
24 Osborne, *Larkin, Ideology and Critical Violence*, 159.
25 Ibid., 165.
26 Rowe, 'Unreal Girls', 82.
27 Castle, 'The Lesbianism of Philip Larkin', 92–3.
28 Motion, *A Writer's Life*, 96.
29 Choi, 'Defensive Homosexuality and Lesbianism', 115.
30 Cooper, *Subversive Writer*, 30.
31 Quoted in Motion, *A Writer's Life*, 88.
32 Isherwood, *Lions and Shadows*, 50.
33 Booth, *Life, Art and Love*, 80.

Chapter 5

1   Motion, *A Writer's Life*, 64.
2   Cooper, *Subversive Writer*, 32.

3   Booth, *Philip Larkin: Writer*, 56.
4   Cooper, *Subversive Writer*, 44; Booth, *Philip Larkin: Writer*, 51.
5   Motion, *A Writer's Life*, 156–7.
6   Booth, *Philip Larkin: Writer*, 50.
7   Ibid., 51.
8   Fenton, introduction to *Lions and Shadows*, x.
9   Bruce Montgomery (as Edmund Crispin), 'An Oxford Group', *Spectator*, 17 April 1964, 525.
10 John Bayley, *The Uses of Division: Unity and Disharmony in Literature* (New York: Viking Press, 1976), 170.
11 A. T. Tolley, *My Proper Ground: A Study of the Work of Philip Larkin and Its Development* (Edinburgh: Edinburgh University Press, 1991), 30.
12 Quoted in Booth, *Philip Larkin: Writer*, 43.
13 Virginia Woolf, *A Writer's Diary: Being Extracts from the Diary of Virginia Woolf*, ed. Leonard Woolf (San Diego: Harcourt, 2003), 59.
14 Osborne, *Radical Larkin*, 37, 36.
15 See, for instance, Tom Paulin, 'She Did Not Change: Philip Larkin', in *Minotaur: Poetry and the Nation State* (London: Faber and Faber, 1992), 233–51.
16 Booth, *Philip Larkin: Writer*, 58.
17 Osborne, *Radical Larkin*, 42.
18 Liz Hedgecock 'New Worlds for Old: Mythology and Exile in the Novels of Philip Larkin', in *New Larkins for Old*, ed. Booth, 104; Booth, *Philip Larkin: Writer*, 55; David Timms, *Philip Larkin* (Edinburgh: Oliver Boyd: 1973), 50.
19 Osborne, *Radical Larkin*, 26–7.

Chapter 6

1   Stan Smith, 'Something for Nothing: Late Larkins and Early', *English* 49, no. 195 (Autumn 2000): 255.
2   Philip Larkin and Bruce Montgomery, 'LIFE WITH PHAIRY PHANTASY: A morality in Pictures Drawn by Mr. P. A. L.', early 1940s, U DPL/4/1.
3   Timms, *Philip Larkin*, 26.
4   Ibid., 28–9.
5   David Lodge, 'The Metonymic Muse', in *Philip Larkin: Contemporary Critical Essays*, ed. Stephen Regan (Basingstoke: Macmillan, 1997), 73.
6   Ted Hughes, 'The Burnt Fox', in *Winter Pollen: Occasional Prose*, ed. William Scammell (London: Faber and Faber, 1994), 8–9.
7   Motion, *A Writer's Life*, 140.
8   Sontag, 'Notes on "Camp"', 286–7.

9. John Betjeman, 'Myfanwy', in *The Best of Betjeman*, ed. John Guest (London: John Murray, 2006), 47–8.
10. Larkin, letter to Lord Tennyson, 29 May 1984, *About Larkin* 41 (April 2016): 18–19.
11. Quoted in James Booth, 'The Girlhood of Philip Larkin', *Standpoint*, 28 January 2019. Available online: https://standpointmag.co.uk/issues/february-2019/critique-james-booth-philip-larkin-brunette-coleman-february-2019/.
12. Charles Baudelaire, 'Femmes damnées: Delphine et Hippolyte', in *The Flowers of Evil*, trans. James McGowan (Oxford: Oxford University Press, 2008), 239–45.
13. Castle, 'The Lesbianism of Philip Larkin', 94.
14. Ibid., 96.
15. Ibid., 97.
16. Quoted in Motion, *A Writer's Life*, 106.
17. Stephen Regan, '*In the Grip of Light*: Larkin's Poetry of the 1940s', in *New Larkins for Old*, ed. Booth, 127.
18. 'All catches alight', 'The moon is full tonight', 'The horns of the morning', 'I put my mouth', 'The bottle is drunk out by one', 'I see a girl dragged by the wrists', 'Love, we must part now: do not let it be', 'Morning has spread again', 'Heaviest of flowers, the head' and 'So through that unripe day you bore your head'. All ten were included in *The North Ship*.
19. Bradford, *The Odd Couple*, 61.
20. Timms, *Philip Larkin*, 26.
21. W. B. Yeats, 'Sailing to Byzantium', in *Yeats's Poems*, ed. A. Norman Jeffares (London: Macmillan, 1989), 301–2.
22. Timms, *Philip Larkin*, 27.
23. Osborne, *Larkin, Ideology and Critical Violence*, 164.
24. Timms, *Philip Larkin*, 34.
25. Anthony Thwaite, 'The Poetry of Philip Larkin', in *The Survival of Poetry: A Contemporary Survey*, ed. Martin Dodsworth (London: Faber and Faber, 1970), 43.
26. Larkin, unpublished ts. letter to John Fuller, 10 August 1977, U DPL2/2/15/59.
27. See Ryan Roberts (ed.), *John Fuller and the Sycamore Press: A Bibliographic History* (Oxford: The Bodleian Library, 2010).
28. Larkin, unpublished ts. letter to John Fuller, 23 August 1977, U DPL2/2/15/59.
29. Larkin, unpublished ts. letter to John Fuller, 11 May 1978, U DPL2/2/15/59.
30. Bate, 'Very Juvenile, This Juvenilia'.
31. Larkin, ts. letter to John Fuller, 12 June 1978, U DPL2/2/15/59.
32. Quoted in Peter Forbes, 'Winning Lines', *The Guardian*, 31 August 2002. Available online: https://www.theguardian.com/books/2002/aug/31/featuresreviews.guardianreview8.

Chapter 7

1. The unfinished drafts of both novels are included in Booth's edition (*TWG*, 277–363, 365–465).
2. Bradford, *First Boredom, Then Fear*, 79.
3. Ibid., 85, 81.
4. Booth, *Life, Art and Love*, 124.
5. Larkin, microfilm copy of Workbook 1, 1944–1950, U DPL/1/1/1. See A. T. Tolley, *Larkin at Work: A Study of Larkin's Mode of Composition as Seen in His Workbooks* (Hull: University of Hull Press, 1997), 4.
6. Larkin, pasted photograph of W. B. Yeats above a pasted ts. of Yeats's poem, 'The Collar-bone of a Hare', October 1944, U DPL/1/1/1.
7. Larkin, ms. draft of 'Wedding-Wind', 26 September 1946, U DPL/1/1/59.
8. Larkin, ms. draft of 'Waiting for breakfast, while she brushed her hair', 15 December 1947, U DPL/1/1/70.
9. Larkin, ms. draft of 'An April Sunday brings the snow', 4 April 1948, U DPL/1/1/72.
10. Larkin, ms. draft of 'Modesties', 13 May 1949, U DPL/1/1/76.
11. Larkin, ms. draft of 'Fiction and the Reading Public', May 1949, U DPL/1/1/78; ms. draft of 'To Failure', 18 May 1949, U DPL/1/1/79.
12. Larkin, ms. list of ex-Forces garments and bedding, opposite a pasted newspaper advertisement for Leicester's Millets store, January 1950, U DPL/1/1/85; pasted newspaper advertisement for properties in Leicester, January 1950, U DPL/1/1/86.
13. Larkin, ms. draft of 'Last of all, when a great war has ended', January 1950, U DPL/1/1/87.
14. Larkin, ms. draft of 'At Grass', 3 January 1950, U DPL/1/1/82; ms. quotation from Henry Mayhew's *London Labour and the London Poor*, January 1950, U DPL/1/1/89.
15. Larkin, ms. draft of 'Deceptions', 20 February 1950, U DPL/1/1/92; poem completed in Workbook 2, 1950–1951, U DPL/1/2: ms. draft of 'Deceptions', 1950, U DPL/1/2/24.
16. Larkin, ms. draft of 'Do not think to step from art's plain room', May 1949, U DPL/1/1/81.
17. Tolley, *Larkin at Work*, 19.
18. Ibid.
19. There is some doubt about the exact inspiration behind 'At Grass': for a fuller account, see Osborne, *Radical Larkin*, 91–2.
20. Motion, *A Writer's Life*, 188.
21. Osborne, *Radical Larkin*, 94.
22. Ibid., 93–4.
23. Booth, *Philip Larkin: Writer*, 108–9.

24 Quoted in Cooper, *Subversive Writer*, 128.
25 William Wordsworth, 'Nuns Fret Not at Their Convent's Narrow Room', in *Poetical Works*, ed. Thomas Hutchinson (London: Oxford University Press, 1971), 199.
26 Booth, *Philip Larkin: Writer*, 109.
27 James Booth, *Philip Larkin: The Poet's Plight* (Basingstoke: Palgrave Macmillan, 2005), 63.
28 Janice Rossen, *Philip Larkin: His Life's Work* (Iowa City: University of Iowa Press, 1989), 89.
29 Joseph Bristow, 'The Obscenity of Philip Larkin', *Critical Inquiry* 21, no. 1 (Autumn 1994): 176.
30 Rossen, *His Life's Work*, 89.
31 Graham Holderness, 'Reading "Deceptions" – A Dramatic Conversation', in *Philip Larkin*, ed. Regan, 90.
32 Stan Smith, 'Margins of Tolerance: Responses to Post-war Decline', in *Philip Larkin*, ed. Regan, 179.

Chapter 8

1 Quoted in Booth, *Life, Art and Love*, 155–6.
2 Quoted in Motion, *A Writer's Life*, 216.
3 Booth, *Life, Art and Love*, 156.
4 Osborne, *Larkin, Ideology and Critical Violence*, 104.
5 Graham Chesters, 'Tireless Play: Speculations on Larkin's "Absences"', in *Challenges of Translation in French Literature: Studies and Poems in Honour of Peter Broome*, ed. Richard Bales (Bern: Peter Lang, 2005), 57–8; Booth, *Life, Art and Love*, 159; Osborne, *Larkin, Ideology and Critical Violence*, 56.
6 Booth, *Life, Art and Love*, 157–8.
7 Osborne, *Radical Larkin*, 67.
8 Cooper, *Subversive Writer*, 125; Osborne, *Radical Larkin*, 69.
9 Cooper, *Subversive Writer*, 127.
10 Osborne, *Radical Larkin*, 69.
11 Palmer, *Such Deliberate Disguises*, 93.
12 Cooper, *Subversive Writer*, 113.
13 Winifred Dawson, 'Photograph Albums Revisited', *About Larkin* 13 (April 2002): 4.
14 Osborne, *Larkin, Ideology and Critical Violence*, 128.
15 Ibid., 80.
16 Ibid., 79.
17 Andrew Swarbrick, *Out of Reach: The Poetry of Philip Larkin* (Basingstoke: Macmillan, 1995), 55.

18 'losel, n. and adj.' and 'loblolly, n.', *OED Online* (Oxford: Oxford University Press, 2020).
19 Palmer, *Such Deliberate Disguises*, 131.
20 Swarbrick, *Out of Reach*, 65.
21 Ibid., 64; Barbara Everett, 'Philip Larkin: After Symbolism', in *Philip Larkin*, ed. Regan, 64.
22 Osborne, *Larkin, Ideology and Critical Violence*, 3.
23 Cooper, *Subversive Writer*, 151.
24 Terry Whalen, 'Philip Larkin and *Lady Chatterley's Lover*: Exploring an Influence', in *New Larkins for Old*, ed. Booth, 119.
25 Lodge, 'The Metonymic Muse', 76.
26 Swarbrick, *Out of Reach*, 2; Steve Clark, '"Get Out As Early As You Can": Larkin's Sexual Politics', in *Philip Larkin*, ed. Regan, 126.
27 Booth, *Life, Art and Love*, 198.
28 Thomas Hood, 'I Remember, I Remember', in *Selected Poems of Thomas Hood*, ed. John Clubbe (Cambridge, MA: Harvard University Press, 1970), 35–6.
29 Osborne, *Larkin, Ideology and Critical Violence*, 137.
30 Ibid., 146.
31 Bradford, *First Boredom, Then Fear*, 127–8.
32 Osborne, *Larkin, Ideology and Critical Violence*, 140.
33 Ibid., 136; Rossen, *His Life's Work*, 40.
34 Osborne, *Larkin, Ideology and Critical Violence*, 135.
35 W. H. Auden, 'In Memory of W. B. Yeats', in *Auden: Poems*, ed. Edward Mendelson (New York: Alfred A. Knopf, 1995), 76–9.
36 Adrian Mitchell, *Poems* (London: Jonathan Cape, 1964), 1.
37 John Wain, letter, *London Magazine*, March 1957, 56.
38 Raphaël Ingelbien, *Misreading England: Poetry and Nationhood Since the Second World War* (Amsterdam: Rodopi, 2002), 21–3.
39 The discussion of 'Church Going' and *Murder in the Cathedral* is a revised version of an earlier article: see 'Larkin's "Church Going": A Source', *Notes & Queries* 61, no. 1 (2014): 146–8.
40 See Larkin, *Early Poems and Juvenilia*, ed. A. T. Tolley (London: Faber and Faber, 2005), 317–46.
41 T. S. Eliot, *Murder in the Cathedral*, in *The Complete Poems and Plays* (London: Faber and Faber, 2004), 239.
42 Ibid.
43 Ibid., 244.
44 Ibid., 281–2.
45 T. S. Eliot, 'Tradition and the Individual Talent', in *Selected Prose*, ed. John Hayward (Harmondsworth: Penguin, 1955), 23.

46 Kingsley Amis, *The Letters of Kingsley Amis*, ed. Zachary Leader (London: HarperCollins, 2000), 399.
47 Michael O'Neill, '"Fond of What He's Crapping On": Movement Poetry and Romanticism', in *The Movement Reconsidered*, ed. Leader, 290.
48 Ibid., 291.

Conclusion

1 Clive James, 'Somewhere Becoming Rain', in *Reliable Essays: The Best of Clive James* (London: Picador, 2001), 34.

Bibliography

Works by Philip Larkin

A Girl in Winter. 1947. London: Faber and Faber, 1957.
'An Incident in the English Camp: A Thoroughly Unhealthy Story, by P. A. Larkin'. 1943. *About Larkin* 12 (October 2001): 5–10.
The Complete Poems, ed. Archie Burnett. London: Faber and Faber, 2012.
Early Poems and Juvenilia, ed. A. T. Tolley. London: Faber and Faber, 2005.
Further Requirements: Interviews, Broadcasts, Statements and Book Reviews, 1952–1985, ed. Anthony Thwaite. London: Faber and Faber, 2002.
Jill. 1946. London: Faber and Faber, 1977.
Letter to Lord Tennyson. 29 May 1984. *About Larkin* 41 (April 2016): 18–19.
Letters Home, 1936–1977, ed. James Booth. London: Faber and Faber, 2018.
Letters to Monica, ed. Anthony Thwaite. London: Faber and Faber, 2011.
The Oxford Book of Twentieth Century English Verse. Oxford: Oxford University Press, 1973.
'Peter'. 1941–2. *About Larkin* 11 (April 2001): 13–23.
Required Writing: Miscellaneous Pieces, 1955–1982. London: Faber and Faber, 1983.
Selected Letters of Philip Larkin, 1940–1985, ed. Anthony Thwaite. London: Faber and Faber, 1992.
'Story I'. 1941–2. *About Larkin* 10 (October 2000): 4–20.
Trouble at Willow Gables and Other Fictions, ed. James Booth. London: Faber and Faber, 2002.

Other works

Ackroyd, Peter. 'Poet Hands on Misery to Man'. *The Times*, 1 April 1993.
Amis, Kingsley. *The Letters of Kingsley Amis*, ed. Zachary Leader. London: HarperCollins, 2000.
Amis, Kingsley. *Lucky Jim*. 1954. Harmondsworth: Penguin, 1977.
Amis, Martin. 'Philip Larkin, His Work and Life'. In *Philip Larkin: Poems Selected by Martin Amis*, ix–xxiii. London: Faber and Faber, 2011.
Auchmuty, Rosemary. *A World of Women*. London: The Women's Press, 1999.
Auden, W. H. *Poems: Auden*, ed. Edward Mendelson. New York: Alfred A. Knopf, 1995.

Bate, Jonathan. 'Very Juvenile, this Juvenilia'. *Daily Telegraph*, 28 April 2002. Available online: http://www.telegraph.co.uk/culture/4727749/Very-juvenile-this-juvenilia.html

Baudelaire, Charles. *The Flowers of Evil*, trans. James McGowan. 1857. Oxford: Oxford University Press, 2008.

Bayley, John. *The Uses of Division: Unity and Disharmony in Literature*. New York: Viking Press, 1976.

Betjeman, John. *The Best of Betjeman*, ed. John Guest. London: John Murray, 2006.

Black, Michael. 'Leavis on Lawrence'. In *F. R. Leavis: Essays and Documents*, ed. Ian MacKillop and Richard Storer, 190–224. London: Continuum, 2005.

Booth, James. 'Editorial'. *About Larkin* 11 (April 2001): 2.

Booth, James. 'The Girlhood of Philip Larkin'. *Standpoint*, 28 January 2019. Available online: https://standpointmag.co.uk/issues/february-2019/critique-james-booth-philip-larkin-brunette-coleman-february-2019/

Booth, James. *Philip Larkin: Life, Art and Love*. London: Bloomsbury, 2014.

Booth, James. *Philip Larkin: The Poet's Plight*. Basingstoke: Palgrave Macmillan, 2005.

Booth, James. *Philip Larkin: Writer*. Hemel Hempstead: Harvester Wheatsheaf, 1992.

Booth, James. 'The Turf Cutter and the Nine-to-Five Man: Heaney, Larkin, and "The Spiritual Intellect's Great Work"'. *Twentieth Century Literature* 43, no. 4 (Winter 1997): 369–93.

Bradford, Richard. *First Boredom, Then Fear: The Life of Philip Larkin*. London: Peter Owen, 2005.

Bradford, Richard. *The Odd Couple: The Curious Friendship between Kingsley Amis and Philip Larkin*. London: The Robson Press, 2012.

Bratton, J. S. 'Girls' Fiction 1900–1930'. In *Imperialism and Juvenile Literature*, ed. Jeffrey Richards, 195–215. Manchester: Manchester University Press, 1989.

Bristow, Joseph. 'The Obscenity of Philip Larkin'. *Critical Inquiry* 21, no. 1 (Autumn 1994): 156–81.

Bucknell, Katherine (ed.). *Christopher Isherwood and Edward Upward: The Mortmere Stories*. London: Enitharmon Press, 1994.

Cadogan, Mary and Patricia Craig. *'You're a Brick, Angela!': A New Look at Girls' Fiction from 1839 to 1975*. London: Gollancz, 1976.

Castle, Terry. 'The Lesbianism of Philip Larkin'. In *The Movement Reconsidered: Essays on Larkin, Amis, Gunn, Davie and Their Contemporaries*, ed. Zachary Leader, 79–105. Oxford: Oxford University Press, 2011.

Chesters, Graham. 'Tireless Play: Speculations on Larkin's "Absences"'. In *Challenges of Translation in French Literature: Studies and Poems in Honour of Peter Broome*, ed. Richard Bales, 47–60. Bern: Peter Lang, 2005.

Choi, Jin-Sung. 'Defensive Homosexuality and Lesbianism in Philip Larkin's Two Girls' School Stories'. *Philip Larkin/British Studies*, special issue of *Hungarian Journal of English and American Studies* 9, no. 1 (Fall 2003): 105–18.

Clark, Steve. '"Get Out As Early As You Can": Larkin's Sexual Politics'. In *Philip Larkin: Contemporary Critical Essays*, ed. Stephen Regan, 94–134. Basingstoke: Macmillan, 1997.

Connolly, Cyril. 'Comment'. *Horizon: A Review of Literature and Art* 1, no. 1 (January 1940): 5–6.

Connolly, Cyril. *Enemies of Promise*. 1938. Chicago: University of Chicago Press, 2008.

Cooper, Stephen. *Philip Larkin: Subversive Writer*. Brighton: Sussex Academic Press, 2004.

Dawson, Winifred. 'Photograph Albums Revisited'. *About Larkin* 13 (April 2002): 4.

Diski, Jenny. 'Damp-Lipped Hilary'. *London Review of Books*, 23 May 2002.

Donoghue, Denis. 'The Hard Case of Yeats'. *New York Review of Books*, 26 May 1977. Available online: https://www.nybooks.com/articles/1977/05/26/the-hard-case-of-yeats/

Earle, Rebecca (ed.). *Epistolary Selves: Letters and Letter-Writers 1600–1945*. Aldershot: Ashgate, 1999.

Eliot, T. S. *The Complete Poems and Plays*. London: Faber and Faber, 2004.

Eliot, T. S. *Selected Prose*, ed. John Hayward. Harmondsworth: Penguin, 1955.

Everett, Barbara. 'Philip Larkin: After Symbolism'. In *Philip Larkin: Contemporary Critical Essays*, ed. Stephen Regan, 55–70. Basingstoke: Macmillan, 1997.

Forbes, Peter. 'Winning Lines'. *The Guardian*, 31 August 2002. Available online: https://www.theguardian.com/books/2002/aug/31/featuresreviews.guardianreview8

Freeman, Gillian. *The Schoolgirl Ethic: The Life and Work of Angela Brazil*. London: Allen Lane, 1976.

Gilroy, Amanda and W. M. Verhoeven. 'Editorial'. *Correspondences*, special issue of *Prose Studies* 19, no. 2 (August 1996): 121–6.

Greenwood, Edward. *F. R. Leavis*. Harlow: Longman, 1978.

Hamilton, Ian. 'Phil the Lark'. *London Review of Books*, 13 October 1988.

Hartley, Jenny. '"Letters are *everything* these days": Mothers and Letters in the Second World War'. In *Epistolary Selves: Letters and Letter-Writers 1600–1945*, ed. Rebecca Earle, 183–95. Aldershot: Ashgate, 1999.

Haughton, Hugh. 'Just Letters: Corresponding Poets'. In *Letter Writing Among Poets from William Wordsworth to Elizabeth Bishop*, ed. Jonathan Ellis, 57–78. Edinburgh: Edinburgh University Press, 2015.

Heaney, Seamus. *Seeing Things*. London: Faber and Faber, 1991.

Hedgecock, Liz. 'New Worlds for Old: Mythology and Exile in the Novels of Philip Larkin'. In *New Larkins for Old: Critical Essays*, ed. James Booth, 97–106. Basingstoke: Macmillan, 2000.

Hill, Geoffrey. 'I Know Thee not, Old Man, Fall to thy Prayers'. Professor of Poetry Lecture. University of Oxford, 5 May 2015. Available online http://media.podcasts.ox.ac.uk/engfac/poetry/2015-05-05_engfac_hill.mp3

Hill, Geoffrey. *Style and Faith*. New York: Counterpoint, 2003.

Holderness, Graham. 'Reading "Deceptions" – A Dramatic Conversation'. In *Philip Larkin: Contemporary Critical Essays*, ed. Stephen Regan, 83–93. Basingstoke: Macmillan, 1997.

Hood, Thomas. *Selected Poems of Thomas Hood*, ed. John Clubbe. Cambridge, MA: Harvard University Press, 1970.

Hughes, Ted. 'The Burnt Fox'. In *Winter Pollen: Occasional Prose*, ed. William Scammell, 8–9. London: Faber and Faber, 1994.

Ingelbien, Raphaël. *Misreading England: Poetry and Nationhood since the Second World War*. Amsterdam: Rodopi, 2002.

Irons, Glenwood (ed.). *Feminism in Women's Detective Fiction*. Toronto: University of Toronto Press, 1995.

Isherwood, Christopher. *Goodbye to Berlin*. 1939. London: Vintage, 1998.

Isherwood, Christopher. *Lions and Shadows: An Education in the Twenties*. 1938. London: Vintage, 2013.

James, Clive. 'Larkin Treads the Boards'. In *The Meaning of Recognition: New Essays 2001–2005*, 92–101. London: Picador, 2006.

James, Clive. 'Somewhere Becoming Rain'. In *Reliable Essays: The Best of Clive James*, 25–34. London: Picador, 2001.

Jardine, Lisa. 'Saxon Violence'. *The Guardian*, 8 December 1992.

Jensen, Morten Høi. 'Larkin's Way'. *Idiom*, 3 April 2012. Available online http://idiommag.com/2012/04/larkins-way/

Johnson, Rebecca. 'Philip Larkin as Brunette Coleman'. *About Larkin* 2 (October 1996): 8–10.

Kirsch, Adam. 'Green Selfconscious Spurts'. *Times Literary Supplement*, 13 May 2005.

Knowles, Murray and Kirsten Malmkjaer. *Language and Control in Children's Literature*. London: Routledge, 1996.

Lawrence, D. H. *The Collected Letters of D. H. Lawrence: Volume II*, ed. Harry T. Moore. New York: Viking Press, 1962.

Leavis, Q. D. *Fiction and the Reading Public*. London: Chatto and Windus, 1932.

Lee, Hermione. 'Dangerous Letters: A Biographer's Perspective'. In *Letter Writing Among Poets from William Wordsworth to Elizabeth Bishop*, ed. Jonathan Ellis, 19–30. Edinburgh: Edinburgh University Press, 2015.

Levi, Peter. 'The English Wisdom of A Master Poet'. In *An Enormous Yes: In Memoriam Philip Larkin 1922–1985*, ed. Harry Chambers, 33–5. Calstock: Peterloo Poets, 1986.

Lodge, David. 'The Metonymic Muse'. In *Philip Larkin: Contemporary Critical Essays*, ed. Stephen Regan, 71–82. Basingstoke: Macmillan, 1997.

Longenbach, James. 'An Imperfect Life: On George and W. B. Yeats'. *Nation*, 18 May 2011. Available online: https://www.thenation.com/article/imperfect-life-george-and-wb-yeats/

Longley, Edna. 'Larkin, Decadence and the Lyric Poem'. In *New Larkins for Old: Critical Essays*, ed. James Booth, 29–50. Basingstoke: Macmillan, 2000.

Maylon, Julie. 'The Other Side of a Friendship: Letters from James Sutton to Philip Larkin'. *About Larkin* 7 (April 1999): 16–17.

Mitchell, Adrian. *Poems*. London: Jonathan Cape, 1964.

Montgomery, Bruce (as Edmund Crispin). 'An Oxford Group'. *Spectator*, 17 April 1964.

Morrison, Blake. 'Philip Larkin: Life, Art and Love by James Booth – Review'. *The Guardian*, 22 August 2014. Available online: http://www.theguardian.com/books/2014/aug/22/philip-larkin-james-booth-review

Motion, Andrew. *Philip Larkin: A Writer's Life*. London: Faber and Faber, 1993.

O'Brien, Sean. 'Philip Larkin: Poems Selected by Martin Amis – Review'. *The Guardian*, 16 September 2011. Available online: http://www.theguardian.com/books/2011/sep/16/philip-larkin-poems-review

O'Neill, Michael. '"Fond of What He's Crapping On": Movement Poetry and Romanticism'. In *The Movement Reconsidered: Essays on Larkin, Amis, Gunn, Davie and Their Contemporaries*, ed. Zachary Leader, 270–91. Oxford: Oxford University Press, 2011.

Orwell, George. 'Boys' Weeklies'. In *Selected Essays*, 175–203. Harmondsworth: Penguin, 1957.

Osborne, John. *Larkin, Ideology and Critical Violence: A Case of Wrongful Conviction*. Basingstoke: Palgrave Macmillan, 2008.

Osborne, John. *Radical Larkin: Seven Types of Technical Mastery*. Basingstoke: Palgrave Macmillan, 2014.

Palmer, Richard. *Such Deliberate Disguises: The Art of Philip Larkin*. London: Continuum, 2008.

Paulin, Tom. Letter. *Times Literary Supplement*, 6 November 1992.

Paulin, Tom. 'She Did Not Change: Philip Larkin'. In *Minotaur: Poetry and the Nation State*, 233–51. London: Faber and Faber, 1992.

Regan, Stephen. 'In the Grip of Light: Larkin's Poetry of the 1940s'. In *New Larkins for Old: Critical Essays*, ed. James Booth, 121–9. Basingstoke: Macmillan, 2000.

Roberts, Ryan (ed.). *John Fuller and the Sycamore Press: A Bibliographic History*. Oxford: The Bodleian Library, 2010.

Rossen, Janice. *Philip Larkin: His Life's Work*. Iowa City: University of Iowa Press, 1989.

Rowe, M. W. 'On being Brunette: Larkin's Schoolgirl Fiction'. *Critical Quarterly* 43, no. 4 (December 2001): 42–58.

Rowe, M. W. 'Unreal Girls: Lesbian Fantasy in Early Larkin'. In *New Larkins for Old: Critical Essays*, ed. James Booth, 79–96. Basingstoke: Macmillan, 2000.

Sagar, Keith. *The Art of D. H. Lawrence*. Cambridge: Cambridge University Press, 1966.

Simons, Judy. 'Angela Brazil and the Making of the Girls' School Story'. In *Popular Children's Literature in Britain*, ed. Julia Briggs, Dennis Butts and M. O. Grenby, 165–81. Aldershot: Ashgate, 2008.

Sims, Sue. Review of *Trouble at Willow Gables and Other Fictions* by Philip Larkin. *About Larkin* 14 (October 2002): 37–9.

Smith, Stan. 'Margins of Tolerance: Responses to Post-war Decline'. In *Philip Larkin: Contemporary Critical Essays*, ed. Stephen Regan, 178–86. Basingstoke: Macmillan, 1997.

Smith, Stan. 'Something for Nothing: Late Larkins and Early'. *English* 49, no. 195 (Autumn 2000): 255–75.

Sontag, Susan. 'Notes on "Camp"'. In *Against Interpretation and Other Essays*, 275–89. London: Eyre and Spottiswoode, 1967.

Swarbrick, Andrew. *Out of Reach: The Poetry of Philip Larkin*. Basingstoke: Macmillan, 1995.

Thwaite, Anthony. 'The Poetry of Philip Larkin'. In *The Survival of Poetry: A Contemporary Survey*, ed. Martin Dodsworth, 37–55. London: Faber and Faber, 1970.

Timms, David. *Philip Larkin*. Edinburgh: Oliver Boyd, 1973.

Tolley, A. T. *Larkin at Work: A Study of Larkin's Mode of Composition as Seen in His Workbooks*. Hull: University of Hull Press, 1997.

Tolley, A. T. *My Proper Ground: A Study of the Work of Philip Larkin and Its Development*. Edinburgh: Edinburgh University Press, 1991.

Underwood, James. '"A Kind of Homosexual Relation, Disguised": Larkin's Letters to Monica Jones'. *English* 65, no. 248 (2016): 38–57.

Underwood, James. 'Larkin's "Church Going": A Source'. *Notes & Queries* 61, no. 1 (2014): 146–8.

Wain, John. Letter. *London Magazine*, March 1957.

Whalen, Terry. 'Philip Larkin and *Lady Chatterley*'s *Lover*: Exploring an Influence'. In *New Larkins for Old: Critical Essays*, ed. James Booth, 107–20. Basingstoke: Macmillan, 2000.

Woolcock, Nicola. 'Poet Larkin's Lesbian Tales "reveal desire to be female"', *Telegraph*, 23 April 2001. Available online: http://www.telegraph.co.uk/news/uknews/1317050/Poet-Larkins-lesbian-tales-reveal-desire-to-be-female.html

Woolf, Virginia. *A Writer's Diary: Being Extracts from the Diary of Virginia Woolf*, ed. Leonard Woolf. San Diego: Harcourt, 2003.

Wordsworth, William. *Poetical Works*, ed. Thomas Hutchinson. London: Oxford University Press, 1971.

Yeats, W. B. *Yeats's Poems*, ed. A. Norman Jeffares. London: Macmillan, 1989.

Index

Principal entries in bold.

Ackroyd, Peter   5
Aldington, Richard   34
Amis, Hilly   170
Amis, Kingsley   97, 125, 170, 185, 192 n.17
 and Brunette Coleman   2, 51–4, 63, 93, 126, 132, 141
 correspondence with PL   7, 13, 40–1, 57
 Lucky Jim   2–3, 96, 143, 146
Amis, Martin   4–6, 7
Amis, Sally   170
Angry Young Men   96
Aristotle   63, 68, 82
Armstrong, Louis   22
Arnold, Matthew   41
Arnott, Winifred (*see* Dawson, Winifred)
Auchmuty, Rosemary   75
Auden, W. H.   88, 119, 123, 180–1
 Auden group   40, 41, 52, 90
 influence on PL   21, 22–3, 25, 26, 60, 120–1, 125
Austen, Jane   79
Auxiliary Territorial Service for Women   67

Barstow, Stan   143
Bate, Jonathan   55, 140
Bateson, F. W.   63
Baudelaire, Charles   48, 50, 68, 75, 81, 129–31, 162
Bayley, John   104
Becket, Thomas   182
Bedtime With Braden (radio series)   180
Beethoven, Ludwig van   22
Belfast   150, 177
Bell, William   133
Betjeman, John   22, 123, 125–6
Blake, William   179
Booth, James   29, 131, 134, 141, 144, 151, 154–5, 157, 159, 162, 178

 on Brunette Coleman   54, 56–7, 58, 62, 68, 80, 89, 131
 on PL's novels   97, 98, 100, 102, 114, 116
 on PL's short stories   40–2, 45, 47, 48, 192 n.11
Born Yesterday (film)   170
Bowman, Ruth   30–1, 141–2, 151, 154, 157
Bradford, Richard   52, 53, 63, 142–3, 179
Bradshaw, Winifred (*see* Dawson, Winifred)
Braine, John   143
Brando, Marlon   57
Bratton, J. S.   71
Brazil, Angela   71, 83–4
Breary, Nancy   57, 83
Brennan, Maeve   6, 7
Brent-Dyer, Elinor   71
Brief Encounter (film)   49
Bristow, Joseph   157
Brooke, Rupert   26
Brown, Ford Madox   19
Brown, Philip   56, 192 n.17
Bruce, Dorita Fairlie   71, 82–4
Bucknell, Katherine   52–3
Burnett, Archie   8–9, 54, 137, 182
Byron, Lord   28

Cadogan, Mary   71, 83–4
Cambridge University   26, 40–1, 52, 65–6, 72, 99, 122
Canterbury Cathedral   183
Canterbury Tales, The (Chaucer)   68
Carswells of Belfast   159
Castle, Terry   51, 57–8, 84, 88, 90, 130, 131
Caton, R. A.   133
Chesters, Graham   162
Choi, Jin-Sung   56, 88
Christie, Agatha   73–4

Churchill, Winston   16, 111–12
Clark, Steve   178
Coleman, Blanche   51
Coleman, Brunette   33, 41, 44, 45, 47, 50,
    51–69, 71–91, 119–40, 141, 144,
    145, 160, 193 n.1
  importance of   2–3, 10–12, 104, 150,
    161, 187
  influence on PL's early poetry   147, 149
  influence on PL's novels   93–5, 98,
    101, 110
  influence on *The Less Deceived*   158,
    161–7, 171, 173, 175–8, 181
  WORKS
  Ante Meridian   53–6, 80, 85, 134, 162,
    195 n.39
  'Ballade des Dames du Temps
    Jadis'   85, **128–9**
  'Bliss'   **125–6**
  'False Friend, The'   86, **125–6**, 133
  'Femmes Damnées'   11, 85, **129–31**,
    133, **139–40**, 147, 161–2, 165, 167
  'Fourth Former Loquitur'   **127–8**, 185
  'Holidays'   **126–7**
  Michaelmas Term at St Bride's   53–6,
    58, **88–91**, 130, 132, 140, 163, 165
  'School in August, The'   **127**
  Sugar and Spice   11, 53–6, 67, 80, 85,
    87, 91, **124–40**, 162
  Trouble at Willow Gables   10, 53–6,
    58, **67–9, 72–84**, 88, 94, 114–15,
    125–6, 129–30, 132, 140, 165
  'What Are We Writing For?'   10,
    53–6, 57, **58–67**, 83, 130, 171, 179
Coleridge, Samuel Taylor   105, 179
Connolly, Cyril   30, 159
  Enemies of Promise   60, 62, 64, 67, 80,
    195 n.39
  Horizon   60, 65, 126
Conquest, Robert   170
Conservative Party   61
Cooper, Stephen   57, 88, 90, 97, 98,
    165–6, 168, 176
Coventry   14, 25, 60, 78, 95, 162, 179–81
  King Henry VIII School   13
Craig, Patricia   71, 83–4
Crispin, Edmund (*see* Montgomery, Bruce)

Daily Telegraph (newspaper)   61

Davie, Ian   133
Davin, Dan   123
Dawson, Winifred   168–9
Day Lewis, Cecil   23, 123, 165
Derrida, Jacques   78–9, 153
Diski, Jenny   55
Donne, John   155
Donoghue, Denis   28
Duffy, Carol Ann   140
Duncan, Ronald   178

Earle, Rebecca   14
Egerton, Ansell   177
Egerton, Judy   177
Eliot, George   182
Eliot, T. S.   3, 28, 65, 68, 123, 176, 182–5
Enright, D. J.   151, 159
Essay on Man (Pope)   68
Essays in Criticism (journal)   63, 145
Everett, Barbara   175

Faber and Faber   95, 120, 137
Faerie Queene, The (Spenser)   66
Fenton, James   103
Financial Times (newspaper)   61
First World War   8, 38, 112, 123
Folly (magazine)   68
Forster, E. M.   112
Fortune Press   133
Frankenstein (Shelley)   105
Freeman, Gillian   83–4
Frost, Robert   182
Fuller, John   139–40, 162

Garbo, Greta   57
Gautier, Théophile   58, 68, 76, 140,
    162–3
Gem (magazine)   61
George VI   16, 111–12
Gilroy, Amanda   14
Gollancz, Diana   53
Gollancz, Victor   53, 54, 146
Green, Henry   105
Greenwood, Edward   65
Gunner, Colin   7, 13

Haffenden, John   5, 163, 168
Hamilton, Ian   5, 159
Hardy, Thomas   168, 182

influence on PL   2, 22, 102, 122–4, 132, 139, 149–50, 187
Harrison, Tony   97
Hartley, Jean   6
Hartley, Jenny   16
Haughton, Hugh   14
Heaney, Seamus   29
Heart of Darkness (Conrad)   42
Hedgecock, Liz   116
Hemingway, Ernest   166
Hickson, Joan   73
Hill, Geoffrey   3–4, 63
Hitchens, Christopher   155
Hitler, Adolf   5
Hogarth Press   34
Holderness, Graham   158
Hood, Thomas   112, 162, 179, 181, 195 n.39
Hopkins, Gerard Manley   17, 41
Hughes, Ted   63, 122
Hughes, Thomas   35, 61
Hull University Philip Larkin Archive   54, 55, 194 n.16
Huxley, Aldous   34

Iles, Norman   192 n.17
Ingelbien, Raphaël   182
Irons, Glenwood   73
Isherwood, Christopher
    influence on PL   22, 25, 52–3
    influence on PL's short stories   33, 37–8, 40–2, 44–6, 90, 103–4, 128
    Lions and Shadows   21, 23–4, 26, 40–1, 46, 52, 89, 146

James, Clive   6, 188
Jardine, Lisa   6
Jensen, Morten Høi   4
Johnson, Rebecca   55
Johnson, Samuel   63
Jones, Monica   7, 27, 31, 142, 150, 155, 167, 172, 177–8
Joyce, James   22, 35–6, 65, 79, 105, 116
Jung, Carl   88

Keats, John   20, 25, 126, 131, 164, 182
Kennedy, Margaret   67, 69, 85, 126
Kirsch, Adam   1
Knights, L. C.   65

Knowles, Murray   72–3

Lady Godiva   78
Lamb, Charles   179
Lansbury, Angela   73
Larkin, Kitty (Catherine)   38, 66
Larkin, Philip
    art and life   25–32, 122–4, 135–7, 138–9, 142–3
    and authorship   23, 33, 40–1, 44–7, 50, 51–3, 77, 94, 98–104, 105, 109, 114, 124, 133, 187
    and (auto)biography   2, 4–6, 7–11, 15, 38, 46, 56, 88, 95–6, 99, 121, 123, 124, 130, 142, 145–6, 150–1, 154–5, 157, 161, 163–4, 169, 174, 177, 178, 186, 187–8
    Brunette Coleman works (*see* Coleman, Brunette)
    and camp   38, 41, 44, 50, 84–7, 89, 125, 128
    and characterization   33, 35, 37–40, 42, 44–5, 47–50, 51, 68, 72–4, 75–9, 95, 97–8, 130
    and class   8, 22, 42–4, 95–7, 111, 155, 157
    and 'Englishness'   16, 19, 48–9, 60–2, 109–12, 116, 134, 143, 179–80
    and femininity   6–7, 47–50, 54, 57, 74, 78, 94–5, 114–17, 136, 139
    and feminism   22, 51, 59, 69, 72–3, 130, 163–4, 165, 168–71
    and gender   4, 8, 22, 51, 59, 62, 67, 68–9, **71–91**, 113, 114–17, 126, 128, 129–31, 134–7, 138–9, 157–8, 163, 164–71, 176–7
    and genre   33, 35–6, 47–50, **51–69**, 71–2, 73–4, 85–7, 126, 131, 161, 171–81
    and jazz   16, 22, 28, 34
    juvenilia   33–6 (*see also* JUVENILIA; SHORT STORIES)
    the 'Larkinesque'   2, 13, 127–8, 136–7, 139, 144, 160–1, 168, 186
    and letters   4–7, 11, **13–32**, 74, 99–101, 106–9, 133 (*see also* OTHER (NON-POETIC) WRITINGS)
    and modernism   8, 22–3, 34, 36, 65–6, 68, 105, 122–3, 142

and nationality 8, 15–16, 49, 109–12, 113, 117, 164
and personae 6–7, 122, 161, 171–81
poetry workbooks 146–50, 151, 154, 160, 162, 167
and politics 6, 8, 22, 28, 61–2, 95, 109–12, 126, 163
and pornography 4, 5, 52, 54, 55–8, 74, 80–2, 88–9
and race 4, 5, 8, 22
reputation 3–4, 22
and Romanticism 25–6, 29, 166, 179–81, 185–6
The Seven 41–2, 90, 100, 192 n.11, 192 n.17
and sexuality 14, 37, 42–4, 47, 48–50, 51, 52, 55–8, 61, 68–9, 71, 76, 80–4, 85–7, 88–9, 94–5, 102, 115–17, 124, 129–31, 134–7
statements on poetry 5, 29, 94, 119–20, 123, 143, 157, 159, 162, 163, 167, 168, 184, 187
'theory of the rupture' 1–2, 119–20, 131, 160
and war (*see* Second World War)
and work 26–9, 34, 172, 173–5
writerly anxieties 20–2, 23–4, 29–30, 31, 46–7, 89, 142, 144–6, 148–9
INDIVIDUAL POEMS
'Absences' 161, **162–4**, 167
'Afternoons' 45, 129, 188
'All catches alight' 121, 198 n.18
'April Sunday brings the snow, An' 147
'Arundel Tomb, An' 128, 185–6, 188
'At Grass' 11, 141, **149–51, 152–4**, 155, 158, 160, 161, 167, 173, 177, 181, 187
'Aubade' 127
'Born Yesterday' 164, **170–1**, 180, 181
'bottle is drunk out by one, The' 198 n.18
'Building, The' 181
'Church Going' 128, 161, **181–6**
'Climbing the hill within the deafening wind' 121
'Conscript' 131
'Dawn' 151

'Deceptions' 11, 45, 113, 121, 141, **149–51, 154–8**, 160, 161, 163, 167, 171, 173, 177, 181, 187
'Dockery and Son' 127, 131
'Do not think to step from art's plain room' 150
'Dry-Point' 162, 163–4
'Dublinesque' 121
'Explosion, The' 45, 121, 188
'Faith Healing' 188
'Femmes Damnées' (*see under* Coleman, Brunette)
'Fiction and the Reading Public' 66, 144–5, 148
'For Sidney Bechet' 121, 188
'Friday Night in the Royal Station Hotel' 127, 188
'Ghosts' 25
'Going' 164
'Heaviest of flowers, the head' 198 n.18
'Here' 143
'High Windows' 145, 155, 163
'Homage to a Government' 112
'Home is so Sad' 5, 127
'horns of the morning, The' 198 n.18
'I dreamed of an out-thrust arm of land' 133
'If, My Darling' 161
'Importance of Elsewhere, The' 112
'I put my mouth' 198 n.18
'I Remember, I Remember' 78, 112, **178–81**
'I see a girl dragged by the wrists' **134–7**, 138, 164, 171, 198 n.18
'Is it for now or for always' 121
'Last of all, when a great war has ended' 149
'Latest Face' 161
'Like the train's beat' 134
'Lines on a Young Lady's Photograph Album' 161, **164–7**, 168, 171
'Livings' 17, 121, 148, 188
'Love Songs in Age' 127, 188
'Love we must part now: do not let it be' 198 n.18
'Maiden Name', 164, **168–70**, 171
'March Past' 112

'MCMXIV'   8, 112
'Modesties'   148
'moon is full tonight, The'   198 n.18
'Morning has spread again'   198 n.18
'Mower, The'   188
'Mr Bleaney'   45, 129, 131, 188
'Mythological Introduction'   133
'Myxomatosis'   **177–8**
'Next, Please'   164
'North Ship, The'   29, 164
'Nursery Tale'   131
'Places, Loved Ones'   161
'Poetry of Departures'   **175–6**
'Posterity'   4
'Reasons for Attendance'   45, 127, 161, **171–3**, 174, 175, 176, 180
'Sad Steps'   127
'Self's the Man'   45
'Skin'   161
'Solar'   155
'So through that unripe day you bore your head'   198 n.18
'Spring'   161, **176–7**
'Stone Church Damaged by a Bomb, A'   133
'Study of Reading Habits, A'   63, 145
'Sunny Prestatyn'   36
'Sympathy in White Major'   140
'This Be The Verse'   56, 78, 145
'Toads'   **173–5**
'To Failure'   148
'To write one song, I said'   121
'Trees, The'   113, 134, 188
'Ugly Sister'   134
'Waiting for breakfast, while she brushed her hair'   **137–9**, 147
'Wants'   164, 179
'Wedding-Wind'   45, 147, 149, 161, 164, **167–8**, 169, 171
'Whitsun Weddings, The'   45, 63, 127, 143, 181, 188
JUVENILIA
Behind the Facade   182
Chosen Poems   54
'Death in Swingtime'   34
'Incidents from Phippy's Schooldays'   35
'It had snowed in the night'   36, 37, 116
'Last Man In (or "How Allan Saved His Side")'   35
'Letter to Myself'   35–6
'Life of a Cog, The'   34
'One O'Clock Jump'   34
'Portrait of the Artist as a Young Frog'   35
'Present Laughter'   34
Seven Poems   54
'Shapes of Clay'   34
'Teddy Bear's Picnic'   34
'Trio'   34
'Vampire Island'   35, 36
NOVELS
Girl in Winter, A   11, 12, 36, 44, 79, 91, 93, 97, **104–17**, 129, 134, 141–2, 144, 150, 158, 163, 165, 171, 178
Jill   11, 44, 55, **93–104**, 109, 110, 114, 115, 132, 141, 144, 165, 178
New World Symphony, A   **142–4**, 145, 146
No For An Answer   **142–4**, 145
OTHER (NON-POETIC) WRITINGS
Letters Home   6
Letters to Monica   6
'LIFE WITH PHAIRY PHANTASY'   120
'note on the freedom of D. H. Lawrence, A'   30–1
'Round Another Point: *Débat*'   144
'Round the Point: *Débat Inédit*'   11, 12, **141–6**, 148, 171–2, 179
Selected Letters   4–6, 22
'Statement'   167, 184, 187
POETRY COLLECTIONS
Collected Poems (1988)   4–6, 7–9, 188
Complete Poems, The   3, 7–9, 29, 182
Early Poems and Juvenilia   1, 8–9
High Windows   139, 181, 188
In the Grip of Light   132, 159
Less Deceived, The   1, 12, 138, 139, 147, 148, 149–50, 153–4, 158, **159–86**, 188
North Ship, The   1, 11, 120, **120–4**, 127, 131, **131–4**, **134–9**, 141, 143, 147, 151, 158, 159, 160, 164, 166, 175, 186

Oxford Book of Twentieth Century English Verse 22, 122–3, 165, 168, 170, 182–3
Whitsun Weddings, The 120, 139, 181, 188
XX Poems 151, 159
SHORT STORIES
'Eagles Are Gone, The' 2, 37, **38–40**, 44–5, 98, 101, 108, 151, 192 n.11
'Incident in the English Camp, An' 10, 33, 37, **47–50**, 51, 52, 95, 104, 110, 112, 114, 115–16, 164, 171
'Maurice' **36–8**, 40, 44
'Peter' 37, **40–7**, 50, 94, 98, 99, 192 n.15
'Story I' 37, **40–7**, 50, 98, 99, 102
Larkin, Sydney 38, 147–8
Lawrence, D. H. 24, 65–6, 114
 art and life 10, 25–6, 27, 30–2, 104, 109, 138
 influence on PL 20–2, 24–5, 34, 105
 Lady Chatterley's Lover 24, 58, 66, 146, 179–80
 Sons and Lovers 24, 103, 167
Layard, John 88–9
Leavis, F. R. 25, 65–7
Leavis, Q. D. 66–7, 145
Lee, Hermione 14
Levi, Peter 3–4
Lodge, David 122, 127, 177
Longenbach, James 27–8
Longley, Edna 26

Mackenzie, Compton 41
MacNeice, Louis 123, 182
Magnet (magazine) 61
Malmkjaer, Kirsten 72–3
Mansfield, Katherine 22, 39, 105
Maugham, Somerset 34
Maupassant, Guy de 68
Maurier, Daphne du 80
Mayhew, Henry 149–50, 154–6
Maylon, Julie 19
Meade, L. T. 166
Milton, John 63, 64, 68, 72, 75, 83
Mitchell, Adrian 181
Montgomery, Bruce 6, 52, 53–4, 88–9, 104, 120, 131
Moore, George 105

Morrison, Blake 4
Motion, Andrew 4–6, 13, 41, 55–6, 60, 80, 82, 88, 94, 98, 124, 131, 151
Murry, John Middleton 25

Nash, Paul 17

O'Brien, Sean 4–5
O'Neill, Michael 185
Orwell, George 67, 69, 76, 88, 101, 182
 'Boys' Weeklies' 59–65, 82–3
Osborne, John 1, 5, 7–9, 78, 87, 111, 115, 116–17, 136, 153–4, 160, 161, 162, 165–6, 169, 170, 171, 175, 179–80
Oxford 18, 139
Oxford Poetry 1942–3 (anthology) 133
Oxford University 60, 142, 165
 Bodleian Library 6, 60, 66, 194 n.16
 and Brunette Coleman 59, 88–9
 English Club 26, 40, 46, 120
 and *Jill* 95–6, 97, 100, 101–3
 and PL 15, 16, 17, 34, 41, 52, 66, 120, 131
 and PL's short stories 33, 36–7, 40, 41, 42–3, 47, 49, 52–3, 90, 95, 122, 146
Oxford University Press 123

Palmer, Richard 1, 2, 55, 167, 174
Paulin, Tom 4, 6, 112
Pearson, Hesketh 24
Peg's Paper (magazine) 26
Petrarch 176
Plato 35
Plaut, Miriam 53–4
Poetry Book Society Bulletin (magazine) 137
Poetry from Oxford in Wartime (anthology) 133, 137
Poet's Choice (anthology) 162
Pound, Ezra 159
Powys, T. F. 65–6
Praed, Winthrop Mackworth 179
Punch (magazine) 178
Pushkin, Alexander 188
Pygmalion 105
Pym, Barbara 139

Queen's University Belfast 169

Regan, Stephen   132
Repton School   26, 40, 42
Rimbaud, Arthur   162
Rochefort Productions (Literary Property) Ltd.   53–4 (*see also* Gollancz, Victor)
Roedean School   62
Rogers, Diccon   166
Rossen, Janice   157, 180
Rossetti, Dante Gabriel   128
Rowe, M. W.   56, 87
Royal Army Service Corps   15
Rugby School   35, 42
Russel, Nick   192 n.17

Sappho   130
Scrutiny (journal)   65–6
Second World War
   and Brunette Coleman works   57, 67, 87, 126, 176
   and *The Less Deceived*   176
   and PL   35–6, 60, 133
   and PL's early poetry   134–6, 149
   and PL's novels   11, 94, 102, 109–12, 115, 116–17
   and PL's short stories   42–3, 47–8, 49
   and Sutton correspondence   15–18, 108
Shakespeare, William   22, 24, 25, 40, 49, 58, 63, 64, 68, 77, 155, 176
Shaw, George Bernard   35, 68
Shelley, Percy Bysshe   126, 179
Sillitoe, Alan   97, 143
Simons, Judy   71, 83–4
Sims, Sue   68
Slade School of Art   15
Smith, Stan   119, 131, 141, 158
Socrates   35
Sontag, Susan   85–7, 125
Spectator (magazine)   184
Spencer, Stanley   19
Spender, Stephen   41
Stephen, Leslie   80
Stevens, Wallace   133
Storey, David   143
Strachey, Lytton   122

Strang, Patsy   177
Sutton, James (Jim) Ballard   1, 7, 10, 12, **13–32**, 40, 104, 108–9, 110, 114, 138, 172
Swarbrick, Andrew   172, 175, 178
Sycamore Press   139–40

Tennyson, Alfred Lord   131, 165
Thomas, Dylan   21, 26–7, 120–1, 123, 133
Thwaite, Anthony   5, 13, 139
Timms, David   116, 121–2, 135–6, 138
Tolley, A. T.   8, 105, 147, 150
Treasure Island (Stevenson)   35

University College, Leicester   142
Upward, Edward   24, 26, 41, 52–3, 89

Verhoeven, W. M.   14
Verlaine, Paul   162
Vicary, Dorothy   57, 84
Villon, François   128, 130–1, 140

Wain, John   97, 143, 182
Waley, Arthur   74
Warhol, Andy   57
Watkins, Vernon   26–9, 40, 120
Waugh, Evelyn   34
Whalen, Terry   176
Whetham, Catherine Durning   58
Wilde, Oscar   105
Willcox, Jimmy   192 n.17
Williams, David   192 n.17
Woolf, Virginia   22, 36, 57, 59, 76, 79, 80, 105–6, 112
Wordsworth, William   155, 164, 179
Wycombe Abbey School   62

Yeats, W. B.
   art and life   27–9
   influence on PL   2, 26–7, 119–23, 125, 135–7, 170, 180, 182
   PL's imitation of   41, 103–4, 128–9, 131, 137–9, 140, 147, 149, 150, 154, 162

www.ingramcontent.com/pod-product-compliance
Lightning Source LLC
Chambersburg PA
CBHW062223300426
44115CB00012BA/2199